Contents

List of tables and figures

List of tables

List of figures

Contributors

Martin A. Andresen is a Professor in the School of Criminology and Director of the Institute for Canadian Urban Research Studies at Simon Fraser University. Professor Andresen's research areas are in policing and mental health, spatial-temporal crime analysis, crime and place, and the geography of crime. His recent publications have appeared in *Policing: An International Journal*, *Policing & Society*, *Policing: A Journal of Policy and Practice*, *Journal of Criminal Justice*, and *Journal of Quantitative Criminology*.

Emma Antrobus is a Criminology Lecturer and researcher with the Australia Research Council Centre of Excellence for Children and Families over the Life Course in the School of Social Science at the University of Queensland. Emma has a background in social psychology and has interests in the legitimacy of social agencies, crime prevention, and youth deviance. Her recent research focuses on randomized controlled trials examining the impact of police behavior and legitimacy, and interventions for young people at risk.

Barak Ariel is a Lecturer in Experimental Criminology at the University of Cambridge and a Senior Lecturer at the Institute of Criminology, Faculty of Law, Hebrew University of Jerusalem.

Craig Bennell, PhD, is a Professor of Psychology at Carleton University in Ottawa, Ontario, Canada, where he teaches classes in forensic psychology and police psychology. He is also Director of Carleton's Police Research Laboratory. He and his students conduct collaborative research with police agencies from across Canada, including the Royal Canadian Mounted Police. He has specific interests in how research can be used to inform police practices and policies, particularly in the areas of use-of-force decision-making, serial crime investigations, and police training.

Sarah Bennett is a Senior Lecturer in Criminology at the University of Queensland. Research interests include evidence based policing, procedural justice and legitimacy, and pathways to preventing offending and victimization. Sarah is a Fellow of the Academy of Experimental Criminology and invests in rigorous research projects and partnerships that directly inform policy and practice.

Brittany Blaskovits is a PhD candidate in Psychology at Carleton University. She received her BA (Hons) in Psychology from the University of Lethbridge in 2012, and her MA in Psychology from Carleton University in 2015. Her current research involves the examination of body-worn cameras on memory during use-of-force events, as well as the practical applications of police investigative techniques (eg behavioral crime linkage analysis).

Anthony A. Braga is a Distinguished Professor in and Director of the School of Criminology and Criminal Justice at Northeastern University. Braga is a fellow of the American Society of Criminology (ASC). He is also a past President and Fellow of the Academy of Experimental Criminology (AEC), and the 2014 recipient of its Joan McCord Award, recognizing his commitment to randomized controlled experiments. Between 2007 and 2013, Braga served as Chief Policy Advisor to former Boston Police Commissioner Edward F. Davis and worked with his command staff and line-level officers on award-winning community policing and crime prevention initiatives. Braga holds an MPA from Harvard University and a PhD in Criminal Justice from Rutgers University.

Tom Cockcroft is Reader in Criminology and Head of Criminology at Leeds Beckett University. His research and publication interests are in the broad area of police occupational culture. His most recent work addresses the impact of new knowledge paradigms on the cultural and structural dynamics of police organizations. He is Visiting Senior Research Fellow at Canterbury Christ Church University.

Gary Cordner is Professor Emeritus at Kutztown University of Pennsylvania and Eastern Kentucky University (EKU). At EKU, Cordner served as Dean of the College of Justice & Safety and also founded and directed the Regional Community Policing Institute and the International Justice & Safety Institute. Before joining EKU, he worked as a police officer and police chief in Maryland. He earned his PhD at Michigan State University.

Ian Hesketh is an organizational psychologist. He is an Honorary Researcher at Lancaster University Management School and a Visiting Fellow at the Open University Business School. He is also a visiting lecturer at several other universities. He holds a PhD in Management and Social Psychology and an MBA from Lancaster University in the UK. He is a Chartered Manager (CMgr) and holds Qualified Teaching, Learning and Skills (QTLS) status with the Society for Education and Training.

Lorelei Hine holds a Bachelor of Social Science from the University of Queensland (UQ). She works in the UQ School of Social Science as a research assistant on a variety of criminology projects. In particular, Ms Hine's work focuses on procedural justice, police legitimacy, and systematic reviews. Ms Hine has contributed to academic articles, industry reports, and populating the Global Policing Database.

Laura Huey is a Professor at the University of Western Ontario, the Director of the Canadian Society of Evidence Based Policing, a member of the College of New Scholars of the Royal Society of Canada, and Senior Research Fellow with the Police Foundation. She is also the London Police Service Research Fellow. Previously, she was a member of the Canadian Council of Academies' Expert Panel on the Future of Canadian Policing and sits on numerous boards and working groups related to policing and community safety.

Hina Kalyal is a PhD candidate in Sociology at the University of Western Ontario. She also holds a PhD in Business Administration. Her research interests include evidence based policing practices and management of strategic change in police organizations.

Peter Martin, PhD, is Assistant Commissioner of the Queensland Corrective Services. In 2010, Peter was inducted into the Evidence-Based Policing Hall of Fame at the George Mason University, Virginia, US. He was awarded the Australian Police Medal on Australia Day 2008 for his contribution to policing and the community of Queensland. He is also the recipient of the Emergency Services Medal, National Police Service Medal, National Medal, and the Queensland Police Service Medal.

Lorraine Mazerolle is an Australian Research Council (ARC) Laureate Fellow (2010–15), a Professor of Criminology in the School of Social Science at the University of Queensland, and a Chief Investigator with the ARC Centre of Excellence for Children and Families over the Life Course. She is a fellow of the American Society of Criminology (ASC), the Academy of Experimental Criminology, and the Academy of the Social Sciences Australia, as well as the recipient of the 2018 Sellin-Glueck Award, the 2016 ASC Division of Policing Distinguished Scholar Award, the 2013 Joan McCord Award, and the 2010 Freda Adler Prize.

Renée J. Mitchell is a Police Sergeant in the Sacramento Police Department and the President of the American Society of Evidence-Based Policing. She is a Police Foundation Fellow, a member of the George Mason Evidence-Based Policing Hall of Fame, a visiting scholar at the University of Cambridge, and a post-doctoral researcher at Hebrew University of Jerusalem.

Alex Murray is Assistant Chief Constable (ACC) of the West Midlands Police. ACC Murray also founded the Society of Evidence Based Policing. The society is made up of police officers, police staff, and research professionals who aim to make evidence based methodology part of everyday policing in the UK. He is the organization's current vice chair and was awarded an Order of the British Empire in 2017 for his services to evidence based policing.

Peter Neyroud is the Deputy Director of the Police Executive Programme and a Lecturer in Evidence-Based Policing in the Jerry Lee Centre for Experimental Criminology at the Institute of Criminology, University of Cambridge. He teaches and supervises police students from across the world. His PhD focused on field experiments in policing. He was a police officer for more than 30 years, serving in Hampshire, West Mercia, Thames Valley (as Chief Constable), and the National Policing Improvement Agency (as chief executive officer).

Lawrence W. Sherman delivered the (Washington, DC) Police Foundation Lecture on evidence based policing that launched the field in 1998. In 2018, he delivered a two-decade assessment of the field at the (London) Police Foundation annual conference, celebrating the major progress in the field across the globe, while posing major challenges and opportunities to come.

Seth W. Stoughton is an Associate Professor at the University of South Carolina School of Law, where he teaches criminal law and procedure, and studies the regulation of policing. His work is informed by his own service as a city police officer and state investigator. He graduated from the University of Virginia School of Law, clerked on the United States Court of Appeals for the Seventh Circuit, and was a Climenko Fellow and Lecturer on Law at Harvard Law School.

Natalie Todak is an Assistant Professor of Criminal Justice at the University of Alabama at Birmingham. She studies policing, with a focus on qualitative and mixed research methods. Currently, her research focuses on police body-worn cameras and de-escalation tactics and training. Her work has been published in leading criminology and criminal justice journals, such as *Criminology*, *Criminology and Public Policy*, *Women & Criminal Justice*, and *Police Quarterly*.

Riley Tucker is a third-year PhD student in Criminology and Justice Policy at Northeastern University. His research is focused on how neighborhood context and social dynamics shape community and individual responses to crime. Additionally, he is concerned with evaluating the effectiveness of various community and individual crime prevention and reduction strategies. He holds a BA in Sociology from Temple University.

Adam D. Vaughan is a Health Policy Fellow with the Michael Smith Foundation for Health Research. Dr Vaughan's primary research focus is on understanding police interactions with the population of persons with severe mental illness and/or substance use problems. He also conducts research in the area of the mental and physical wellness of emergency responders. Recent publications of his work can be found in *Policing: An International Journal, Journal of Forensic & Legal Medicine*, and *The Journal of Workplace Behavioral Health*.

Tom Walker is a member of the Royal Canadian Mounted Police (RCMP) and is the Officer in Charge of the RCMP's National Use of Force Unit. Most of his experience is in operational policing and use-of-force training. Presently, Thomas is an MA candidate in forensic psychology at Carleton University.

Emma Williams is the Director of the Canterbury Centre for Police Research at Canterbury Christ Church University. She was a senior researcher at the Metropolitan Police Service for 12 years and at the Ministry of Justice for two years as a principal researcher in the Criminal Justice Reform Programme. She has experience of operational and action research focused on the needs of the practitioner. Emma is the south-east coordinator of the Society of Evidence Based Policing in the UK.

An introduction

Laura Huey

University of Western Ontario and Canadian Society of Evidence Based Policing

Renée J. Mitchell

American Society of Evidence Based Policing

One of the questions that both of us have been asked over the past few years is: "What on earth made you get started on this evidence based policing (EBP) stuff?" This question has variously been asked with tones of skepticism, wonder, casual or pointed interest, and/or a certain degree of head shaking. Although our routes to becoming advocates for a movement that promotes the use of quality research in policing are very different—Renée started as a police officer and Laura as an academic researcher—we shared a common belief early on. That belief can succinctly be captured in the phrase: "we suck."

For Laura, the pivotal moment came when asked to sit on an expert panel of the Canadian Council of Academies (CCA, 2014). The panel was tasked with the following mandate: predict the future of Canadian policing models based on the available research. There was only one small problem: chronic underfunding of Canadian policing research over the previous 30 years meant that the panel was unable to answer many basic, yet highly important, questions about contemporary policing. Predicting the future based on the Canadian work available would therefore be a nearly impossible task. Indeed, subsequent research into the size and scope of the canon of published Canadian policing studies revealed significant gaps in almost all aspects of policing, including training, recruitment, public oversight, operational issues, and others (Huey, 2016). The Canadian Society of Evidence Based Policing was launched in April 2015 as an effort to reinvigorate domestic policing research and spur home-grown innovation in the field.

Renée learned about EBP through a serendipitous meeting at a police conference with Jim Bueermann, the now-retired chief of Redlands Police Department and the current President of the Police Foundation. Learning that she was about to embark on a Fulbright scholarship with the London Metropolitan Police Service (Met), Jim connected Renée with Lawrence Sherman (the godfather of EBP) at the University of Cambridge, and Cambridge became Renée's host university and Lawrence her mentor. The Fulbright experience allowed her to learn about research methodology from Betsy Stanko's research team at the Met and EBP from Lawrence at Cambridge. At this time, she had been an officer for 12 years before she had ever even heard the term or knew that there was research on policing. Renée prided herself on being a progressive, educated police officer and could not believe that she had spent this long in her career not knowing about police research. It was in that moment that she realized "I suck." She knew policing had a long way to go when it came to advancing research in the field and had no idea where to start. With good academic mentors supporting her, she went on to implement her own research in the field (hot spots), do a couple of TEDx talks on the topic, and founded the American Society of Evidence Based Policing.

Why EBP, specifically? Why not just simply hoist a banner calling for more research, as some scholars have done? For both of us, the answer is simple: what makes EBP powerful is its emphasis on meaningful reciprocity—a central tenet of EBP is that it is important to grow knowledge within, outside, and across organizations through the sharing of information, local knowledge, and skills. While many academics recognize policing as a public good, and this somehow translates into unrestricted access for researchers to conduct projects as they see fit, they forget that *research is also* a public good. Research as a public good entails the creation of research products that can benefit the public by being actionable, useful, accessible, and, one might add, moderately intelligible (ie readable by more than three people, each trained in an obscure, specialist language). It should also impose on the researcher a commitment to pass along both research knowledge and skills to one's collaborators— after all, researchers benefit immensely from the time, energy, patience, and willingness to share cultural and local knowledge of the police officers with whom we engage.

Although we have been focusing on knowledge sharing as key tenet of EBP, it is, we believe, only one of four such guiding principles. As you will see in the pages that follow, as with nearly everything in life, there are multiple definitions of EBP. Fortunately, despite any real or perceived differences, each contains the following beliefs:

1. scientific research has a role to play in developing effective and efficient policing programs;
2. research produced must meet standards of methodological rigor *and* be useful to policing;
3. results should be easily translatable into everyday police practice and policy; and

4. research should be the outcome of a blending of police experience with
    academic research skills (Telep and Lum, 2014; Sherman, 2015).

It is these beliefs that readers will find interwoven throughout the various
chapters of this book.

Speaking of which, why this book? Over the past 10 years, the field of
EBP has grown substantially, evolving from what many saw as a novel idea
at the fringes of policing to increasingly becoming a core component of
contemporary policing research and practice. In support of this contention,
we need only look at the proliferation of EBP-themed studies, conferences,
research networks, research products, journals, graduate programs, and
voluntary associations (with Societies of Evidence Based Policing in the UK,
Australia, Canada, and the US), as well as, in due course, its likely inclusion
within university and college programs. We decided that the time was therefore
ripe to craft an introduction to EBP that would provide readers with a greater
sense of some of the concepts, ideas, and topics that animate the field of
EBP. To do so, we opted for an edited collection in the hopes that readers
would both enjoy and benefit from exposure to a variety of perspectives and
experiences from a diverse array of EBP practitioners.

We have divided this book into four parts: *key ideas*; *research methods*; *current
and emerging research areas*; and *experiences in EBP*. In organizing the chapters in
this way, we have tried to make it easier for readers to pick and choose among
topics of interest. Police practitioners, for example, might find chapters on
experiences in EBP or on emergent topics of immediate interest, whereas
some students and researchers might be more interested in key ideas or research
methods. In any event, we have tried to include something for everyone!

Key ideas

In this section, our authors explore the concepts and ideas that they see as
central to EBP and its practice. Renée J. **Mitchell** begins this section with
a brief introduction to EBP, as well as to some of the resources available to
practitioners and researchers alike. As EBP advocates, we have occasionally run
into some confusion about what EBP is and how it can be used. Identifying
and addressing some of these misconceptions is the focus of a research note by
Laura **Huey** and colleagues, a note that draws on the results of a recent study
of EBP practice across Canada. One principle among key concepts found
within EBP is Sherman's (2013) Triple-T approach to policing research, which
places equal weight on three distinct phases of a sound research program: the
targeting of problems; the *testing* of interventions; and the *tracking* of results
over time. We are fortunate to be able to include an informative overview of
the Triple-T approach by Lawrence **Sherman** himself, who explains that,
when "taken together, the Triple-T framework" that he elaborates upon

can provide significant insights for police decision-making that connect directly to better outcomes on every issue from recruitment to the police shootings of citizens. In the next chapter, Anthony **Braga** and Riley **Tucker** draw much-needed attention to the critical importance of crime analysis in informing evidence based decision-making. As these authors note, program evaluation is important for understanding "what works" in EBP, but so, too, is strategic crime analysis, which can play a key role in developing and supporting problem-oriented approaches to crime and community safety issues. Criminal justice—including the development and use of research to inform practice—operates within legal frameworks. Thus, if legislators and other public policymakers fail to understand and appreciate the importance of scientific-based forms of knowledge when crafting statutes and regulations, the ultimate usefulness of the research we create becomes highly limited. This is also the case with respect to judicial decision-making. Understanding and applying the relevant research on policing can help guide judicial decision-making and, in turn, potentially shape positive policing practice, but only if judges are exposed to the EBP approach. This concern is the focus of Seth **Stoughton**'s chapter.

Research methods

While much attention has been placed on the use of randomized control trials as the "gold standard" technique in EBP, the reality is that researchers and practitioners use a diverse array of research methods to answer the range of questions (and often thorny problems) with which police agencies grapple. In this section, contributors discuss not only the use of various methods in policing research (including qualitative research and systematic reviews, among others), but also, more importantly, some of the outstanding issues facing policing researchers. To begin these discussions, we turn to Emma **Williams** and Ian **Hesketh**, who discuss the use of social media as an avenue through which to gain access to not only police as potential participants, but also to police thoughts, feelings, and experiences through social media posts, blogs, and so forth. When people reference EBP, there is sometimes a tendency to think of it solely in terms of policing actions that are based on some form of research (which, unfortunately, frequently means one or two studies). When practitioners reference EBP, they are focusing on the *evidence base* as a whole, that is, the sum of all of the available studies on a given topic. In his chapter on systematic reviews, Peter **Neyroud** reminds us of the important role that rigorous reviews of the evidence base on selected topics can play in generating sound decision-making. For those with an interest in systematic reviews but a fear of anything remotely statistical, Neyroud also thoughtfully provides an easy to walk through overview of what systematic reviews are, and how they can be used. The importance of building evidence bases in policing research is highlighted in another chapter in this section by Craig **Bennell** and Brittany **Blaskovits**. In "Conducting open research in the policing field," these researchers discuss the open science movement and the potential effects of this movement on making policing research not only more accessible, but also more open to replication. Replication—the deliberate retesting of a study or experiment under exact or very similar conditions to confirm results—is what allows researchers to build a solid evidence base in any given area. The final chapter in this section is from Emma **Williams** and Tom **Cockcroft**, who examine the increasing role that police practitioners are playing in developing and conducting research. Following the EBP philosophy, these authors argue that academics need to involve police practitioners in all stages of research, including in the process of implementation, so that the impact of the research will not be limited due to a lack of understanding of both the institutional and cultural contexts of police work. Rounding out this section is a timely and important chapter by Barak **Ariel**, who speaks to the enduring quantitative–qualitative divide in research, reminding us that we need both approaches—singly and in combination—if EBP is going to reach its fullest potential as an important source in the development of policy and practice based on sound research.

Current and emerging research areas

The overarching goal of EBP is to understand "what works" in order to produce policies, practices, and programs that not only help policing to become more effective and efficient, but moreover increase community safety and well-being. To that end, EBP practitioners work on a number of important issues, from how to increase community satisfaction with police ("procedural justice") to how to most effectively deploy front-line personnel to deal with localized crime ("hot spot policing"). Within this section, we feature discussions with leading experts, who offer insights into both current areas of EBP research focus and emergent topics. Leading off this section is a chapter by Sarah **Bennett**, Lorraine **Mazerolle**, and colleagues, drawing on experiences of their work testing the use of procedural justice (PJ)-focused interventions with the Queensland Police. These researchers explain not only how they conducted randomized controlled trials into whether PJ-based techniques of interacting with the police can influence citizen perceptions of police legitimacy, but also highlight some of the challenges that they faced. For those seeking to learn more about how to engage in and test the effects of hot spot policing—the effective allocation of officers to high-crime areas—we also include a chapter from Renée J. **Mitchell**, who—as a police officer and then for her own academic research—has conducted hot spot studies in several cities. Mitchell walks readers through issues ranging from "officer presence" to explaining some of the subtleties found within the current literature on hot spot policing. A topic of much interest to police executives is the issue of mental health service calls, which continue to generate significant resource demands on urban agencies. Most of these calls do not generate official crime statistics and therefore remain largely "uncounted" when assessing the volume of and/or costs associated with police work. Adam **Vaughan** and Martin **Andresen** begin the process of unpacking the costs associated with mental health calls, demonstrating a methodology that can easily be replicated by police agencies across the globe. Another important area of research that has generated too little attention focuses on the question of how to embed "change" within police organizations and empirically evaluate the results (the "tracking" element of Sherman's Triple-T). Two topics of significant interest to policing agencies are de-escalation and body-worn cameras. In her chapter, Natalie **Todak** explores both topics by examining the potential benefits of using video footage to better understand the elements of skilled policing, particularly in real or potential conflict situations.

Experiences in EBP

As we have noted, a central concern of EBP entails recognizing the importance of drawing on practitioner experience in constructing testable solutions to policing and community safety problems. After all, it is the police practitioner who will frequently be involved in implementing new policies and programs. In this section, police practitioners relate their experiences of EBP, the knowledge they have gained, and the lessons learned. Thus, the chapters in this section will be especially appealing to those interested in the question of how to embed EBP within an agency. To help us move this discussion forward, we begin with Peter **Martin**'s chapter on the "inevitability of EBP," in which he argues for strong and effective leadership and dedicated funding to move the EBP agenda forward. Martin also notes, and this is highly important, that today's leadership needs to begin the process of training and mentoring successive generations of officers who are committed not only to police science, but to science more broadly defined. Drawing on the UK experience, and particularly on the facilitating role of the UK College of Policing and the Society of Evidence Based Policing in promoting EBP, Alex **Murray** writes on the need for structural forms of support for EBP, as well as home-grown efforts. Gary **Cordner**, who is working with the National Institute of Justice (NIJ) on initiatives aimed at improving the internal research capacity of police agencies, discusses a new NIJ program: the Law Enforcement Advancing Data and Science (LEADS) agencies. This is an innovative program within which the NIJ assists agencies seeking to become more "evidence based" through the creation and sharing of implementation tools and measures, as well as other materials, to help police services embrace better data collection, analytics, and research-based decision-making.

References

CCA (Canadian Council of Academies' Expert Panel on the Future of Canadian Policing Models [Beare, Dupont, Duxbury, Huey et al]) (2014) *Policing Canada in the 21st century: New policing for new challenges*, Ottawa, Ont: Council of Canadian Academies.

Huey, L (2016) "What one might expect: a scoping review of the Canadian policing research literature." Available at: http://ir.lib.uwo.ca/sociologypub/36/

Sherman, L.W. (2013) "The rise of evidence based policing: targeting, testing, and tracking," *Crime and Justice*, 42(3): 377–451.

Sherman, L.W. (2015) "A tipping point for 'totally evidenced policing': ten ideas for building an evidence based police agency," *International Criminal Justice Review*, 25(1): 11–29.

Telep, C.W. and Lum, C. (2014) "The receptivity of officers to empirical research and evidence based policing: an examination of survey data from three agencies," *Police Quarterly*, 17(4): 359–85.

SECTION I:
Key ideas

1

A light introduction to evidence based policing

Renée J. Mitchell

American Society of Evidence-Based Policing

Introduction

As discussed in greater detail in Chapter Two, one thing that advocates of evidence based policing (EBP) understand is that EBP is not a particularly well-understood concept by many. One cause of confusion is the term "evidence." Historically, evidence in policing relates to clues—that is, physical evidence of a legal case—rather than to research evidence. Introducing a new concept to a profession is always difficult, but the term "evidence" carries much more meaning to police. When introducing the term "evidence based" to medicine, social work or to any other field, the word "evidence" does not carry quite as much significance. The dual meaning of "evidence" for policing might make it an even more difficult concept to embrace. For example, during a police patrol hot spots study, only 24% of the front-line officers surveyed had heard the term "evidence based policing," even though the Crime Analysis Sergeant had explained what EBP was during roll-call trainings (Lum et al, 2012). It is unknown whether officers did not associate the term "evidence based" with research findings or whether they just tuned out during the training. Either way, officers should understand what EBP means and how to access it. This chapter aims to clear up some of that confusion.

This chapter gives a superficial overview of EBP. It skims the surface of police research to give someone new to EBP an idea of what is available to him or her as an officer, a police manager, a student, or even a civilian. It examines the convergence of different EBP definitions and, using the UK College of Policing definition, explores the strengths and weaknesses of different research methodologies. Without delving too deeply, I review the EBP tools available to the public and explain the EBP societies that work to advance EBP out in the field. For those who are interested in taking an active role in promoting EBP, in the pages that follow, I discuss academic–practitioner partnerships and taking a leadership role to promote a future of rigorously evaluated police practices and programs. Hopefully, some of this information will provide the EBP novice with a starting point for their learning.

Definition of EBP

In his analysis of scientific revolutions, Thomas Kuhn (2012) sets out the stages that occur to create a paradigm shift. Of these, Kuhn's "pre-paradigm" stage best describes where we are at with EBP. At the pre-paradigm stage, there are multiple theories or definitions being discussed among experts, from which the scientific community will eventually move towards a general consensus (Kuhn, 2012: 61). This is approximately where we are at with EBP. To illustrate, here are three working definitions of EBP:

> Evidence based policing is the use of the best available research on the outcomes of police work to implement guidelines and evaluate agencies, units, and officers using the best research. (Sherman, 1998: 3)

> Evidence based Policing is an approach in which police officers and staff work with academics and other partners to create, review, and use the best available evidence to inform and challenge policing policies, practices, and decisions. (UK College of Policing, 2018)

> Evidence based policing means that research, evaluation, analysis, and scientific processes should have "a seat at the table" in law enforcement decision making about tactics, strategies, and policing. (Lum and Koper, 2017: 3)

Notice that none of these definitions mentions data. Although data is a foundational building block of science, EBP is not data. We build hypotheses from the data and test them through research, producing findings that are termed "evidence."

Another common misunderstanding has to do with the word "base." While you can base decisions on the results of one study, we do not recommend this and, in fact, EBP advocates typically take a much broader understanding of what it means to be "evidence based." When we use the term "evidence bases," we are referring to the overall body of knowledge—evidence—developed from multiple studies examining the same research questions or issues (Greenhalgh, 1996). For example, when we say "hot spots policing works," we can assert this with some confidence because this conclusion rests on the results of the accumulation of all the hot spot studies completed to date (Braga et al, 2017). When enough research accumulates, a systematic review or meta-analysis will be completed on the subject area. This type of analysis will be discussed later in the chapter.

One important component of the College of Policing definition is the officer and staff working in partnership to "create, review, and use" the best available evidence, which is what the chapters of this book maintain. This is a critical juncture in the development of the EBP definition. The practitioner has to be included in the development of EBP. The College of Policing is the only definition that includes the practitioner. The chapters in this book were written by academics, practitioners, and "pracademics,"[1] demonstrating that first-line officers can and should have a say in how police practices are evaluated (Huey and Mitchell, 2016). EBP was developed from evidence based medicine (EBM), which has three fundamental principles; one principle of EBM is "evidence alone is never sufficient to make a clinical decision" (Guyatt et al, 2002: 8). Without the involvement of the practitioner, the EBP paradigm will be difficult to implement and maintain.

Using the "best available evidence"

If we use the College of Policing definition for the purposes of this chapter, then we have to ask: what determines the "best available evidence?" The UK College of Policing (2018) describes this as follows:

> "best available" evidence will use appropriate research methods and sources for the question being asked. Research should be carefully conducted, peer reviewed and transparent about its methods, limitations, and how its conclusions were reached. The theoretical basis and context of the research should also be made clear. Where there is little or no formal research, other evidence such as professional consensus and peer review, may be regarded as the "best available", if gathered and documented in a careful and transparent way.

The UK College of Policing states that the research question should determine the type of research method to be used. This is an important point because it validates the use of quantitative, qualitative, and mixed methodological approaches to answering policing research questions.

When examining quantitative research, it is a little bit easier to make assessments of the quality of research data because previous researchers have already developed evaluation tools to help guide decision-makers. Of these, I am going to focus on the Maryland Scientific Methods Scale (Maryland SMS). The Maryland SMS rank-orders research from 1 (weakest methods) to 5 (strongest methods) based on the quantitative methods used. The levels are as follows:

> Level 1: Correlation between a prevention program and a measure of crime at one point in time.

> Level 2: Measures of crime before and after the program, with no comparable control condition.

> Level 3: Measures of crime before and after the program in experimental and comparable control conditions.

> Level 4: Measures of crime before and after the program in multiple experimental and control units, controlling for other variables that influence crime.

> Level 5: Random assignment of program and control conditions to units. (Farrington et al, 2002: 13–21)

The fundamental goal behind quantitative-based forms of EBP is to find causal links between police interventions and crime or calls for service reductions. As evaluations move from a 1 to 5 on the Maryland SMS, the strength of the causal link increases due to reducing the number of threats to internal validity. Internal validity refers to the question "Does a change in X cause a change in Y?" (Farrington et al, 2002: 14). There are many variables that influence crime and calls for service. The goal is to construct the research method to find, as narrowly as possible, the link between X and Y. For example, a level 1 type of research is surveying officers after completing a training course. This measures the correlation between the training and the officers' opinions at one point in time. This is a weak research method because we have no indication if the officers' opinions changed from before they took the course. We do not know if the course influenced the officers' opinions. A level 2 research project would be the same training with pre- and post-surveys of the officers' opinions; this would be two measures at two points in time, but would have no comparison group. A level 3 research project would be comparing post-surveys of two or more groups of officers that received the training. The idea of a strong research methodology is to eliminate as many variables as possible that can affect the assumption that X causes Y. A level 4 research project would compare the pre-/post-surveys of the training group to a control group (no training). It would try to match the two groups as closely as possible on all variables that could influence the effects of the training, such as age, rank, time of service, or education level. The randomized controlled trial is the "gold standard" of research and is a level 5 methodology. The randomization eliminates selection bias and has the highest level of internal validity. The internal validity comes from randomly assigned individuals, groups, or areas. When the treatment and control groups are randomly assigned and there are outcome differences between the groups, then it can be said that the intervention *caused* the outcome.

The Maryland SMS has limited application for the UK College of Policing definition of EBP. The Maryland SMS does not have the capability to rank research that does not attempt to find a causal link. Police shootings are an area of research that cannot be randomized. The type of research methodology would depend on what question you are asking about police shootings. If trying to determine a causal link between use-of-force training and police shootings, then a comparison group between a shoot/do not shoot group may be found. If trying to determine why some officers shoot and some do not, then the research methodology might consist of interviewing officers about the context of the shooting, their mindset during the shooting, their physical ability, their past use-of-force incidents, and other variables that would influence their decision. Analyzing the interviews could determine if there were any variables that made one person more likely to shoot. This would possibly fall into a level 1 on the Maryland SMS or may not even make it to level 1. Police shootings, in addition to other issues in law enforcement, may not be viable for randomization, which is why the UK College of Policing advocates for the best methodology to be matched with the research question. The idea is to use the most rigorous research method possible to evaluate a hypothesis and to understand which methodologies are more rigorous than others.

In relation to qualitative research methods, there are (so far) no comparable evaluation tools or scales. In large part, this is because qualitative research does not aim to address causal questions, and so rank-ordering research methods based on questions of validity and reliability are less important. That said, qualitative researchers do pay an equally significant amount of attention to these issues and their importance in determining qualitative data. In making assessments of the merits of research evidence produced by colleagues, they also look at sample size (Did the researcher interview only two people out of a possible 2000?), the fit between the questions posed and the methods used, whether the findings are actually grounded in the data, how samples were located (Is there a self-selection bias that could skew the data and results?), and a host of other issues that might bias results (Did the researcher identify any areas of personal or other bias?).[2]

Overall, police officers should be knowledgeable consumers of research. Police management make decisions about what new software to buy, what training to employ, and what crime interventions to deploy. As stated by Neil deGrasse Tyson (2017): "To be scientifically literate is to empower yourself to know when someone else is full of shit." Being comfortable in critically evaluating programs, projects, and procedures through a scientific lens helps determine where to spend taxpayers' monies. Police departments are often the largest portion of a city's budget. Allocating police resources inefficiently can drain a city's coffers. Wisely choosing interventions that reduce crime or calls for service while spending less money is simply a better business model. Being scientifically astute allows police managers to decide which interventions have scientific support and which ones do not. Besides understanding how to evaluate a research project on its strengths and weaknesses, police managers should also understand how systematic reviews and meta-analyses fit into this determination.

One way of examining the evidence base for a topic is to search for a systematic review or a meta-analysis. A systematic review is an examination of all the research on a specific topic or question using predetermined eligibility criteria (Campbell Collaboration, 2017). A meta-analysis is like a systematic review but uses statistical analysis to determine the overall effect size of the cumulative research. An effect size is exactly like it sounds: a number determining how much effect the intervention had on the outcomes (crime, calls for service, recidivism). An effect size ranges from −1 to 1. A small effect is a .10, a medium effect is a .30, and a large effect is a .50. The systematic review of hot spots shows a small effect of .20 over 25 separate studies (Braga et al, 2014). An overview of all the systematic reviews in crime and justice can be found on the Campbell Collaboration's website.[3] There are 41 separate systematic reviews on the Campbell Collaboration's website under the crime and justice section. Topics include such areas as juvenile delinquency, police legitimacy, interview and interrogation methods, and problem-oriented policing (Campbell Collaboration, 2017). Many of the systematic reviews include plain-language summaries: two-page documents that explain the overall findings without the analytic and academic jargon. The Campbell Collaboration website is a good starting point for reviewing the academic literature.

The tools of evidence based research

There are a handful of tools that a practitioner can use to research evidence based approaches to police problems. These include the Evidence based Policing Matrix, the UK College of Policing Crime Reduction Toolkit, Crimesolutions.gov, the Problem Oriented Policing (POP) Center and the Police Foundation's Evidence based Policing phone app. Each tool has its strengths and weaknesses. One way to start problem-solving a police issue would be to use each of the tools to determine which one best suits the problem at hand.

The Evidence based Policing Matrix is a visual tool that maps the crime prevention studies that meet a Maryland SMS level 3 scientific standard onto a three-dimensional chart (CEBCP, 2017). The Matrix is maintained by the Center for Evidence based Crime Policy at George Mason University. The Matrix maps the studies three-dimensionally on three areas: the scope of the target; the specificity of the intervention; and the level of proactivity. The website explains how the studies are mapped, how the success of studies is determined, and where the "realm of effectiveness" is located. The site is easy to navigate. The symbols located within the Matrix denote whether the study had a backfire effect, positive effect, had no significant effect, or had mixed effects. When a cursor hovers over one of the symbols, the citation for that study will pop up. When the study title is clicked, the website will take you to a short overview of the study that discusses what the study was evaluating, the study methodology, and the results of the study.

Another easy web tool to use is the UK College of Policing Crime Reduction Toolkit. The structure of the website of this program based on the "effect, mechanism, moderators, implementation, and economic costs" (EMMIE) framework (What Works Centre for Crime Reduction, 2017) created by researchers at University College London: "effect" evaluates whether the intervention reduces crime or not; "mechanism" explains how the intervention works; "moderators" explain the circumstances in which the intervention works; "implementation" discusses what conditions to consider when implementing the intervention locally; and the "economic costs" section discusses the direct and indirect costs of the interventions. The website is searchable by the crime intervention type. It also has filters that can be applied to look at only the most successful interventions by type of crime. The Crime Reduction Toolkit, like the Matrix, has a short overview of each of the studies using the EMMIE framework. The Crime Reduction Toolkit website is user-friendly and easy to navigate.

The National Institute of Justice maintains the Crimesolutions.gov website.[4] This website evaluates over 500 police practices and programs. This website is useful as you can sign up to receive alerts. The alerts are sent when programs or practices are given an overall effectiveness rating. The website rates programs and practices as effective, promising, or no effect. This website also gives a summary of the program but is not as thorough as the Crime Reduction Toolkit website.

The POP Center is one of the longest-running websites and has the most in-depth guidance. The POP Center has created over 70 problem-specific guides. The POP Center does not focus specifically on evidence based approaches; thus, it is up to the reader to determine the level of evaluation that was conducted to determine whether the intervention is evidence based. The strength of the POP Center is the in-depth problem-specific guides written by experts in the field. None of the other websites contain crime-specific guides.

The last tool is the Police Foundation's Evidence based Policing app. This app was developed by the Police Foundation in conjunction with George Mason's Center for Evidence based Crime Policy and the International Association of Chiefs of Police. This app is constructed in the same way as many of the other EBP tools, giving the user access to research projects aimed at crime reduction, community trust, or organizational strategies. It also gives the user summaries of key studies in policing. This application is a phone-based app created for the front-line officer to use in the field. It is free and easy to use.

These websites are a good starting point for someone who is new to EBP. They give a good overview of how research is evaluated, what makes one research project stronger than another, and what works, what does not, and what looks promising. After a few hours on the websites, users will have a much better idea of the workings of EBP.

The societies of EBP

Another way to gain a foundational understanding of EBP is to join one of the EBP societies. There are EBP societies in the UK, America, Canada, Australia/New Zealand, and Spain.[5] The societies support each other but are not connected under an international umbrella. Each organization works to support its members through conferences, websites, research briefs, connecting practitioners with academics, and connecting members to each other. Connecting with other people who are knowledgeable about EBP is important. EBP is an emerging area in policing. Not many people have a thorough understanding of what EBP is, how to use it, and why it is important to the field. Building relationships with other pracademics, academics, and officers allows EPB knowledge to diffuse across the profession. These relationships are invaluable to an organization as the academic–practitioner relationship can lead to future ideas for research.

Academic–practitioner relationships

Academic–practitioner relationships come in a lot of different forms. There are casual relationships where a practitioner may have questions about a topic and they contact the academic for information. Academics do not have a thorough understanding of all police research. Most academics have a narrow field of research that they understand deeply. If the academic does not know the answer, they may connect the practitioner to another researcher who knows the topic area. Some relationships are more formal, as when an academic has a research project grant-funded with an agency. This relationship may have specific requirements for both the academic and the practitioner due to the grant. The relationship may only last over the course of the research project funded by the grant. If desired, the relationship can continue beyond the course of the grant and can be beneficial to both parties. The practitioner can help the academic connect with other agencies in order to pursue other avenues of research. The practitioner can also add credibility to an academic's presentation of research to other agencies. The academic can provide guidance to the practitioner on future evaluations or on purchases of new software. Practitioners can also learn from the academic about which evidence based practices work and which ones do not. The practitioner–academic relationship can be beneficial to both sides if each party tries to advance what is good for the agency and the scientific field at the same time.

What evidence based practices work?

There are a multitude of police programs and practices across the profession but we have no idea if most of them work. Here are some of the programs that have shown positive results for crime reduction: hot spots policing, focused deterrence, problem-oriented policing, directed patrols to reduce gun crime, using DNA for property crime cases, and focusing efforts on improving police legitimacy (Telep and Weisburd, 2012). Problem-oriented policing and directed patrols are a readily understood concept in policing and there are chapters of this book covering hot spots policing and police legitimacy; thus, a brief description of focused deterrence and the use of DNA for property crimes will be covered here.

Focused deterrence is an intervention that has been used to reduce violent crime, drug market activity, and gang crime by focusing on repeat offenders (Braga and Weisburd, 2012). The theory (deterrence) behind the intervention is that punishment should be certain, swift, and severe (Blumstein et al, 1978; Nagin, 1998; Apel and Nagin, 2011), with severity losing weight over the last several years (Nagin et al, 2015). The intervention focuses on repeat or violent offenders, making it clear that if they do not stop their behavior, they will be dealt with swiftly and certainly. The offenders are then offered social services to help them get out of the criminal lifestyle, whether it be gangs, violent crimes, or drugs. This approach appears to lower the recidivism rates of some offenders and reduce crime in the area where the intervention is focused (Braga and Weisburd, 2012). More often, this approach is used to reduce the harm to the community than to save one or two offenders from a life of crime.

The use of DNA evidence for property crimes is not a common practice in the US when compared to the UK. In a multi-site study, processing DNA evidence for property crimes showed an increase in suspect identification and arrest. Of the suspects arrested, many of them had twice the rate of offenses compared to offenders arrested through normal means (Telep and Weisburd, 2012). Although these results did not translate to lower property crime rates over the five sites evaluated, if the arrests continue to remove the top property offenders from the streets, the results may eventually translate to overall property crime reductions. Property crimes have one of the lowest solvability rates (Telep and Weisburd, 2012). Increasing the clearance rate for property crimes would be a benefit to any police department.

Why be evidenced based?

In this chapter, I have attempted to provide a general overview of EBP. What I have yet to do is explain why there is a need to be evidence based in policing. The importance of EBP lies in the premise that police should have an ethical duty to employ the best evidence based practices that reduce crime and calls for service while doing the least amount of harm to the community (Mitchell and Lewis, 2017). If police managers do not have a grasp of whether they are using the city's resources in the most effective and efficient way, then they are not using taxpayers' monies wisely. What duty does the police department owe to the public? Is public safety a sacred cow that is given a wide berth without determining cost, effectiveness, efficiency, or harm to the public, or should the police be held to a higher standard? Evaluating interventions should be part of standard police practice.

I am not alone in this view. Richard Nisbett (2015) has expressed similar views on the importance of being evidence based:

> Society pays dearly for the experiments it could have conducted but didn't. Hundreds of thousands of people have died, millions of crimes have been committed, and billions of dollars have been wasted because people have bulled ahead on their assumptions and created interventions without testing them before they were put into place.

In short, we must continue to rigorously evaluate our current practices. Police managers should understand what EBP is, how to apply it, and how to evaluate current practices. Understanding EBP is important for the future of policing and our communities.

Notes

[1] Practitioner–academics.

[2] For an excellent example of a discussion on assessing quality in qualitative research, see Meyrick (2006).

[3] Available at: https://www.campbellcollaboration.org/library.html

4   Available at: https://www.crimesolutions.gov/programs.aspx

5   See: http://www.AmericanSEBP.com, http://www.can-sebp.net and http://www.anzsebp. com

References

Apel, R. and Nagin, D. (2011) "General deterrence: a review of recent evidence," in J.Q. Wilson and J. Petersilia (eds) *Crime and Public Policy*, New York, MY: Oxford University Press, pp 411–36.

Blumstein, A., Cohen, J., and Nagin, D. (eds) (1978) *Deterrence and incapacitation: Estimating the effects of criminal sanctions on crime rates*, Washington, DC: National Academy of Sciences.

Braga, A.A. and Weisburd, D.L. (2012) "The effects of focused deterrence strategies on crime: a systematic review and meta-analysis of the empirical evidence," *Journal of Research in Crime and Delinquency*, 49(3): 323–58.

Braga, A.A., Papachristos, A.V., and Hureau, D.M. (2014) "The effects of hot spots policing on crime: An updated systematic review and meta-analysis," *Justice Quarterly*, 31(4): 633–663.

Braga, A.A., Turchan, B., Hureau, D., and Papachristos, A.V. (2017) "Hot spots policing and crime prevention: an updated systematic review and meta-analysis," paper presented at the annual meeting of the American Society of Criminology, November, Philadelphia, Pennsylvania.

Campbell Collaboration (2017) Available at: https://campbellcollaboration. org/

CEBCP (Center for Evidence-Based Crime Policy) (2017) "Evidence based Policing Matrix." Available at: http://cebcp.org/evidence based-policing/ the-matrix/

DeGrasse Tyson, N. (2017) Twitter communication.

Farrington, D.P., Gottfredson, D.C., Sherman, L.W., and Welsh, B.C. (2002) "The Maryland Scientific Methods Scale," in L. Sherman, D.P. Farrington, B.C. Welsh, and D.L. MacKenzie (eds) *Evidence based crime prevention*, London and New York: Routledge, pp 13–21.

Greenhalgh, T. (1996) "Is my practice evidence based?" *BMJ: British Medical Journal*, 313(7063): 957.

Guyatt, G., Rennie, D., Meade, M., and Cook, D. (eds) (2002) *Users' guides to the medical literature: A manual for evidence based clinical practice*, Chicago, IL: AMA Press.

Huey, L. and Mitchell, R.J. (2016) "Unearthing hidden keys: Why pracademics are an invaluable (if underutilized) resource in policing research," *Policing: A Journal of Policy and Practice*, 10(3): 300–307.

Kuhn, T.S. (2012) *The structure of scientific revolutions*, Chicago: University of Chicago Press.

Lum, C. and Koper, C. (2017) *Evidence based policing: Translating research into practice*, New York, NY: Oxford University Press.

Lum, C., Telep, C.W., Koper, C.S., and Grieco, J. (2012) "Receptivity to research in policing," *Justice Research and Policy*, 14(1): 61–95.

Meyrick, J. (2006) "What is good qualitative research? A first step towards a comprehensive approach to judging rigour/quality," *Journal of Health Psychology*, 11(5): 799–808.

Mitchell, R.J. and Lewis, S. (2017) "Intention is not method, belief is not evidence, rank is not proof: ethical policing needs evidence based decision making," *International Journal of Emergency Services*, 6(3): 188–99.

Nagin, D.S. (1998) "Criminal deterrence research at the outset of the twenty-first century," *Crime and Justice*, 23(1): 1–42.

Nagin, D.S., Solow, R.M., and Lum, C. (2015) "Deterrence, criminal opportunities, and police," *Criminology*, 53(1): 74–100.

Nisbett, R.E. (2015) *Mindware: Tools for smart thinking*, New York: Farrar, Straus and Giroux.

Sherman, L.W. (1998) "Evidence-based policing," *Ideas in American Policing*, Washington, DC: Police Foundation.

Telep, C.W. and Weisburd, D. (2012) "What is known about the effectiveness of police practices in reducing crime and disorder?" *Police Quarterly*, 15(4): 331–57.

UK College of Policing (2018) "What is evidence-based policing?" Available at: http://whatworks.college.police.uk/About/Pages/What-is-EBP.aspx (accessed July 12, 2018).

What Works Centre for Crime Reduction (2017) "Crime Reduction Toolkit." Available at: http://whatworks.college.police.uk/toolkit/About-the-Crime-Reduction-Toolkit/Pages/About.aspx

2

Targeting, testing, and tracking: the Cambridge Assignment Management system of evidence based police assignment

Lawrence W. Sherman

Universities of Cambridge and Maryland

Introduction

In the two decades since the Police Foundation in Washington first published the phrase "evidence based policing" (EBP) (Sherman, 1998), the "EBP" phrase has been used with increasing frequency in English-speaking nations. At the same time, the meaning of EBP has become increasingly muddy. There is little clarity, for example, about how to embed EBP in the daily decision-making of police agencies, let alone what it means for a decision to be "evidence based." The purpose of this chapter is to show how EBP can be used thousands of times every day in police operations by applying the three key concepts of EBP: targeting, testing, and tracking.

The plan of this chapter is to start with the finished product: an organizational model of an evidence based police agency, called the Cambridge Assignment Management (CAM) system. We then show how the Triple-T decision framework (Sherman, 2013) fits into that model, which is a 2017 product of my seminars with senior police leaders in the Cambridge University Police Executive Programme. The CAM system is designed to operate a police agency very differently from current models of policing (which can be called business as usual [BAU]). Unlike the predominantly reactive BAU model, the CAM system creates a systematic balance between proactive and reactive strategies for preventing crime and harm. CAM uses good data-analytic local evidence, and global research evidence (Sherman, 1998), to target, test, and track the allocation of police resources (Sherman, 2013), *both* reactively and proactively. The theory of using EBP in this way is that *the CAM system should yield much greater reductions in harm to victims and communities than BAU systems produce, for the same amount of money and police officers*.

While the CAM model of an EBP agency is still only a proposal, parts of it are already in operation in different British police agencies. The goal of CAM is to make EBP as much an automated system as a police call centre to which citizens make 999 (or 911) calls asking for a police car to be dispatched. The CAM system may also raise police decision-making to a more professional level, giving greater case-by-case discretion to police commanders and supervisors (and less to civilian telephone operators and dispatchers). Combining the best use of agency data and research from around the world, CAM uses algorithms to advise experienced police leaders and officers of the best options for action. CAM thus leaves final decisions neither to clerks nor to computers, but to highly trained police professionals. If implemented as described here, the adoption of CAM would be *supporting* a change in the ways in which police use good evidence for decisions, not just demanding it.

Policing with the CAM system

The CAM system is a process for allocating police resources according to a strategic plan for using the best evidence available for each decision to do, or not to do, something that they could do. CAM requires that a senior police leader provide strategic direction for such resource allocation decisions at all times (24 hours a day, 365 days per year). Working from a decision-making resource management centre, the commander would be tightly linked to the call centre and investigative and response units. This system, unlike BAU, allows the commander to achieve a continuous and evolving balance between reactive and proactive policing. As Figure 2.1 shows, it places the 999 (911 in US) and 101 (311 in US) call-centre function on the outer rim of policing, rather than at the core. It makes the minute-by-minute requests for service from the public only one source of information about harm in the community, rather than the primary source. That, in turn, allows the sense of urgency of someone complaining to be balanced against the needs and vulnerability of someone who is *not* complaining—but who may be at much greater risk of much greater harm—as identified by intelligence, algorithms, and other ways of targeting proactive policing.

CAM redresses the problem in policing of combining assessments of three distinct factors in resource allocation: threat, harm, and risk. If we define threat as how *soon* harm may happen, define risk as how *likely or probable* the harm is to happen, and the harm level as the *severity* of harm that may happen, we can use prior evidence to predict a separate score for each element. Yet, without that systematic evidence for targeting resources, threat–harm–risk combinations are merged subjectively by police dispatchers into a single decision. Past experience shows that in balancing those three elements of assessment, threat (immediacy) usually wins, at the expense of risk and harm taking a back seat.

The task of the evidence based algorithms processing every possible target for police actions is to *predict which targets have the highest risk of the highest harm today*, and which fail to meet some triage-driven threshold of limited resources. As the workload limitations may vary widely from one day to the next, there is great benefit in having a senior commander make real-time judgments about where to set the threshold. In the long run, even those judgments may be informed by evidence based forecasting. However, even in the long run, we will always need experienced professionals to decide what not to do as well as what to do. Applying the concept of a "power few" of the highest risk, highest-harm targets, police agencies can create evidence-based algorithms to provide a prioritized list of such power few individuals to the senior commander on each shift. Yet, the commander must make the final call, especially when surveying the whole landscape of police duties at any given moment.

The task of the senior commander at the centre of a CAM system is to use evidence based algorithms and other information to focus resources on overall *reductions* in harm, and not just rapid *responses* to reported threats. The commander's job would not be to decide where each officer should be working at every moment. Rather, the CAM operations commander would make hourly or even minute-by-minute strategic adjustments in resource allocations between proactive and reactive policing. This level of control would protect proactive policing from being diverted into reactive responses that may have far less value for harm reduction.

A classic example of this diversion is the interruption of problem-oriented policing (POP) plans for disrupting patterns of crime and harm (Goldstein, 1979, 1990). Neighborhood police teams that identify and target such patterns (with places, offenders, or victims) often complain that they cannot carry out the plans due to the constant risk of interruption of their proactive steps by a CAD assignment to answer a call for service. In a CAM system, a strategically focused operations commander can decide the number of POP operations that can be protected from dispatch assignments at any given time. This would give more strategic direction to dispatchers who would otherwise ignore the benefits of POP work since it is "not my job."

Similarly, assignments of follow-up investigations to neighborhood police teams could be balanced against the crime preventive work that such teams can do by patrolling crime and harm hot spots (Sherman and Weisburd, 1995; Telep et al, 2014; Ariel et al, 2016; Mitchell, 2017). The Kent Police, for example, have introduced one key element of the CAM system with an Evidence based Investigative Tool (E-BIT) for selecting out cases of non-domestic violence that, as good research by Kent Police showed (McFadzien and Sherman, 2017), are highly unlikely to produce a sanctioned detection. Based on the evidence based algorithm from research on over 1,000 cases, the Kent E-BIT for assessing the solvability of each case screens out approximately 70% of such cases to be closed after the initial investigation. From a CAM perspective, the E-BIT is not just advising what *not* to do; rather, it is implicitly advising what *better* things police can do with their time to prevent crime. However, as always, the E-BIT does not make the decision; a police professional would actually make each decision. The basis for the decision would be both the computerized assessment of the likely solvability of the case and other possible considerations, such as offender or victim characteristics in the case. The E-BIT assessment, for example, could be balanced against another tool which shows that the suspect in the case is a very dangerous offender. That fact could make the case much more valuable in harm prevention. Similarly, if the victim in the case is a repeat victim suffering high total levels of harm, the decision might be to investigate the case as a means of helping to safeguard that particular victim.

The core skill of operational resource management with CAM is a balancing act: learning how to divide investments in preventing harm across the three key types of targets for proactive police prevention activities—places, offenders, and victims. There is relatively little evidence from police research that allows CAM to compare the benefits of preventive activities for each type of target. Yet, the logic of CAM should lead police agencies to develop such evidence. This can be done by tracking the links between resource investment and harm reductions for each type of target. However, those investments can be made better from the outset with better predictive evidence for proactive policing.

The CAM system requires four major categories of evidence based prediction to support the operations commander:

- EBIT: evidence based investigative targeting for assessing the solvability of each case that could be given further investigation.
- EBPAT: evidence based place assignment targeting for high-risk crime harm locations.
- EBOT: evidence based offender targeting of the most harmful known offenders currently at liberty in the policing jurisdiction.
- EBVAT: evidence based victim assistance targeting to the individuals suffering the most harm from crime in the jurisdiction.

Figure 2.1 shows that all four of these predictive tools can come together in a single decision-making hub called a resource management center. That center can also combine these separate streams into EB-HART: evidence based harm assessment resource targeting. The EB-HART would be developed as the

Figure 2.1: CAM: evidence based resource allocation

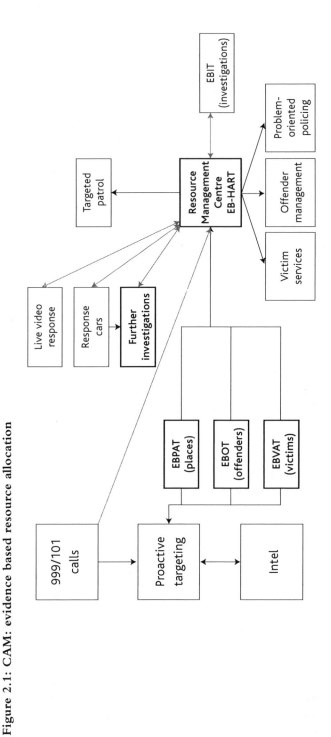

final stage of a CAM system, built from the extensive tracking of the links between resource investments and reductions in predicted harm guided by the four supporting predictive systems (EBPAT, EBOT, EBVAT, and EBIT).

Other elements of the CAM system also draw on new technologies, but they are less central to a police cultural shift to EBP. One key example is the testing of a video response unit, in which police would use the Skype features of smart phones owned by such a high proportion of the populations in the UK, US, and other countries. Instead of consuming substantial amounts of time for response cars driving to a location, the CAM system could assign a call to a video unit that would immediately Skype to complainants to see them, and even see a crime scene. This might lead to a final disposition without any car being dispatched, or a decision that a police car should go to the scene immediately, or that an investigator should make an appointment, relying on evidence from the Differential Police Response (DPR) experiments in the US in the early 1980s (McEwen et al, 1986).

The Triple-T foundation

Underlying the operation of the CAM system is the Triple-T framework of EBP (Sherman, 2013): *targeting*, *testing* and *tracking*. Both the demand for and uses of research evidence have become clustered around this strategic framework of three key principles:

1. Police should conduct and apply good research to selectively *target* their scarce resources on predictable concentrations of harm from crime and disorder (a "power few").
2. Once they choose their high-priority targets, police should use *tests* of police methods to help choose what works best to reduce harm.
3. Once police agencies use research to *target* their *tested* practices, they should generate and use internal evidence to *track* the daily delivery and effects of those practices, including the publicly perceived legitimacy of policing.

The growing focus on these three decisions has given shape to another three-part conception of the police mission, developed under the leadership of former Chief Constable Chris Sims of the West Midlands Police (see Figure 2.2). In the "big picture" of policing, there is a democratic consensus that the police must be both responsive and preventive, as well as trustworthy. Building trust requires engagement and reassurance. That, in turn, requires police success in predicting and preventing serious harm. However, when harm does occur, the police must be responsive in resolving and terminating the harm as quickly as possible, preferably with offenders brought to justice. Reading Figure 2.2 from left to right, we see the police seeking trust by both prevention and response.

Figure 2.2: Big picture of policing

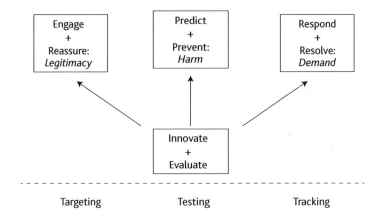

Reading across the bottom of Figure 2.2, we see the three foundations of EBP: selectively *targeting* scarce resources for greatest effect; *testing* what works best to achieve large effects; and *tracking* to measure and ensure that the police are doing what works best with those targets. Those foundations constrain all new innovations to satisfy not only a "what works" requirement, but also a requirement that police focus on high-priority tasks for harm reduction, and implement what they plan to do. These concepts and their relationships are woven throughout the CAM system for guiding police operations, with all its predictive algorithms and decisions.

Targeting resources

As Figure 2.3 shows, there are three key components of evidence based targeting decisions: identifying a power few, making predictions; and using triage to make decisions. These components are defined as follows:

- *The power few* is the small percentage of all the possible units of any distribution (ie places, offenders, victims, gangs) that recently *have accounted* for the majority of all the phenomena of interest, such as crimes, injuries, or crime harm (Sherman et al, 1989, 2016; Sherman, 2007, 2013; Dudfield et al, 2017).
- *Predictions*, for present purposes, are forecasts of the risk (defined as percentage likelihood) of any particular unit in a population (of offenders, victims, or places) experiencing a particular event in a specific period of future time, such as over the next year, month, or two years. This risk can be linked to any level of severity of harm of the predicted events, such as murder only (Berk et al, 2009), domestic abuse (Berk et al, 2016), or any crime at all.

Figure 2.3: Triple-T for EBP

Targeting	Testing	Tracking
Power few	Sample	Measure
Prediction	Comparison	Feedback
Triage	Integrity	Correction

- *Triage* is a decision to select some units (places, offenders, or victims) for attention while ignoring or postponing most other units due to insufficient resources for attending to all requests with adequate care. It is foremost a moral principle by which utilitarians value achieving overall harm reduction by investing in those units for which most benefit can result, as compared to doing very little for everyone but almost nothing well enough to make a difference.

The core point for targeting resources with these EBP concepts is that:

- the power few of the recent past may not be the power few of the immediate future;
- only predictions can identify a future power few, not just recent history; and
- triage is essential for reducing total harm.

A crime harm index

The most precise targeting of police resources requires a finely calibrated measure of not just risk of an event, but the severity of an event. Assessments of severity are often confounded by the frequency of events, which leads to many inaccurate predictions. One way to solve that problem is to use a crime harm index (Sherman, 2007, 2013; Sherman et al, 2016). A weighted index for all crimes associated with any targeting unit—offenders, places, or victims—can be achieved by a simple calculation. First, the index adds up the number of offences of each type (murder, burglary, car theft, etc). Second, it multiplies the number of offences of each type by the number of days of recommended incarceration for an offence of that type, holding constant the characteristics of each individual offender. Third, it adds up the results of all multiplications of offences by days of recommended incarceration across all offence types. The final sum is the "weight" of the index.

The applications for targeting are substantial. One police agency has already used the Cambridge Crime Harm Index to show that 4% of the victims in one year suffered 85% of all crime harm (Dudfield et al, 2017). Another agency is developing a power few list of the most harmful offenders over the preceding 12 months at the end of each month, which has strong predictive power for at least the next year in the future. Rather than using intuition, impressions, or biases in selecting such high-priority lists, the computerized algorithms for generating a precisely calculated list can provide much more accurate predictions.

Testing for outcomes

EBP requires high standards for drawing conclusions about "what works." These standards help define the huge difference between "trying" and "testing" an idea. Many police agencies say that they have "evidence" that a police practice "works" because they have "tried" it. Yet, in most cases, there is no good evidence of *impact on outcomes* gained from "piloting" a new practice just for "trying it out." The minimal standards of evidence from the kind of test that should be used to guide policy require the three elements listed in Figure 2.3: sample, comparison, and integrity. These concepts are defined as follows:

- *Samples* are the selected units of a larger population on which a policy, program, or practice is tested. Samples need to be as "representative" as possible of the larger population to which the tested actions would be applied. If the test sample is, for example, substantially worse, or better, or older or younger than the larger population, it is not a good basis for testing actions that might then be used with the larger population. Samples also need to be large enough and homogeneous enough to provide what statisticians call "statistical power," or the capacity to see a difference that is truly there. A bad sample is like a weak microscope: it does not allow you to see what is really going on.

- *Comparisons* are samples that are similar to the test samples but are given no police actions or even different police actions. The comparison of this sample to the test sample can reveal a difference in trends or harm levels, showing which sample did better (and by how much). In some cases, it can show that a police practice had no effect, or even had a backfiring effect. If there is no comparison sample, the only test possible is a before-and-after-action comparison of the test sample over time. The problem with that single-sample approach is that crime or harm goes up and down for many reasons, such as weather, economic trends, technology, or illicit drug use. Unless there is a comparison sample, any changes in the test sample over time can be merely due to chance.

- *Integrity* is a concept in testing that refers to whether the action was carried out as the policy required. If patients are supposed to take pills but they do not, the test of the effects of the pills lacks integrity. If police are supposed to patrol hot spots for 15 minutes but they only stay for seven minutes, that test lacks integrity. Even worse, if there are to be no extra patrols in some locations (for a comparison sample) but extra patrols occur, that test also lacks integrity. Without integrity, there is no (or much less) validity of the conclusions of any test.

Tracking police outputs and outcomes

Three key issues shape the growth of tracking police outputs and outcomes. One is how police leaders *measure* what police officers do. A second is how they *feed back* comparative measures of performance across officers to the officers themselves. The third is when and how to make *corrections* when tracking data show that police are not delivering the actions required with integrity. These three concepts are defined as follows:

- *Measures* in EBP tracking are ways of counting how much of anything the police are doing, often in relation to how much crime or harm is changing in response to police actions. We call what police do the *outputs* of police work, such as minutes of patrol presence, the number of street checks, the number and location of traffic tickets, minutes spent interviewing victims and suspects, and so on. The effects of these outputs on public safety and justice are called *outcomes*, arguably occurring as a result of certain outputs (or a lack of enough outputs). Whether or not those outputs should cause good outcomes is a matter for testing. However, for tracking, the key question is whether previously tested outputs have been delivered as assigned. For commanders to lead resource-allocation decisions, they require constant and precise measures of both police outputs and outcomes.

- *Feeding back* consists of supervisors or managers telling units and individual officers what they have produced in a given time period, relative to other units or officers—and potentially in relation to outcomes. It is rare in policing, unlike in medicine and in investment banking, for professionals to be told what their individual delivery of outputs has been. However, doing so is essential to ensuring the precise delivery of policing actions that are cost-effective. In testing terms, feedback is needed to create *integrity* as regards delivering what has been tested. Thus, when units or individuals are not doing what works, they need to be told that so that they will change their actions in order to create integrity. How that is done is itself a matter for testing. Telling them face to face, for example, was more effective than email messages in one recent test in London (De Brito and Ariel, 2017).

- *Correction* of failures to deliver required outputs can be accomplished in a variety of ways, ranging from carrots to sticks. There is little relevant research on what methods of correction work best. One example was reported in a recent Cambridge study of 10 local commanders in a non-UK police agency. After four of them consistently received feedback that the units under their command were not delivering the required number of (GPS-measured) proactive patrol minutes in high-violence hot spots, the four local commanders were transferred to other units. While the transfers corrected the integrity of police actions in that agency, a recent UK example in relation to turning on police body-worn video cameras (Drover and Ariel, 2015) had more mixed results.

The Triple-T in CAM

For over two decades, I have discussed EBP with enthusiastic police professionals. Thousands of them have joined the new, independent societies of EBP in the UK, Australia, New Zealand, Canada, and the US. What they all agree about EBP is that it is hard to do. The difficulty comes on many levels, starting with skepticism about the value of research evidence to inform experience and intuition. Yet, the greatest difficulty of all may lie in attaching evidence based analysis to every decision to assign police to particular actions.

This chapter defines the basic elements of a new system for attaching evidence to decisions. It shows how "big data" can be used to target police assignments (or not—with triage) based on predictions of the greatest concentrations of harm, using algorithmic advice for each case to manage both the proactive and reactive policing of places (EBPAT), offenders (EBOT), and victims (EBVAT). It shows how predicting investigative success with EBIT can reduce the wasting of resources on unsolvable cases, putting more police time into crime prevention or the investigation of more solvable cases. It shows how knowledge of "what works" from testing done in other agencies, such as the EBP Matrix (Lum et al, 2011; Lum and Koper, 2017), can be incorporated into decisions about what officers can or must do for both proactive and reactive assignments. It shows how tracking data can be brought back to a resource management centre for feedback and correction. Most of all, the chapter provides a blueprint for the much more precise management of policing actions and priorities in an era of budget cuts, allowing police to make transparent decisions in support of legitimate and effective policing.

What this chapter does not do is to spell out how to put these parts together in detail. That task must be accomplished in the field, through learning by doing. However, with the parts themselves on view for trials, we may now be in the position of the Wright brothers when they had glider wings, an engine, a propeller, and a steering system. Now, let us see if this plane can fly.

References

Ariel, B., Weinborn, C. and Sherman, L.W. (2016) "'Soft' policing at hot spots—do police community support officers work? A randomized controlled trial," *Journal of Experimental Criminology*, 12(3): 277–317.

Berk, R., Sherman, L., Barnes, G., Kurtz, E., and Ahlman, L. (2009) "Forecasting murder within a population of probationers and parolees: a high stakes application of statistical learning," *Journal of the Royal Statistical Society: Series A (Statistics in Society)*, 172(1): 191–211.

Berk, R.A., Sorenson, S.B., and Barnes, G.C. (2016) "Forecasting domestic violence: a machine learning approach to help inform arraignment decisions," *Journal of Empirical Legal Studies*, 13(1): 94–115.

De Brito, C. and Ariel, B. (2017) "Does tracking and feedback boost patrol time in hot spots? Two tests," *Cambridge Journal of Evidence Based Policing*, 1(4): 244–262.

Drover, P. and Ariel, B. (2015) "Leading an experiment in police body-worn video cameras," *International Criminal Justice Review*, 25(1): 80–97.

Dudfield, G., Angel, C., Sherman, L.W., and Torrence, S. (2017) "The 'power curve' of victim harm: targeting the distribution of crime harm index values across all victims and repeat victims over 1 year," *Cambridge Journal of Evidence Based Policing*, 1(1): 38–58.

Goldstein, H. (1979) "Improving policing: a problem-oriented approach," *Crime & Delinquency*, 25: 236–58.

Goldstein, H. (1990) *Problem-oriented policing*, New York, NY: McGraw-Hill.

Lum, C. and Koper, C.S. (2017) *Evidence-based policing: Translating research into practice*, Oxford, UK: Oxford University Press.

Lum, C., Koper, C.S., and Telep, C.W. (2011) "The evidence based policing matrix," *Journal of Experimental Criminology*, 7(1): 3–26.

McEwen, J.T., Connors, E.F., and Cohen, M.I. (1986) *Evaluation of the differential police response field test*, Washington, DC: US Department of Justice, National Institute of Justice.

McFadzien, K. and Sherman, L. (2017) *Statistical investigative triage: Predicting non-domestic minor assault and public order offence case outcomes at investigative assignment*, Cambridgeshire: Cambridge Centre for Evidence Based Policing.

Mitchell, R.J. (2017) "The Sacramento hot spots policing experiment: an extension and sensitivity analysis," unpublished PhD Dissertation, Institute of Criminology, University of Cambridge.

Sherman, L.W. (1998) *Evidence based policing*, Washington, DC: Police Foundation.

Sherman, L.W. (2007) "The power few: experimental criminology and the reduction of harm," *Journal of Experimental Criminology*, 3: 299–321.

Sherman, L.W. (2013) "The rise of evidence based policing: targeting, testing, and tracking," *Crime and justice*, 42: 377–451.

Sherman, L.W. and Weisburd, D. (1995) "General deterrent effects of police patrol in crime 'hot spots': a randomized, controlled trial," *Justice Quarterly*, 12: 625–48.

Sherman, L.W., Gartin, P.R., and Buerger, M.E. (1989) "Hot spots of predatory crime: routine activities and the criminology of place," *Criminology*, 27(1): 27–56.

Sherman, L.W., Neyroud, P.W., and Neyroud, E. (2016) "The Cambridge Crime Harm Index: measuring total harm from crime based on sentencing guidelines," *Policing: A Journal of Policy and Practice*, 10(3): 171–83.

Telep, C.W., Mitchell, R.J., and Weisburd, D. (2014) "How much time should the police spend at crime hot spots? Answers from a police agency directed randomized field trial in Sacramento, California," *Justice Quarterly*, 31(5): 905–33.

3

Problem analysis to support decision-making in evidence based policing

Anthony A. Braga
Northeastern University

Riley Tucker
Northeastern University

Introduction

Evidence based policing is based on the simple idea that law enforcement agencies should apply research knowledge to help guide strategic and tactical decisions. In his seminal essay on evidence based policing, Sherman (1998) suggested two dimensions of the approach that would improve feedback systems in police practices and facilitate learning in police agencies. First, police decisions should be rooted in the results of scientifically rigorous evaluations of law enforcement tactics, strategies, and policies. Second, internal and external resources should be used to generate and apply analytical knowledge to guide police decision-making. Decisions about what strategies and tactics to employ in any given situation should consider research evidence and analysis, as well as officer discretion, experience, and knowledge of the law and standard operating procedures (Lum and Koper, 2017). A substantial amount of effort has been made to develop stronger knowledge bases on "what works" in policing to guide the advancement of evidence based models (see, eg, Lum et al, 2011). However, our understanding of the role of problem analysis in implementing and sustaining the evidence based policing model in law enforcement agencies is still developing (Lum, 2013).

Problem-oriented policing seeks to identify the underlying causes of crime problems and to frame appropriate responses using a wide variety of innovative approaches (Goldstein, 1979, 1990). Problem-oriented policing is considered an evidence based practice as the available scientific evidence suggests that the approach generates crime and disorder reduction impacts when applied to targeted problems (Weisburd et al, 2010). Relative to increasing police presence and enforcement actions, problem-oriented interventions have been shown to generate more potent crime prevention impacts when used to address crime hot spots (Braga et al, 2014). The basic problem-oriented policing framework also undergirds focused deterrence strategies, which have been found to be effective in reducing crime committed by highly active groups of offenders (Braga and Weisburd, 2012). The analysis of identified problems and response assessment phases of the problem-oriented policing model fit well with analytical knowledge generation and program evaluation activities advanced by evidence based policing advocates. The lessons learned about the value of conducting strong problem analyses can be particularly beneficial to the continued development and implementation of evidence based policing.

It is important to note here that Sherman (1998) and Goldstein (1979, 1990) intended evidence based policing and problem-oriented policing, respectively, to be general approaches that could be applied to a wide range of police business problems. This includes non-crime problems such as personnel issues, budgetary concerns, and police–community relations. Most research and practical experience, however, has focused on applying these approaches to addressing crime and disorder problems (Braga, 2008; Lum and Koper, 2017). As such, this chapter largely draws upon these knowledge bases in making the argument that problem analysis should be considered a central activity in the evidence based policing model.

Problem analysis plays a key role in the successful adoption of evidence based policing within law enforcement agencies in two related ways. First, analysis aids implementation by tailoring proven tactics and strategies to local contexts and operational environments. Crime problems and organizational capacities can vary in important ways across jurisdictions and the crime prevention potency of proven programs can be undermined if implementers are not responsive to salient differences. In turn, experimentation with evidence based practices in varying settings contributes to our knowledge on the conditions and circumstances under which these interventions are successful in preventing crime. Second, analysis can provide important descriptive evidence to guide and focus new approaches when police are faced with emergent crime issues and there is a lack of empirical evidence on effective strategies and tactics. As evidence based policing advocates suggest (Lum and Koper, 2017), descriptive research evidence on crime problems provides police decision-makers with some much-needed information on innovative, and plausibly effective, ways to address new crime control challenges.

Problem analysis

The analysis phase of problem-oriented policing challenges police officers to analyze the causes of problems behind a string of crime incidents or substantive community concern (Eck and Spelman, 1987; Goldstein, 1990). Once the underlying conditions that give rise to crime problems are known, police officers develop and implement appropriate responses. It is worth differentiating problem analysis from traditional crime analysis. A survey of American police departments found that crime analysts tend to conduct tactical analyses, which are focused on short-term problems and day-to-day operations, such as target profile management, case management, and patrol strategy analysis (O'Shea and Nicholls, 2003). Tactical analyses are largely descriptive; they identify crime trends but do not explain the reasons for those trends. Conversely, problem analysis utilizes strategic analyses, focused on the long term rather than day-to-day operations, in order to identify the underlying causes of problems and the long-term solutions to address those problems (Boba, 2003).

According to the Centre for Problem-Oriented Policing (no date), the key elements of problem analysis are:

- identifying and understanding the events and conditions that precede and accompany the problem;
- identifying relevant data to be collected;
- researching what is known about the problem type;
- taking inventory of how the problem is currently addressed and the strengths and limitations of the current response;
- narrowing the scope of the problem as specifically as possible;
- identifying a variety of resources that may be of assistance in developing a deeper understanding of the problem; and
- developing a working hypothesis about why the problem is occurring.

These key elements of problem analysis outline a process where officers identify a specific problem and seek out diverse sources of information and data that can help them unravel the causes of that problem. By gaining a deep understanding of criminogenic factors and how agency policies succeed or fail to address those conditions, agencies can develop new strategies that effectively address specific crime problems.

Although the problem-oriented approach has demonstrated much potential value in preventing crime and improving police practices, research has also documented that it is very difficult for police officers to implement problem-oriented policing strategies (Clarke, 1998; Cordner, 1998; Braga and Weisburd, 2006). There is a tendency for officers to conduct only a superficial analysis of problems and then rush to implement a response. Goldstein (1990: 98–9) describes this as the problem of "ensuring adequate depth" in the analysis. To help avoid shallow problem analyses, officers should be paired with crime analysts, academic research partners, and "pracademics" (ie skilled officers with academic training) (Braga, 2008; Huey and Mitchell, 2016). Ensuring adequate problem analyses will better support police decision-making in the adoption of existing evidence based practices and the development of innovative responses to emergent crime problems.

The importance of problem analysis in the implementation of evidence based practices

When knowledge about successful crime prevention programs in one field setting is disseminated to others, there is a tendency for police officers to blindly adopt these "proven" responses rather than conducting the necessary problem analysis to determine whether the program fits well with the nature of the crime problem as it manifests itself in the operational environments of their cities. As suggested by Ekblom (1997), the fact that a crime prevention measure has proven successful in past circumstances does not guarantee its appropriateness in the future. On the surface, the problems may look similar. However, the circumstances may be different, the causal mechanisms might be different, and, therefore, the resulting outcomes could be very different. In his examination of the Crime and Disorder Reduction Partnerships mandated by the Crime and Disorder Act 1998 in England and Wales, Hough (2006) suggests that mistaking tactics for strategy caused the failure of the local police and their partners to produce crime prevention gains.

Implementation is critical to the development of the evidence based policing model in law enforcement agencies. It is not enough to evaluate what strategies work best when implemented properly under controlled conditions. Ongoing research is necessary to determine the results that particular police agencies are achieving by applying (or ignoring) the recommended practices. Some critics of the evidence based paradigm claim that it fails to adequately account for local context and conditions in reaching conclusions about what works (or does not work) (Moore, 2006; Sparrow, 2011; Greene, 2014). The main thrust of this argument is that unless local context and conditions are investigated, undue weight may be ascribed to any effects of the police intervention on the outcome of interest (usually crime prevention); taking account of local context and conditions in the implementation of new strategies is an important component of the evidence based policing model.

An ongoing challenge to the evidence based movement is the development of an accessible body of scientific evidence on what works best in crime prevention that can guide local police in targeting risk factors and tailoring recommended practices to local context and conditions (Welsh, 2006). Proactive efforts are necessary to direct accumulated research evidence into policy and practice via national and community guidelines. These guidelines can focus particular police agencies on in-house evaluations of what works best across agencies, units, victims, and officers. Local police departments can then apply problem analysis to best position their agencies to adopt evidence based practices. Detailed information on the local crime problem and its setting can be matched with proven practice, and modifications to recommended crime prevention strategies can then be made as needed. The combination of basic research on what works and ongoing analyses of crime problems that generate additional evidence on varied applications of specific strategies creates a feedback loop (Sherman, 1998; Lum and Koper, 2017). This process increases the amount of information available that documents how police agencies might obtain the best crime prevention effects. The review of this accumulated body of evidence may lead to the further development of practical strategy guidelines that take law, ethics, and community culture into account.

Sherman (1998) offers the policing of domestic violence as an illustration of the evidence based policing paradigm, which serves as an excellent cautionary tale about the need to do upfront analytical work in order to ensure that practices fit local context. The large body of available research evidence on police practices in dealing with domestic violence offers a fair and scientifically valid approach for holding police agencies, units, and officers accountable for the results of police work, as measured by repeated domestic violence against the same victims. The research revealed that police practices vary greatly in their implementation and that these variations generate differing results for repeat offending against victims. Even when varying practices are controlled for, responses to arrest vary by offender, neighborhood, and city. For instance, a series of experiments revealed that mandatory arrest and prosecution policies reduce domestic violence in some cities but increase it in others, reduce domestic violence among employed people but increase it among unemployed people, and reduce domestic violence in the short run but can increase it in the long run (Sherman, 1992a). The experiments also suggested that the police can predict which couples are most likely to suffer future violence.

Given local variations in domestic violence problems, the police need more options than simply mandatory arrest and subsequent prosecution. Rather than a one-size-fits-all policy, the evidence suggests specific guidelines to be used under different neighborhood conditions and the absence or presence of the offender (Sherman, 1992a, 1998). Structured police discretion that allows officers, after receiving training, to select from a range of approved options based on their assessment of the situation could be substituted for mandatory arrest laws. The available evidence could also support guidelines about listening to suspects' side of the story before making arrest decisions. Other policy options could include giving the police enhanced arrest powers in misdemeanor domestic violence cases that they did not witness, issuing arrest warrants for domestic violence offenders who are not present or flee the scene, and the development of special police units and policies that focus on chronically violent couples. Upfront problem analysis facilitates police decision-making on what policies and practices should be adopted in their jurisdiction. Furthermore, as the police implement and evaluate these new approaches in varying environments, they contribute to and continually refine the body of research evidence on best practices in dealing with the problem of policing domestic violence.

Problem analysis as scientific evidence to support new police practices

In his critical examination of evidence based policing, Sparrow (2009, 2011) examined the nature of analytic support required by modern operational policing. He advanced the idea that police departments employing multiple crime control strategies need to safeguard against rigid adherence to any particular approach that could result in a diminished capacity to respond to new and evolving crime and disorder problems. Police departments need to be creative and versatile rather than stagnant and inflexible. Crime problems need to be deconstructed through analysis and responses need to be tailored to underlying conditions and local community needs. Through institutional dedication to ongoing problem analysis, this view is completely compatible with an evidence based policing model. Police decision-makers need scientific information to help them figure out "What is going wrong?" when faced with new challenges that require an innovative response. Two classic examples from the crime prevention literature that illustrate the value of problem analysis in dealing with emergent crime problems are presented here.

In 1985, local police began an effort to address burglaries on the Kirkholt estate, a large local authority-owned estate in Rochdale, England, that had a domestic burglary rate twice as high as the national total (Forrester et al, 1988). After conducting interviews with burglars and burglary victims, as well as their neighbors, several patterns emerged from the data. First, analysis found that 49% of burglaries on the Kirkholt estate involved thefts from prepaid gas and electricity meters. Second, a pattern of repeat victimization was revealed: a residence that had previously been a victim of burglary was four times as likely to be victimized as a residence that had not been previously victimized. To address the problems of meter thefts and repeat burglary victimizations, the agency settled on four major policy initiatives: (1) remove prepaid meters from residences; (2) conduct security surveys of victimized residences; (3) develop a Community Support Team who would provide emotional support to victims and connect them to external organizations; and (4) facilitate neighborhood watch cocoons.

Upon implementing the policies, the agency created an electronic monitoring system that collected data on burglary offenders and victims by using members of the Community Support Team to conduct interviews. After a seven-month intervention period, analysis suggested that the Kirkholt estate experienced an 80% drop in multiple burglary victimizations and a 47% drop in burglaries overall, suggesting that the newly implemented policies served their purpose. The agency found further evidence that the intervention was responsible for the decreased burglary rate by comparing the burglary rate in Kirkholt to that in Langley, an area that did not receive the intervention. The Kirkholt Burglary Project illustrates how problem analyses conducted with novel data sources and variables are not only relevant to the identification of factors that drive crime problems, but also play an important role in evaluating whether or not new policies are effectively achieving their goals.

In 1998, as part of a larger effort to introduce problem-oriented policing practices, the Charlotte-Mecklenberg Police Department in North Carolina started a program that sought to address the problem of construction site thefts, which had arisen amid a housing boom (Clarke and Goldstein, 2002). In collaboration with academic researchers, the Charlotte-Mecklenberg research team chose to focus on thefts of appliances because the items stolen were often high-value but were easier for police to trace than other items that might be stolen from a construction site, such as lumber, scrap metal, and tools. The first step of this project was to create a data set of appliance thefts using past incident reports. Upon conducting an analysis of the appliance thefts, the research team found appliances that plug in to electrical outlets were far more likely to be stolen than appliances hard-wired into the building. Thus, the research team further defined the crime problem as thefts of plug-in appliances from construction sites.

Efforts to understand the factors that drive plug-in appliance thefts included the evaluation of risk factors using a data set built from certificates of occupancy—documents issued by the county that represent completed construction projects—as well as interviews with builders to evaluate their security practices. Analysis showed that some builders who delayed the installation of appliances had not experienced any thefts at their construction sites. The department recruited 12 building companies to participate in a six-month experiment that delayed the installation of all plug-in appliances and posted notices that there were no appliances on the premises. The research team evaluated the degree to which builders complied with these policies. Over 8,000 in-person checks were made to verify whether builders were complying with the crime reduction strategy. For the 12 builders participating in the program, the average builder delayed installation at 78% of their construction sites, compared with an average compliance rate of 43% for non-participating builders, suggesting that the agency intervention successfully impacted construction security practices. Following the experiment, analyses found that there was a 50% reduction in appliance burglaries compared with the two years prior, and that builders who delayed the installation of appliances effectively limited the risk of appliance theft.

Conclusion

A major contribution of the evidence based policing movement involves the important task of determining whether specific innovative policing programs generated crime reduction impacts. Rigorous evaluation research generally attempts to isolate causal relationships between programs and outcomes through the use of comparison groups and statistical controls (Shadish et al, 2002). Clearly, conducting isolated tests of specific interventions is critically important in developing a body of knowledge on "what works" in police crime reduction (Weisburd and Neyroud, 2011). However, in practice, research findings should be used to inform a general approach to crime reduction that includes a diverse set of proven practices but can also be flexible enough to understand new crime problems and develop appropriate interventions to address the risky situations, dynamics, and people that cause problems to recur (Sparrow, 2009, 2011). Police departments should be developing a strategic orientation to crime reduction rather than simply adopting specific programs and tactics that risk stifling innovation. The existing research evidence suggests a police crime prevention approach that focuses on identifying and addressing the "precipitating" causes of specific crime problems, engages the community and a broad range of governmental and non-governmental partners, and uses a diversity of tools and strategies, including but certainly not limited to law enforcement actions (National Research Council, 2004; Weisburd and Eck, 2004).

Developing and maintaining a strong analytical capacity within police departments is clearly essential to strategic crime prevention in an evidence based policing model (Sherman, 1998; Lum and Koper, 2017). A focused approach to crime reduction requires identifying high-risk situations, people, and places (Braga, 2008; Sherman, 1992b). It also requires developing an understanding of the underlying conditions that cause these identifiable risks to persist. Measuring whether implemented crime prevention strategies seem to be generating the desired crime reduction impacts is also important so that ineffective police strategies can be discontinued and more appropriate interventions can be developed. This orientation obviously puts a premium on systems of data collection and analysis, as well as on developing the human capital within police departments to carry out such analytic work. By virtue of their representation as patterns within commonly available criminal justice databases (such as arrest data, crime incident data, and calls for service data), these risks are easily identifiable through simple analysis. Through the collection of other data (such as offender and victim interviews) and more sophisticated analysis (such as social network analysis and geo-temporal analytics), the underlying conditions and dynamics associated with the genesis and continuation of these recurring problems can be understood. Training police officers in problem analysis, hiring civilian crime analysts, and developing strategic partnerships with external researchers will better position police departments to implement evidence based policing.

Problem-oriented policing is an evidence based approach to addressing recurring crime problems that complements the adoption of a broader evidence based policing model in law enforcement agencies. The adequate analysis of crime problems supports police decision-making in an evidence based model by tailoring proven crime prevention programs to local conditions and by providing much-needed descriptive evidence to inform innovative crime prevention practices when new crime problems emerge and existing crime problems evolve. As suggested by Lum (2013: 12), analysis "lies at the heart" of developing focused interventions and is therefore an important requirement for police departments carrying out evidence based strategies.

References

Boba, R. (2003) *Problem analysis in policing*, Washington, DC: Police Foundation.

Braga, A.A. (2008) *Problem-oriented policing and crime prevention* (2nd edn), Monsey, NY: Criminal Justice Press.

Braga, A.A. and Weisburd, D. (2006) "Problem-oriented policing: the disconnect between principles and practice," in D. Weisburd and A. Braga (eds) *Police innovation: Contrasting perspectives*, New York, NY: Cambridge University Press, pp 133–54.

Braga, A.A. and Weisburd, D.L. (2012) "The effects of focused deterrence strategies on crime: a systematic review and meta-analysis of the empirical evidence," *Journal of Research in Crime and Delinquency*, 49: 323–58.

Braga, A.A., Papachristos, A.V., and Hureau, D.M. (2014) "The effects of hot spots policing on crime: an updated systematic review and meta-analysis," *Justice Quarterly*, 31: 633–63.

Center for Problem-Oriented Policing (no date) "The SARA model." Available at: http://www.popcenter.org/about/?p=sara (accessed August 15, 2017).

Clarke, R.V. (1998) "Defining police strategies: problem solving, problem-oriented policing and community-oriented policing," in T. O'Connor Shelley and A.C. Grant (eds) *Problem-oriented policing: Crime-specific problems, critical issues, and making POP work*, Washington, DC: Police Executive Research Forum.

Clarke, R.V. and Goldstein, H. (2002) "Reducing theft at construction sites: lessons from a problem-oriented project," in N. Tilley (ed) *Analysis for crime prevention* (Crime Prevention Studies, vol 13), Monsey, NY: Criminal Justice Press.

Cordner, G. (1998) "Problem-oriented policing vs. zero tolerance," in T. O'Connor Shelley and A.C. Grant (eds) *Problem-oriented policing: Crime-specific problems, critical issues, and making POP work*, Washington, DC: Police Executive Research Forum.

Eck, J.E. and Spelman, W. (1987) *Problem-solving: Problem-oriented policing in Newport News*, Washington, DC: U.S. National Institute of Justice.

Ekblom, P. (1997) "Gearing up against crime: a dynamic framework to help designers keep up with the adaptive criminal in a changing world," *International Journal of Risk Security, and Crime Prevention*, 2(3): 249–65.

Forrester, D., Chatterton, M., Pease, K., and Brown, R. (1988) *The Kirkholt burglary prevention project, Rochdale*, London: Home Office.

Goldstein, H. (1979) "Improving policing: a problem-oriented approach," *Crime & Delinquency*, 25: 236–58.

Goldstein, H. (1990) *Problem-oriented policing*, Philadelphia, PA: Temple University Press.

Greene, J.R. (2014) "New directions in policing: balancing prediction and meaning in police research," *Justice Quarterly*, 31: 193–228.

Hough, M. (2006) "Not seeing the wood for the trees: mistaking tactics for strategy in crime reduction initiatives," in J. Knutsson and R.V. Clarke (eds) *Putting theory to work: Implementing situational prevention and problem-oriented policing*, Monsey, NY: Criminal Justice Press, pp 139–62.

Huey, L. and Mitchell, R. (2016) "Unearthing hidden keys: why pracademics are an invaluable (if underutilized) resource in policing research," *Policing*, 10(3): 300–7.

Lum, C. (2013) "Is crime analysis 'evidence based'?" *Translational Criminology*, Fall: 12–14.

Lum, C. and Koper, C. (2017) *Evidence based policing: Translating research into practice*, New York, NY: Oxford University Press.

Lum, C., Koper, C., and Telep, C. (2011) "The evidence based policing matrix," *Journal of Experimental Criminology*, 7: 3–26.

Moore, M.H. (2006) "Improving police through expertise, experience, and experiments," in D. Weisburd and A. Braga (eds) *Police innovation: Contrasting perspectives*, New York, NY: Cambridge University Press, pp 322–38.

National Research Council (2004) *Fairness and effectiveness in policing: The evidence*, Committee to Review Research on Police Policy and Practices, Committee on Law and Justice, Division of Behavioral and Social Sciences and Education, Washington, DC: The National Academies Press.

O'Shea, T. and Nicholls, K. (2003) "Police crime analysis: a survey of US police departments with 100 or more sworn personnel," *Police Practice and Research*, 4(3): 233–50.

Shadish, W., Cook, T., and Campbell, D. (2002) *Experimental and quasi-experimental designs for generalized causal inference*, Belmont, CA: Wadsworth.

Sherman, L. (1992a) *Policing domestic violence*, New York, NY: The Free Press.

Sherman, L. (1992b) "Attacking crime: police and crime control," in M. Tonry and N. Morris (eds) *Modern policing* (Crime and Justice Series, vol 15), Chicago, IL: University of Chicago Press.

Sherman, L.W. (1998) *Evidence based policing* (Ideas in American Policing Series), Washington, DC: Police Foundation.

Sparrow, M. (2009) "One week in Heron City (parts A and B)," *New Perspectives in Policing*, Washington, DC: National Institute of Justice, U.S. Department of Justice.

Sparrow, M. (2011) *Governing science: New perspectives in policing*, Washington, DC: National Institute of Justice, U.S. Department of Justice.

Weisburd, D.L. and Eck, J. (2004) "What can police do to reduce crime, disorder, and fear?" *Annals of the American Academy of Political and Social Science*, 593: 42–65.

Weisburd, D.L. and Neyroud, P. (2011) "Police science: toward a new paradigm," *New perspectives in policing*, Washington, DC: National Institute of Justice, U.S. Department of Justice.

Weisburd, D., Telep, C., Hinkle, J., and Eck, J. (2010) "Is problem oriented policing effective in reducing crime and disorder?" *Criminology & Public Policy*, 9: 139–72.

Welsh, B.C. (2006) "Evidence based policing for crime prevention," in D. Weisburd and A. Braga (eds) *Police innovation: Contrasting perspectives*, New York, NY: Cambridge University Press, pp 305–21.

4

The legal framework for evidence based policing in the US

Seth W. Stoughton
University of South Carolina

Introduction

Police officers do not typically enjoy paperwork. Writing reports is widely viewed as a mind-numbingly tedious part of the job, one that often requires officers to spend hours providing redundant recitations of the same information on different forms. A simple low-level arrest may give rise to an incident report, an arrest report, a probable cause affidavit, a use-of-force report, an evidence report, a criminal intelligence report, an entry on an activity log, and so on. Officers who are purportedly supposed to be responding to calls for service or engaging in proactive policing instead spend a substantial portion of each work day bogged down with report writing and other administrative tasks. Why? Why would police executives require officers to spend so much time and effort on such an unpleasant task?

With a few notable exceptions, there are no statutes or other legal mandates that obligate officers to provide voluminous records of their activities. However, while "law" is definitively not the answer, the legal system is—at least, it is a large part of the answer. Police reports play a crucial role in a variety of legal proceedings. Criminally, the reports are central to a prosecutor's decisions about whether to file charges and which charges to file, the defense attorney's development of trial strategy, and the officer's ability to refresh their memory before testifying. Civilly, the reports are a vital component of resolving any claims leveled against the officer, from complaints of excessive force to accusations of theft. In short, even without any statutory requirements, the legal system still provides a range of incentives that encourage officers to create a robust written record of their observations and actions. Without those incentives, officers simply would not put the time and effort into documenting their activities.

Police reports provide a useful contrast to evidence based policing practices. As with written reports, there are no legal mandates that require evidence based policing. However, unlike written reports, the legal system provides little in the way of incentives. If anything, the contemporary legal system discourages the widespread adoption of this promising methodology. This is not to say that legal incentives are necessary to prompt the adoption of evidence based policing, nor that they are sufficient to ensure that every police agency does so. Some agencies will put themselves on the forefront by adopting evidence based practices even in the absence of appropriate incentives from the legal system—indeed, they have already done so. In the same vein, some agencies will resist evidence based practices even after there are clear legal benefits. Most agencies, however, will fall between these two extremes, as unlikely to rush toward adoption as they are to resist all pressures. It is precisely these agencies—which likely make up the bulk of the profession— that require incentives such as those that the legal system can provide before they shift to evidence based policing. This chapter examines the existing legal framework for evidence based policing in the US, identifying three areas in which contemporary constitutional and sub-constitutional law create obstacles to evidence based policing and exploring how reforms to the legal system could instead create incentives.

First, constitutional decision-making by the Supreme Court is often predicated on the justices' understanding of police practices and the environment in which officers operate. The Court has proven willing to rely on its own factual assumptions even when there is a noticeable lacuna of evidence that support its assertions. With the improved availability of information, evidence based policing can offer the Court and other judicial decision-makers a more robust and accurate understanding of the world that they are regulating. In the same vein, courts can inspire police agencies to adopt evidence based practices by relying more heavily on reliably gathered data rather than anecdotes and speculation.

Second, when officers testify, they are often asked to provide both their first-hand observations and their professional opinions about various matters. Such opinions, including expert opinions, are typically grounded in officers' "training and experience." In many cases, however, that training and experience may not support the inference of reliability that expert testimony properly demands. With a rigorous and methodologically sound approach to developing information, opinions grounded in evidence based practices and instruction would be substantially more dependable than opinions based on more traditional forms of instruction.

Third, and finally, the legal rules that restrict or permit the introduction of a variety of other forms of evidence can be leveraged to encourage evidence based policing practices. In the absence of an evidence based approach to analyzing forensic evidence, eyewitness identification, interrogation procedures, and other sources of information, policing as an industry has had little reason to keep abreast of best practices. Through their adoption of an evidence based inquiry, courts are in a position to create incentives that could dramatically improve police procedures.

Judicial presumptions about policing

The constitutional rules that regulate policing in the US do not allow officers to use their coercive authority without reason. The Supreme Court has made clear that official intrusions into liberty, privacy, and autonomy must be based on more than mere hunches, subjective beliefs, and speculation; instead, they must be justified by objectively reasonable conclusions grounded in specific and articulable facts. This makes good sense. Constraining the power of government vis-a-vis the citizenry is fundamental to the concept of democratic freedom in the US. Yet, the Court does not hold itself to the same standard when it goes about developing the constitutional rules that regulate policing. When the Court creates, modifies, or eliminates a legal doctrine, it acts on its understanding of policing, an understanding that is eminently observable in judicial opinions in the form of factual assertions. Those assertions include generalizations about the environment in which officers work, descriptions of common police practices, statements about officer motivations, predictions about how officers will respond to proposed legal rules, and so on. Unfortunately, the Court often fails to base its factual assertions on any reliable authority. Instead, as legal scholar David L. Faigman (1991: 45) has written, "[M]ost constitutional fact-finding depend[s] on the [Court's] best guess about the matter."

I do not mean to suggest that the Court's unsupported factual assertions are invariably incorrect; that is certainly not the case. There are any number of examples where the Court's failure to identify the source of its information is easy to overlook because the underlying suppositions are unobjectionable generalizations. For example, the Court was entirely right when it wrote:

> Police officers engaged in the dangerous and difficult tasks associated with protecting the safety of our communities not only confront the risk of physical harm but also face stressful circumstances that may give rise to anxiety, depression, fear, or anger. (*Jaffee v. Redmond*, 1996)

In the same vein, the Court was doubtlessly correct when it observed: "[t]hat most law enforcement officers are armed is a fact well known to the public" (*United States v. Drayton*, 2002). On other occasions, the Court has made commodious assertions that are far more specific. For example, the Court concluded that, as a rule, 15 to 20 seconds was "sufficient" for the occupant of a home, alerted to the presence of officers outside, to "get to the bathroom or the kitchen to start flushing [narcotics] down the drain" (*United States v. Banks*, 2003). Although the accuracy of that assertion may be fairly debated in any specific case, it is, on its face, at least plausible.

However, not all the Court's assertions can be taken at face value. There are also a number of legal doctrines that the Court has built on shaky factual foundations. In several contexts, for example, the Court has held that the inherent dangerousness of police activity can be mitigated by allowing officers to establish and exercise "unquestioned command" over the individuals with whom they are interacting (*Muehler v. Mena*, 2005; *Brendlin v. California*, 2007; *Arizona v. Johnson*, 2009). Police scholars and policing commissions, however, have identified how an officer's expectations of and demands for compliance—often referred to in policing as "command presence"—can give rise to avoidable conflicts, increasing the danger to officers and civilians alike (Stoughton, 2017). Other important doctrines have been similarly predicated on highly questionable factual suppositions, including the rules that regulate consent searches, the use of force, and the admissibility of unlawfully gathered evidence. Further, the Court has regularly both rejected proposed rules that it believes would hamper effective policing and justified its articulation of a rule with the explanation that it would *not* impede law enforcement efforts, often with very little attempt to gather reliable information about what effective policing may or may not require (Stoughton, 2014).

The body of constitutional case law amply demonstrates the Court's willingness to rely on unsupported factual propositions of its own devising. As Kenneth Culp Davis (1986) observed more than 30 years ago: "When the Court lacks the needed information, it usually makes guesses." Those guesses hardly encourage the adoption of evidence based policing. Indeed, it may stand as a disincentive: why would an agency, practitioner, or academic dedicate the time, effort, and money to developing an empirically sound understanding of policing if the single most important constitutional law-making body in the country will blithely reject reliable findings in favor of its own unsupported presumptions?

Buried in the challenge is a kernel of opportunity. The Court *can* correct its inaccurate factual assertions. It has already done so. For almost 30 years, officers were permitted to search the passenger compartment of a vehicle after arresting a vehicle occupant because, the Court originally believed, it was necessary for officer safety: arrestees were thought to be in a position where they could easily reach into the vehicle to obtain a weapon (*New York v. Belton*, 1981). Eventually, the Court relied on multiple lower court cases and an academic treatise in coming to the conclusion that its earlier beliefs were "unfounded" and "faulty"; instead, the Court wrote, "it will be the rare case in which an officer is unable to fully effectuate an arrest so that a real possibility of access to the arrestee's vehicle remains" (*Arizona v. Gant*, 2009).

Further, the Court has demonstrated that it is entirely capable of avoiding inaccuracy altogether by basing its assertions on reliable authorities that arise out of policing itself. In *Miranda v. Arizona*, the case that gave rise to the now-famous "*Miranda* Warning" that officers must provide prior to custodial interrogations, the Court discussed both historical and contemporary interrogation practices, bolstering its descriptions with citations to six police training manuals, three books about policing, eight academic articles, three news articles, reports by two different commissions that studied policing, and 23 prior cases in federal and state courts (*Miranda v. Arizona*, 1966). When the Court developed the *Miranda* Warning itself, it drew on interrogation procedures used by the Federal Bureau of Investigation (FBI), as well as the laws regulating police interrogations in England, Scotland, India, and Sri Lanka (then known as Ceylon) (*Miranda v. Arizona*, 1966). Similarly, in the Court's groundbreaking foray into the constitutionality of officers' use of deadly force, the Court rejected the common law rule that authorized officers to use deadly force to prevent the escape of fleeing felons in large part because, it concluded, officers simply did not need that authority. It based that conclusion on: policies at the FBI, the New York Police Department, and 44 other police agencies; research by the Boston Police Department's Planning and Research Division and by the International Association of Chiefs of Police; and the industry best practices suggested by the Police Foundation and the Commission on the Accreditation for Law Enforcement Agencies (*Tennessee v. Garner*, 1985).

To best incentivize the widespread adoption of evidence based policing practices, the Supreme Court should hew to the path it charted in *Miranda v. Arizona* and *Tennessee v. Garner*: basing its factual assertions about policing on empirically sound studies and knowledge reliably developed within the profession itself. Doing so would create a strong incentive for agencies, professional associations, and reformers to support their legal arguments with empirically valid research. That, in turn, would lead to more efficacious rule-making by the Supreme Court.

Officers as experts

The rules of evidence in US courts draw a distinction between lay witnesses and expert witnesses. Lay witnesses testify primarily about their own perceptions; they are permitted to offer their opinion only when the opinion is rationally based on their own perceptions and the opinion is helpful in clarifying their testimony or resolving a factual question (Federal Rule of Evidence 701). A lay witness's opinion must be grounded in "reasoning familiar in everyday life" (Advisory Committee Notes to Federal Rule of Evidence 701). For example, a lay witness who was testifying about a fight could describe the incident (relying on their first-hand perception) and identify which one of the combatants was the aggressor (by using everyday reasoning to form an opinion based on their first-hand perception). Expert witnesses, in contrast, are permitted to offer opinions grounded in their scientific, technical, or other specialized knowledge, skill, experience, training, or education. Experts need not have any first-hand knowledge of the events about which they are forming an opinion; instead, they contribute to the jury's understanding of the incident by providing insights "from a process of reasoning which can be mastered only by specialists in the field" (Advisory Committee Notes to Federal Rule of Evidence 702). A medical expert testifying about the fight could, for example, opine on whether a particular blow was likely to cause serious bodily harm, while a vision scientist or cognitive psychologist could testify as to whether, given distance and lighting, the lay witness could really have seen and properly remembered what they testified about.

Police officers regularly testify as both lay witnesses and experts, and "[c]ourts have often struggled to draw definitive lines between law and expert police opinion testimony" (Stoughton, 2015: 447). Consider, for example, that in the scope of a trial for drug dealing, an officer's testimony might reflect watching a hand-to-hand transaction, concluding that an individual was a drug dealer, arresting the individual, finding drugs on the arrestee, and concluding that the arrestee was carrying a quantity of drugs that is consistent with dealing but not personal use. In some jurisdictions, the entirety of an officer's testimony may constitute lay testimony; in others, the officer would have to qualify as an expert before offering opinions about criminal behavior or drug quantities.

That distinction matters. Anyone with first-hand knowledge can be accepted as a lay witness, but courts actively vet expert witnesses' qualifications to ensure that the witness truly is an expert. The legal system puts tremendous weight on experts' shoulders; they can rely on information that would not be admissible in court and render opinions without any first-hand knowledge precisely because the legal system trusts them to be able to do so reliably. Courts, then, are supposed to ensure that the witness's purported expertise satisfies that heavy burden. For experts who are testifying on the basis of scientific or technical knowledge, this requires a relatively straightforward, if multifaceted, analysis that focuses on, among other things, whether the witness's opinion is "based on sufficient facts or data," whether it is "the product of reliable principles and methods," whether the expert's methodology has been "reliably applied … to the facts of the case," and so on (Federal Rule of Evidence 702). The Advisory Committee notes suggest a series of additional considerations that can help a judge determine whether proffered expert testimony is reliable, including whether the witness made an unfounded jump from premise to conclusion, whether the expert has accounted for alternative explanations, and so on.

Some police expert testimony can be described as scientific or technical—accident reconstruction or the manufacture of narcotics, for example—but most of it falls under a different category: "specialized knowledge." Unfortunately, there is no straightforward analysis that courts can use to readily identify individuals who have sufficiently reliable and specialized knowledge such that they should be accepted as experts. In the context of policing, courts tend to abandon the multi-factor analysis used for scientific and technical experts and instead recite the number of years of experience an officer has, their current and former job assignments, and any special training that the officer has received. Training and experience serve as the foundations of police expertise because the courts accept them as reliable.

This approach can be problematic; a substantial amount of police training is simply not empirically valid, and officers' experiences are often colored by motivated reasoning and other cognitive biases. Police training in the United States is heavily anecdotal; in some ways, it more closely resembles an oral tradition than a formal mechanism for passing along reliable information. Researchers have not studied every aspect of policing, yet what research there is tends to be ignored or discounted in police training. Within the culture of policing, information that originates on the street is inherently more reliable than information from other sources, especially academic studies (Harris, 2012). The lack of a reliable foundation should be deeply troubling; a court would be remiss if it qualified a witness as an expert based on their incidental exposure to casual information over the course of their careers, yet that is how a significant amount of knowledge is disseminated in policing.

As with the Supreme Court's factual assertions about policing, it is probably the case that a significant proportional of "cop knowledge" is accurate, but the mechanism through which information is developed and transmitted not only makes verification difficult, but also almost guarantees the introduction and perpetuation of inaccuracy. In the March 2014 issue of the *American Bar Association Journal*, for example, the President of the New York City Patrolmen's Benevolent Association described how officers could identify a person carrying a weapon: "[T]hey tend to be heavy on one side. They're nervous and repeatedly tap the area." Maybe, but that inherently empirical assertion was made without any attempt at validation—we do not know, for example, how often people engage in the same behaviors when they are not carrying a weapon or how often people who are carrying a weapon *do not* engage in those behaviors. That, of course, is only the tip of the iceberg. Popular police-oriented media publications like *American Police Beat* and *Police Magazine* are filled with unsupported and often questionable factual assertions. Formal police training includes instruction on: how to recognize criminal activity, deception, and imminent violence; how to interact with juveniles, civilians from other countries, and individuals of different socio-economic classes; patrol tactics that can reduce crime; hand-to-hand combative techniques that can overcome resistance; and mindsets that can promote officer safety, just to name a few.

The judicial tendency to qualify officers as experts on the basis of their vacuously stated "training and experience" fails to satisfy the requisite level of reliability that expert testimony demands. Further, it fails to provide any incentive, and may create a disincentive, to adopt an evidence based approach to policing. This, too, is a problem that can be addressed. A more searching judicial inquiry could distinguish between expert testimony that is grounded in some reliable methodology and that which is grounded in the traditional perpetuation of unreliable information. By demanding that proffered police experts establish that there is a reliable basis for their opinions, the courts could create an incentive for officers and agencies to adopt evidence based practices that can withstand judicial scrutiny.

Validating investigative methods

The criminal justice system has, over the years, evolved an ever-more sophisticated understanding of the types and sources of information that should be accepted as evidence. Hundreds of years ago, trial by combat or by ordeal were believed to constitute reliable evidence upon which the legal decisions of the day could be based. More recently, forensic disciplines such as bite-mark analysis, hair and fiber comparison, tool-mark analysis, and ballistics were believed to offer definitive proof. In 2009, the National Research Council—which is made up of members of the National Academy of Sciences, the National Academy of Engineering, and the Institute of Medicine—released a more than 300-page report that sent shockwaves through the criminal justice world. Titled *Strengthening forensic science in the United States: A path forward*, the report strongly criticized a range of forensic investigative techniques, concluding that "many forensic tests ... have never been exposed to stringent scientific scrutiny" (National Research Council, 2009: 42) By 2017, hundreds of convicted criminals had been exonerated by DNA—which is not without its own limitations but is generally an exception to the bunk and nonsense that permeates traditional forensic "sciences." Those exonerations have proven a range of traditional, non-forensic investigative techniques to be less reliable than the legal system has long assumed.

The contemporary conception of reliable evidence offers another path through which the legal system does not, but could, incentivize evidence based policing. The legal system will always lag behind the most current scientific research. In part, that is because the legal system prioritizes stability; judges are likely to wait for a scientific consensus to emerge before they begin to revise long-held assumptions. The lag may also be partially explained by the mechanism through which law is developed; courts act only in the context of the cases before them, and it may simply take time for the appropriate cases to make their way through the judiciary. Accepting those caveats as true, the legal system can also create incentives for evidence based policing by insisting that investigative techniques are validated, or at least have not been called into question, by methodologically rigorous study.

There is substantial room for improvement. The procedures that officers use in day-to-day investigations and with the very best of intentions can contribute to inaccurate results. Interview and interrogation training can leave officers with the belief, often presented explicitly, that they can not only reliably identify deception, but also conduct interrogations without contributing to the risk of false confessions (Wilson, 2010; Reid & Associates, 2014). Police training can inculcate the belief that police canines simply *do not* make mistakes or, at least, do not have false positives in the field (*Illinois v. Caballes*, 2005). Outdated investigative procedures can lead officers to conduct simultaneous, non-blinded photographic line-ups or to put undue weight on a cross-race identification by an eyewitness. Officers can be both innocently ignorant and intentionally dismissive of a compelling body of scientific evidence that calls all of these investigative techniques into question (Harris, 2012).

Reforms have been suggested, and even adopted to a limited extent, within policing, but policing as an industry accepts change only slowly. In 2011, for example, the Virginia Department of Criminal Justice Services promulgated a model policy for photographic line-up procedures. Based on scientific research, it outlined the reasons for reform and laid out how agencies could implement blinded, sequential line-ups that would improve the accuracy of eyewitness identifications. Two years later, only 6% of almost 150 surveyed agencies had adopted the model policy; 85% of agencies relied on outdated policies and about 20% did not have a policy in place at all. Those results might well have been different, and adoption much more widespread, if attorneys and judges had been more attuned to and skeptical of outdated, inherently less reliable investigative techniques. Through statutory law, judicial opinions, or changes to the rules of evidence, the legal system has the opportunity to incentivize the development and adoption of evidence based investigative practices.

References

Arizona v. Gant (2009) 556 U.S. 332, 350–51.

Arizona v. Johnson (2009) 555 U.S. 323, 325.

Brendlin v. California (2007) 551 U.S. 249, 258.

Davis, K.C. (1986) "Judicial, legislative, and administrative lawmaking: a proposed research service for the Supreme Court," *Minnesota Law Review*, 71: 1–15.

Faigman, D.L. (1991) "Normative constitutional fact-finding: exploring the empirical component of constitutional interpretation," *University of Pennsylvania Law Review*, 139(3): 542–5.

Harris, D.A. (2012) *Failed evidence: Why law enforcement resists science*, New York, NY: NYU Press.

Illinois v. Caballes (2005) 543 U.S. 405, 410 (Souter, J., dissenting).

Jaffee v. Redmond (1996) 518 U.S. 1, 11 n.10.

National Research Council (2009) *Strengthening forensic science in the United States: A path forward*, Washington, DC: The National Academies Press. Available at: https://doi.org/10.17226/12589

Reid & Associates (2014) "Interrogation." Available at: http://www.reid.com/educational_info/criticinterrogation.html (accessed September 13, 2014).

Miranda v. Arizona (1966) 384 U.S. 436, 445–55, 483–9.

Muehler v. Mena (2005) 544 U.S. 93, 98.

New York v. Belton (1981) 453 U.S. 4543, 460.

Stoughton, S.W. (2014) "Policing facts," *Tulane Law Review*, 88(5): 847–98.

Stoughton, S.W. (2015) "Evidentiary rules as police reform," *Miami Law Review*, 69: 429–68.

Stoughton, S.W. (2017) "Principled policing: warrior cops & guardian officers," *Wake Forest Law Review*, 611: 652–8.

Tennessee v. Garner (1985) 471 U.S. 1, 19–22.

United States v. Banks (2003) 540 U.S. 31, 40.

United States v. Drayton (2002) 536 U.S. 194, 205.

Wilson, G.I. (2010) "Perspective on Neurolinguistic Programming (NLP)," *Police Chief*, 40: 40–51.

5

Identifying some misconceptions about evidence based policing: a research note

Laura Huey
University of Western Ontario

Brittany Blaskovits
Carleton University

Craig Bennell
Carleton University

Hina Kalyal
University of Western Ontario

Tom Walker
Carleton University

Introduction

This research note is informed by analysis of answers ($n = 149$) to an open-ended question appended to a survey conducted on police receptivity to empirical research. The purpose of the study was to replicate Telep and Lum's (2014) receptivity research with Canadian policing agencies. We developed a modified version of the Telep and Lum survey[1] that included three open-ended questions not found in the original version. These questions were intended to help us more thoroughly explore awareness of evidence based policing (EBP) and the extent to which respondents value this approach and feel that it should be used in relation to their work and the work of their organizations.

Answers to the question "Would you consider evidence based policing to be a good approach for your department?" were initially coded and analyzed to help us explore knowledge and/or awareness of EBP. We then reanalyzed comments in which the respondent did not demonstrate knowledge of EBP, looking to identify themes that might help practitioners better understand where knowledge gaps exist or misconceptions. In the following pages, we present the six themes that we uncovered.

Methods

Recruitment

Given the difficulties associated with securing decent response rates for online surveys, we felt that approaching a higher number of participating agencies would be beneficial to achieving a larger sample size. For the sake of regional and other diversity, we sought participation from agencies in seven provinces and included a mix of municipal and regional police services. Therefore, whereas the original Lum, Telep, Koper, and Grieco (2012) pilot study, and subsequent Telep and Lum (2014) follow-up study, drew on samples of one and three police agencies, respectively, the decision was made to ask seven municipal and regional police agencies ($n = 7$) across Canada to participate.

Senior command staff at selected police agencies were contacted by email and asked if their service would participate in the survey. We defined participation as agreeing to send out an internal email to all employees describing the survey, its goals, that it was anonymous, and how to access it online. The survey was posted online in October 18, 2016 using Qualtrics and it remained active until February 1, 2017. Follow-up emails were sent prior to the survey being discontinued.

Data collection

The original survey consisted of five parts (Lum et al, 2012; Telep and Lum, 2014). Section 1 explored officers' knowledge of both policing evaluation research and EBP more generally. The second part asked officers for their views on science and scientific research. Section 3 asked officers about their openness to innovation, including new techniques and strategies. This was followed by Section 4, which explored views on higher education and its relative merits within the field of policing. The survey concluded by asking for demographic and institutional information.

Respondents were advised that they would remain anonymous, that details of their survey would not be shared with their employer, and that they could skip any questions they chose. In total, 586 individuals completed the survey. Of these, 352 sworn officers and civilian employees ($n = 352$) answered open-ended question #2: "Would you consider evidence based policing to be a good approach for your department?"

Data analysis

Once the survey data were collected in SPSS, a second version was created in Excel and sent to a team member for an exploratory, inductive coding. Through this initial coding, it was seen that, once simple "yes," "no," "maybe," and "unsure" responses were removed, the remaining answers provided richer details as to the relative degree of knowledge of EBP held by respondents. The result was a data set of 149 responses ($n = 149$). These responses were then reread and placed into one of two categories: "demonstrates some knowledge/awareness of EBP" and "demonstrates no knowledge/awareness of EBP." Decisions as to what category a response would be placed into were made based on whether the response clearly referenced some aspect of the collection, analysis and/or use of *research* in policing. We were also helped by the fact that many participants simply stated that they did not know what it was.

Drawing on the first coding results, a decision was made to recode the data using a more, focused approach centered on the theme of "knowledge." This entailed identifying themes based on recurrent patterns in responses and then attempting to identify related sub-themes and map them to develop a larger "picture" of what the data were telling us about officer "knowledge" of EBP. To ensure a degree of reliability in our coding and results, all coding was independently verified by another team member. A third team member reviewed the manuscript to ensure that all figures are accurately reported.

Initial results

> Question: "Would you consider evidence based policing to be a good approach for your department?"

> Response received: "Possibly, but I would like to see more analysis and/or evidence of what this strategy would entail."

Of the 149 comments analyzed, we found that 42 ($n = 42$) evidenced some knowledge of EBP (see Table 5.1). For example, one respondent opined that "research and evidence based policing provide a concrete foundation to gear policing strategies." Another replied that "policing strategies based on scientifically conducted, and peer-reviewed studies make far more sense than relying on old-fashioned systems based on tradition." An officer from

Table 5.1: Knowledge of EBP

	n
Demonstrates little to no knowledge/awareness of EBP	107
Demonstrates some knowledge/awareness of EBP	42
Total	149

a different agency stated that "I believe scientific study has a definite role to play in analyzing the effectiveness of policing methods and tactics."

Conversely, 107 ($n = 107$) clearly stated that they: (1) did not know what evidence based policing was; (2) were confused by the meaning of the word "evidence" in this context; and/or (3) provided other indicators that demonstrated a lack of knowledge. The most common answers in this group included: "not sure what is meant by this term" and "DONT KNOW WHAT THIS IS." Other examples in this category are discussed among the themes presented in the following.

In short, the responses analyzed here indicate that most participants who responded to this open-ended question in some detail were unfamiliar with the concept of EBP. In the next section, we examine some of the themes that emerged in their comments. The identification of these themes can, we believe, help EBP proponents address what might be common misconceptions among police practitioners.

Themes identified from the data

In this section, we draw on the thematic analysis we employed to help us better understand gaps in knowledge of EBP. In particular, we wanted to know more about what police officers, who were not familiar with the concept thought it might mean and where there might be misconceptions or misapprehensions that could be addressed through future knowledge mobilization efforts. In total, we identified five themes worth further attention.

Legal evidence, not research

One of the biggest sources of confusion is rooted in the name. The term "evidence based policing" is derived from an earlier, similar movement: evidence based medicine (Sherman, 1998). In medicine, evidence refers to results achieved from rigorously designed research. In the policing environment, evidence has traditionally meant something entirely different: a fact that meets standards of admission into a set of legal proceedings.

Not surprisingly, then, some individuals who lacked knowledge of EBP misunderstood the concept of evidence and its use in this context: "If I knew what it was," one respondent acknowledged, "Isn't all policing evidence based????" Another agreed that EBP is a good approach because "that is what I use to determine how an event occurred and who is at fault." Another replied: "I don't know what other method could be used. Court oversight examines and weighs 'evidence'." One officer thought that EBP was "common sense": "As a police officer or investigator it is our job to follow the evidence and let the evidence dictate the course of the investigation." Still another worried that the emphasis on evidence could be problematic because "There are some investigations that have no evidence at all other than the allegation that's been made. Evidence takes time to gather and is not always available at the time it's needed, ex. DNA evidence." Some did, however, seen the benefits if it meant that "with CCTV or other evidence you won't need witness accounts to corroborate what occurred."

EBP = cops taken off the streets

A key component of identifying "what works" in EBP is centered on the effective and efficient allocation of policing resources. A raft of studies— from hot spot policing to foot patrol evaluations—have all been directed at determining what strategies and programs use resources wisely, without producing crime displacement and other backfire effects (Weisburd et al, 2011; Slothower et al, 2015). While it is the case that a strategy implemented on the basis of one or more of these studies could result in police officers being reallocated, or assigned new or different tasks, we are not aware of any case in which a study resulted in police officers being removed from patrol or other front-line duties. This was, however, a concern of some respondents.

One respondent wanted to see "more details on implementation" but was concerned that EBP might entail removing police officers from the community: "People still want to see a cop at the door when they call," he advised. More specifically, some participants worried that front-line officers might be reallocated from patrol or community responsibilities, or new officers simply assigned away from patrol to work in offices generating research. As one expressed this concern:

> "The onus is placed on general patrol officers, who are already incredibly overwhelmed/worked with calls for service. We are over specialized and do not have enough boots on the ground. Cops on corners, stop crime—not cops in offices researching new policing tactics."

This concern was shared by another officer, who advised:

"I am a huge advocate of not removing policing agencies from close contact with the community it serves. There must be a balance. Removing oneself from community stakeholders to 'hide' behind a computer is, in my opinion, a flawed strategy."

EBP increases workload

Despite the fact that EBP is not about increasing workload or cost inefficiencies, but rather about ensuring that existing systems and processes—whether crime-control strategies or human resources decisions—are effective and efficient, some participants expressed concerns that EBP would increase officer workload and/or policing costs. As can be seen in one of the comments cited earlier, some members felt that their agencies were "overwhelmed" with calls for service. This view was expressed by an officer from the same city, who stated: "we need to get more staff in the reactive component ... as the city is tied down due to calls for service."

An illustrative example of the "inefficiency concern" was found in the following statement: "I don't know much about this strategy but it sounds like it would involve a great deal of leg work prior to implementing any strategy. How cost effective would that be?" Others cited "lack of resources" as a barrier to adopting an evidence based approach: "the theory is practical, however the lack of resources do not support its effective application." Another officer thought that EBP might be "somewhat" useful but worried whether there would be "appropriate resources to use." Still another expressed concerns over the possibility of an extra work burden that might render police less efficient: "Would the paperwork alter our ability to serve the public? How would this approach change our workflow? Would it hamper our ability to provide information to prosecutions (in a timely manner)?"

EBP = less or no community policing

EBP is an approach that can work well in combination with other major policing philosophies, notably, with problem-oriented and community policing models (Bueermann, 2012). It is not a total or absolute vision in the sense that its adoption necessarily requires an organization to abandon reliance on these other models. Indeed, many police services have found that EBP and community policing can be highly complementary. Unfortunately, this message may have failed to gain wider traction among Canadian police audiences. This suggestion is based on the fact that some respondents stated that they would only be supportive of EBP if their organization did not abandon their community policing approach.

One participant wrote that "As long as the community based policing still plays an underlying role," he would view EBP as a valuable approach for his organization. Another similarly replied "Yes" to EBP but that its use "also needs to include aspects of community policing." Yet another officer thought that EBP would be a "great approach" if used as "an extension of community-based policing." While a fourth individual thought that there was "no doubt every police department or service should use evidence based policing to support their presence and implications," she was concerned that EBP might actually inhibit community policing because "EBP does not allow police to fully integrate themselves in the community as policing is a 'sense,' a 'gut instinct,' a commitment to the community!"

EBP is not effective

As we have stated throughout, much of the focus of EBP is on increasing effectiveness and efficiency, particularly (but not exclusively) on issues of crime control. However, this message has also failed to translate to a wider audience as one a major theme of several of the comments received was the perceived *in*effectiveness of EBP strategies and programs in addressing crime and disorder.

In essence, respondents whose comments fell under this theme perceive their world as too fluid and/or complex to be accurately captured in data. As one explained: "Statistics are not an accurate reflection of actual crime and disorder." This view was shared by an officer in another service: "Policing is a dynamic, fluid response to volatile often unknown circumstances. Due to this nature, no amount of statistics or analysis can accurately or effectively assist in the deployment of resources or the profiling of crime." Someone else disagreed about the utility of EBP in assisting with resource-allocation issues but similarly thought that those changes would have little effect: "I believe it is a good model in that it puts resources in the right places ... but ... it will not improve the crime rates we have here." One explanation for why reliance on research evidence could have little effect on crime rates was offered by an officer in a different city: "only incarceration works at minimizing crime in a noticeable way. Evidence based policing and any other form of resource allocation will only be effective at disrupting trends or displacing crime." Some felt that EBP would be a good approach but only "when combined with traditional approaches to policing" because it is not "practical." Another could give only qualified support to EBP because it is "a reactive approach" and is thus limited in its potential effectiveness.

EBP lacks officer input

We received fewer comments about the last theme that arose; however, we include it here as we felt it important to highlight. A core principle of EBP is that the research produced should be a product of the experience of police officers and the academic skills and knowledge of the researcher (Sherman, 2013). Part of the job of EBP practitioners is to ensure that officers and civilians in relevant roles throughout an organization are engaged with the research-creation process in a meaningful way, and that this expectation is embedded in how we communicate what EBP is and how it can be used. Some respondents were unaware of this condition, which was reflected in their comments. The most illustrative example came from a participant who was not supportive of the idea of EBP because "I find that when academics try to mold policing without actually having experienced it for themselves, the solutions that are brought forward are either impractical or unrealistic."

Conclusions

Since its introduction in 1998, the EBP approach has generated a significant volume of research and knowledge mobilization activity. Since 2010 alone, we have seen the development of four national EBP societies,[2] the recent launch of a new journal,[3] and a host of workshops and annual meetings. Each of these activities has helped to generate a global membership of over 5,000 police and civilian police employees in one or more of the societies, with that number growing daily. All of this would seem to suggest that knowledge and awareness of EBP is becoming increasingly mainstream within policing circles. Findings presented in this research note indicate, however, that EBP practitioners need to do a better job of communicating what EBP is and is not to policing audiences.

There is some good news, though. The focus of our research has been on Canadian police services. In Canada, EBP is a much more recent arrival compared with the UK and Australia, for example, whereas the UK Society of Evidence Based Policing was founded in 2010, the Canadian version launched in 2015. EBP-themed workshops, articles, videos, and other modes of knowledge exchange only really began in Canada in 2016. Thus, it is hardly surprising that significant knowledge gaps remain. The utility of this research note is in providing some insights into how to respond to those gaps and, perhaps more importantly, to any misconceptions and misunderstandings that might exist.

Notes

[1] We had to revise questions about rank structure that were not appropriate for Canadian municipal police services.

² In the UK, Canada, the US, and Australia and New Zealand.
³ *Police Science*, launched by the Australia–New Zealand Society of Evidence Based Policing in 2016.

References

Bueermann, J. (2012) "Being smart on crime with evidence based policing," *NIJ Journal*, 269: 12–15.

Lum, C., Telep, C., Koper, C., and Grieco, J. (2012) "Receptivity to research in policing," *Justice Research and Policy*, 14(1): 61–95.

Sherman, L. (1998) *Evidence based policing. Ideas in American policing*, Washington, DC: Police Foundation.

Sherman, L. (2013) "The rise of evidence based policing: targeting, testing, and tracking," *Crime and Justice*, 42(1): 377–451.

Slothower, M., Sherman, L., and Neyroud, P. (2015) "Tracking quality of police actions in a victim contact program: a case study of training, tracking, and feedback (TTF) in evidence based policing," *International Criminal Justice Review*, 25(1): 98–116.

Telep, C. and Lum, C. (2014) "The receptivity of officers to empirical research and evidence based policing: an examination of survey data from three agencies," *Police Quarterly*, 17(4): 359–85.

Weisburd, D., Hinkle, J., Famega, C., and Ready, J. (2011) "The possible 'backfire' effects of hot spots policing: an experimental assessment of impacts on legitimacy, fear and collective efficacy," *Journal of Experimental Criminology*, 7: 297–320.

SECTION II:
Research methods

6

"Not all evidence is created equal": on the importance of matching research questions with research methods in evidence based policing

Barak Ariel

Hebrew and Cambridge Universities

Introduction

Evidence based policing (EBP) has enjoyed continuous growth in recognition and implementation since Sherman originally used the term in 1998 (Sherman, 1998). At its core, EBP is a paradigm that means using the best "research to guide practice and evaluate practitioners. It uses the best evidence to shape the best practice" (Sherman, 1998: 4). For many, the "best evidence" approach often means experiments, and particularly randomized controlled field trials (in medicine, see Haynes, 2002; in education, see Burtless, 2002; in criminology, see Sherman, 2009). The random assignment of "units" in their natural environment—police officers, time, victims, suspects, shifts, or cases—into treatment and control conditions is assumed by most scholars to be the strongest research design for measuring causal estimates. As much of the work conducted thus far "on" and in the name of EBP has been about measuring the efficacy and the cost-effectiveness of various policing tactics, then experiments are, indeed, the most promising research methodology that science has to offer (Shadish et al, 2002). There are strong merits for using randomized trials, which most criminologists consider the "gold standard" of impact evaluation research.

However, the focus—or perhaps overemphasis—on randomized controlled field trials can be linked to three debilitating consequences for the growth of EBP. First, there are more non-experimental criminal justice scholars than there are experimentalists, and attributing a "second-to-best" status to this important scholarship enterprise is alienating. To consider the seminal work of notable scholars such as Westley Skogan, John Braithwaite, Sir Anthony Bottoms, or Gloria Laycock as "lesser" than experimental findings would be taking a superfluous purist approach. Second, conducting a randomized controlled field trial is operationally challenging and difficult to execute with sound rigor, which makes them less palatable to police chiefs. The life cycle of a chief does not always align with the time it takes to plan, execute, and analyze a randomized controlled field test. Third, and perhaps most crucially, there are certain questions that are not meant to be answered using an experimental approach because not all questions posed by EBP researchers are about impact: studies on perceptions, emotions, and processes, for example, are critical for our understanding of the world, but they do not necessarily require the random assignment of units into treatment and control conditions.

Conducting an experiment is not an end goal by itself; research questions ought to be answered with the appropriate research methods, and not the other way around. Over a century of "research-methods theories" have been developed, and science has a rather robust layout for marrying research questions and the ways in which these queries can be answered. The more pertinent definition of EBP should therefore be using the most *appropriate* research design to collect evidence that will guide practitioners and continually evaluate practice.

To discuss these issues, we must first go back to the fundamentals: "fitting" the research question to the research design is not a matter of preference, but rather a logical, deductive process with a set of guiding rules. Similarly, preference toward a certain design is not a political phenomenon; it is a formal decision-making process, which balances between the research question, research goals, and realpolitik and feasibility considerations. Through a wide range of case studies, this chapter illustrates that experimental designs are, in principle, the gold standard for impact evaluation research, but only when a certain set of conditions is met. Similarly, observational research has a special place in EBP for the discovery of new ways of understanding policing. Therefore, there should not be a conceptual war between EBP scholars.

This chapter is meant to lay out the broad methodologies that are most fitting for the broad types of questions in EBP. This discussion can illustrate how EBP benefits from each category for different types of research questions. A special emphasis will be given to causal designs, but it will be shown that causal studies include other designs beyond the randomized field methodology, such as pre-experimental designs, quasi-experimental designs, and natural experiments, all of which are critical for our understanding of what works, what does not, and what is promising. The benefits and shortcomings of each design will also be explored.

Back to basics: contextualizing EBP designs as a methodological choice

When embarking on an EBP program, how should researchers decide which is the most fitting and cost-effective approach to answering the research question? This dilemma is less concerned about the substantive findings that arise from an EBP program—although it may serve as a good starting point to reflect on past experience—and more concerned about the ways in which such a dilemma can be answered empirically and structurally. While some of the chapters of this book deal with practical findings from rigorous studies with real policy implications, a more fundamental question should be: how do we choose the research design that is most suitable to nullify the null hypothesis of no effect?

We rarely find two research designs that are identical (Ethridge, 2004: 20). However, there are basic types of models that are widely recognized in research, and anybody who has been trained with a research-methods course was exposed to these designs to some degree or another (see, eg, Hagan, 2013; Jupp, 1989). Based on these categories, we know that some designs are appropriate for a particular type of research question but not others (De Vaus, 2001). As such, a decision tree can help us decide early on which type of design is paramount for a certain research question given the defining parameters of the study. We can start by classifying research based on the causal links that the study purports to explore (Bryman, 2015: 73).

Step 1: exploratory EBP

As shown in Figure 6.1, at the bottom of the causality scale, we find exploratory studies. These are studies in areas that can be considered *terra nullius* in the body of knowledge of the phenomenon they are investigating: unchartered territories in a relatively new research venture (see Stebbins, 2001). This type of study is more diffused, with loosely defined key terms and objectives as there are no implicit hypotheses that the research is attempting to address. In fact, most exploratory studies are focused on detecting possible hypotheses for *future* studies to explore more robustly. For instance, a new drug rehabilitation program that focuses on new cognitive, behavioral, or neurological processes, which has never been trialed before, should be explored within the confounds of a pilot, rather than an expensive or elaborate test (eg Lackner et al, 2016;

Figure 6.1: Broad categorization of EBP research methods

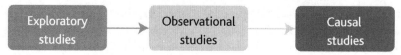

Rivera et al, 2017). There are both theoretical and practical considerations here. It may be that the treatment program is relatively expensive or resource-intensive. Researchers and policymakers should not invest heavily in a new intervention that may turn out to be unsuccessful in reducing drug use (for reviews, see Cartwright, 2000; Farrington et al, 2001). A fact-finding study will not provide a meaningful effect-size estimate for planning subsequent studies given the imprecision that characterizes data in small samples. Safety, efficacy, and effectiveness are also not fully evaluated in these pilot studies (Leon et al, 2011: 626) as these sorts of questions are answered through a different set of research methods.

Similarly, the type of intervention may be immature from a theoretical perspective, and may therefore be difficult to explain and subsequently generalize to patients outside the pilot parameters (Bachman and Schutt, 2013: 259). Indeed, in some basic studies, certain theories "pop up"—even in a profound way—but unless the theories are properly assessed in a deductive process, it cannot be said that they explain, predict, or expound the evidence in a valid or reliable way.

Exploratory research is chiefly interested in gaining a broader level of understanding about the relevant variables that may or may not play a part in the success of the studied phenomenon. These studies are meant to lay out the patterns and concentrations that can be found in the data. By implication, the types of statistical tools that researchers should consider for this kind of design are reflective of the study design: descriptive statistics rather than inferential statistics (Leon et al, 2011). Exploratory studies are usually not based on probability (representative) samples, and the exploration of the data is not therefore meant to conclude generalizable findings about the population from which the samples were drawn.

Unfortunately, there are far too many implemented interventions in the criminal justice system based on crude pilot tests (for a review, see Poyner, 1993). Admittedly, some basic testing of the intervention is better than non-evidence based applications in the criminal justice system; however, the basic EBP model should advocate the implementation of policies that were tested more than once, or at least based on rigorous designs, rather than an exploratory analysis of existing data.

Step 2: observational EBP

As shown in Figure 6.1, the second step of EBP designs consists of observational studies. These designs are intended to provide a rich description of a group of cases or situations where the studied phenomenon is relatively established (see Mann, 2003; Jupp, 1989). Given the level of maturity of the theory behind these studies, they allow the researchers to discover patterns and concentrations based on prior research, rather than start from scratch (as in the case of exploratory designs). Consequently, the researcher can observe links between variables and specific trends in the data, and relay these findings to other studies or populations that are relevant to the study. Studies such as Sutherland's (2012) study on parental socio-economic status is useful in providing a (more) complete description of the distribution of such variables related to the initiation of substance abuse by young people. Similarly, Tankebe and Ariel (2016) administered a survey of police officers in police departments where body-worn cameras were introduced in order to quantify the scattering of responses about officers' views on these devices. This descriptive study links between these perceptions and officers' perceptions on self-legitimacy, a more mature area of theory and research. The findings can illustrate the possible association between previous experiences with officers' supervisors and perceptions of the legitimacy of introducing body-worn cameras. They can also model the ways in which perceptions of police effectiveness are associated with legitimacy perceptions among body-worn camera-equipped officers—an area of growing attention.

Critically, however, much like the exploratory studies, observational studies are not causal (Grimes and Schultz, 2002). They may include in-depth analysis of a phenomenon, and the richness of data may lead some to conclude that a large data set could help in determining cause and effect. However, observations alone are not meant to infer causality because causality means something very specific in science. Even though observational studies can estimate temporal sequencing between variables—for example, that criminal behavior follows traumatic childhood experiences (Wilcox, Richards, and O'Keeffe, 2004; see also, more broadly, Sampson, 2010)—that is not enough to show that the former causes the latter. Observations are crucial for our understanding of the ways in which such variables are correlated with one another. They are also useful in laying out predictive models based on a set of factors that calculate the possible variations in the predicted variable. However, they are not causal models in the strict sense of the word. In the victim–offender cycle hypothesis, for example, there may be additional factors beyond traumatic experiences that are necessary conditions for criminal behavior to take place; after all, the majority of childhood victims do not go on to commit violent crimes, even though the majority of violent offenders experienced traumatic events in their childhood (Burton et al, 1997).

Step 3: causal EBP

To infer causality, more is needed than to observe relationships between variables. To be able to declare a causal relationship between variables, we turn to the third family of studies depicted in Figure 6.1. These are studies where the researcher can safely conclude that variations in the independent variable(s)

(IVs) *cause* variations in the dependent variables (DVs). Observational studies are not intended for this, and should not be interpreted as such. They are fitting for exploring the data and to observe associational relationships between variables and groups within the data set, but they are not meant to confirm causal relationships.

In science, causality means something quite specific, and scholars are usually in agreement about three minimal conditions for declaring that a causal bond exists between the IVs and DVs: (1) that there is a correlation between the two variables; (2) that there is a temporal sequence whereby the IVs precede the DVs; and (3) that alternative explanations are safely removed from or controlled for in the stated mechanism (for a more elaborate discussion, see Lewis, 1974; see also the premier collection of papers on causality edited by Beebee et al, 2009). Whereas observational studies such as Tankebe's (2009) enterprise on legitimacy are valuable at indicating the relative role of procedural justice (PJ) for police legitimacy, they may not be in a good position to firmly place PJ as a causal antecedent to legitimacy (as the chronological ordering of the two variables is difficult, if not impossible, to lay out within the confounds of a questionnaire) (on concerns about the inability of surveys to show causality, see Marsh, 1979: 294–7). Similarly, longitudinal studies can show a significant (and negative) correlation between age and criminal behavior (Hirschi and Gottfredson, 1983; Sweeten et al, 2013), and while they can firmly illustrate the temporal sequence between age and crime, they are not able to sufficiently rule out alternative variables (outside of the age factor) to the hypothesized link between age and crime (Gottfredson and Hirschi, 1987). Group-based trajectory analyses are incredibly pertinent to showing how certain clusters of cases or offenders change over time (Haviland et al, 2007; Nagin and Odgers, 2010), yet there may be more variables that explain crime (eg resilience, social bonds, and internal control mechanisms, to name a few—which often go unrecorded and therefore cannot be controlled for in the statistical model), rather than the clustering variable per se. As clearly laid out by Wikström (2008: 128):

> [i]f we cannot manipulate the putative cause/s and observe the effect/s we are stuck with analyzing patterns of association (correlation) between our hypothesized causes and effects. The question is then whether we can establish causation (causal dependencies) by analyzing patterns of association with statistical methods. The simple answer to this question is most likely to be a disappointing "no."

Thus, we ought to be careful in concluding casualty from observational studies (but compare McGue et al, 2010).

Under the bonnet of research methods: a closer look at the fit-for-purpose dilemma

Of course, there are many types of research designs in science. Breaking them down into "qualitative" versus "quantitative" is overly crude given the wealth of designs that EBP scholars may consider (Fielding and Schreier, 2001); thinking one approach is superior for an entire discipline (eg Tewksbury, 2009) seems inappropriate as research methods follow the research question, and not vice versa. Within the three broad families of designs—exploratory, observational, and causal—there are many specific blueprints for excavating findings that are useful for EBP scholars. Figure 6.2 shows the prominent designs, and scholars may find this decision tree useful when considering the types of methods that are best fitting given their research program—even though some of the most influential studies in EBP implemented mixed methods, thus benefiting from a wide range of methodologies for a growing range of questions (eg the early place-based studies produced several influential answers that continue to dominate contemporary EBP [see, eg, Koper, 1995; Sherman and Weisburd, 1995; see also Shaw, 1995; Sherman and Rogan, 1995]).

This decision tree is accommodating for those considering fitting the research method to the research question in the most optimal way. As shown, the first dilemma that scholars must address is whether they are involved in the administration of the tested intervention. In some instances, the researchers directly oversee the implementation of the manipulation, and in other cases, the researchers are in cooperation with the professional treatment provider; however, the critical point is that the researcher can provide some sort of a declaration about who will or will not be given a certain level of dosage of the treatment (eg Ariel et al, 2016, 2017a; see also Mitchell, 2017), as well as how the allocation procedure was decided, executed, and managed. In other cases, it might be that the researcher is directly involved in the assignment of interventions in treatment groups but is removed from the immediate administration of the manipulation—as is the case in many policing experiments (for a review, see Sherman, 2010). However, there is still a direct and prospective involvement of the researcher in the process. If the researcher is not involved in the administration of the intervention, and the collection of data has already taken place, then the majority of study designs are deemed retrospective and non-causal. There are some exceptions to this rule; however, as will be shown, the majority of the methods of retrospective studies are not intended to infer causality. Therefore, the primary question—"Who administered the intervention?"—creates a fundamental branching within EBP.

When the research area is relatively new, then it is likely to be considered an exploratory study that looks at existing data in order to establish *future* hypotheses (shown on the top right-hand side of Figure 6.2). As noted earlier, the level of information that exists in this research area does not merit a causal research design since there are no inductive or deductive hypotheses

Figure 6.2: Decision tree model

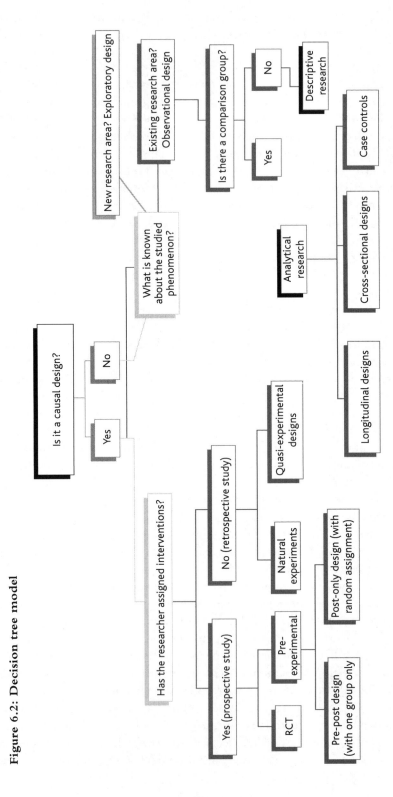

that can be properly tested. These are the fact-finding designs, and are at the lowest level of validity—despite being incredibly important for scientific exploration: they diagnose problems and subsequently guide us as to what we need to focus on.

Next, again as we noted earlier, we have the observational designs. Here, we have studies where researchers fully describe the data. This does not mean the physical observation of participants or events (observations can thus also be the research tool, not just the design), but in-depth analysis of existing data sets, historical or archival (eg Barnham et al, 2017; Bland and Ariel, 2015). By focusing on factors and causes, and addressing the five W's—the what, who, where, when, and why/how of crime and the response to it—EBP advances in ways that define what the appropriate targets for effective crime policies are (Sherman, 2013). Within this, it is easy to see why case definitions, persons, places, time, and causes/risk factors are all critical units of analysis in observational EBP when scholars are interested in discerning the patterns and concentrations in the data. These methods are therefore useful in generating possible hypotheses that explain crime, deviance, and the response to these social phenomena, often using large sets of data (eg Dudfield et al, 2017). They are also useful in identifying the risk factors that may reduce these issues (or increase them, as the research question might be about increased risk) (see, eg, Button et al, 2017).

However, to characterize the relationship between the causes, exposures, and outcomes, EBP scholars need to turn to another line of research methodology: analytical research. What characterizes analytical research more than anything is the existence of a comparison group. Comparisons are essential if researchers wish to point out how causes and effects relate to one another. This line of inquiry can be used when the researcher wishes to show that a group of offenders are more likely that another group to benefit from a particular intervention (eg Gibson et al, 2017), or to illustrate that exposure to a certain treatment is associated with a reduced risk of harm compared with another group of offenders. In other words, analytical research is useful in identifying cases that are correlated with an outcome of interest but not with other types of cases. For example, criminologists might be interested in particular attributes that are associated with future offending when found in higher frequencies in certain offenders (Button et al, 2017). When these attributes are found in lower frequencies in other offenders—that is, the comparison group—then recidivism would be elevated. The detection of these attributes, or factors, can be used in identifying the appropriate targeting approaches of effective future interventions.

There are a number of observational study designs that are aimed at observing causes and effects. In practical terms, the way in which it is done is by observing the frequency, rate, or prevalence of a set of attributes (or just one) in the group of interest, and often comparing the same in a comparison group (for a review, see Fleiss et al, 2013: ch 9). The "comparison" group comprises a different set of cases altogether, or the same group of interest over time.

One of the most common designs in observational EBP research is the longitudinal, or cohort, design. Cohort studies refer to the study of a set of units—places, individuals, or cases—over a period of time. Formally, cohort studies usually observe the degree of exposure to the outcome variable of interest—crime, harm, arrests, or victimization figures—in a studied sample at several "waves." There are two types of cohort studies and they are equally important in EBP. In some cohort studies, the researcher follows up on the cases "into the future." These are studies in which the researcher tracks cases prospectively as they enter the study. For example, longitudinal studies such as those by Laub and Vaillant (2000) and West et al (1973) are now classic examples in EBP in which offenders are observed over time in order to understand the risk factors associated with criminal behavior. Antrobus, Thompson, and Ariel (2018) is another example in which police officers are followed at several junctures in order to understand change over time when some officers are exposed to training in PJ while a comparison group of officers is not exposed to the training. These studies are different from cohort studies in which the outcome variable of interest (eg recidivism) and the exposure to the factors have both already occurred—or retrospective cohort studies. These studies are arguably more common because the data already "exist," and the researcher is essentially observing archival data on the exposed and unexposed cases, thus saving resources. However, the benefits of a prospective longitudinal study cannot be overstated as these studies are able to place controls over the data-collection process. For example, it is common for police departments to change regulations, for data-collection mechanisms to change over time, or for crime-recording practices or the data-entry processes to vary for operational reasons. A prospective study is in a better position to control these changes, or at least to be able to identify and quantify them more fully, than a retrospective study.

Next, we have case control studies. Some may refer to these studies as causal but, in the strict sense, they are not. The researcher classifies the units based on the degree of exposure, for example, those that have and those that have not experienced the treatment. By doing so, the researcher would then try to understand what makes the two groups different from one another. For instance, a researcher may follow up on a cohort of offenders who were recently released from prison; some would subsequently return to prison within five years of their date of release, and some would not. The researcher can then try to observe the two groups of released prisoners in an attempt to identify what factors were present in the recidivist group but not present in the non-recidivist group. Such factors may be a particular rehabilitation program, age differences, crime types, or any other feature that the researcher hypothesizes may lead to a reduction in recidivism. Thus, those "exposed" to this feature of interest can be said to be affected by it, which, in turn, reduces the risk of recidivism. Conversely, lacking this feature as a comparison case increases the risk of recidivism.

The "holy grail" of impact evaluations: causal research

Notwithstanding the importance of diagnostic and observational studies, most practitioners are keen to understand "what works" and "what does not work" in day-to-day crime policies. After all, in the grand scheme of things, exploratory studies lead to more comprehensive observational research, and observational studies ought to lead to the proper testing of IVs. Eventually, we will need to move away from studies on perceptions about the relationship between PJ and legitimacy to asking questions about how PJ tactics can substantively change police legitimacy (in whichever form "legitimacy" is operationalized in real-life settings) (see Nagin and Telep, 2017; see also the responses by Murphy and Tyler, 2017; Tyler, 2017). What is not agreed, however, is what *type* of causal research is optimal under certain realpolitik conditions.

Several types of research methodologies can be used in the exploration of causes and effects. Standard research-methods textbooks can be consulted for more details (eg Shadish et al, 2002). These include experiments, natural experiments, and quasi-experimental designs. The common feature in these study types is the attempt to answer an empirical, quantifiable question in EBP: the identification of causes, effects, mechanisms, or risk factors causally linked to targeting crime. For example, impact evaluations are, by definition, causal studies, and therefore much of the discussion on the appropriateness of different research designs centers on these types of studies (Hanges and Wang, 2012).

The decision tree in Figure 6.2 shows that the first fundamental branching of causal EBP research is whether or not the researcher is involved in the administration of the treatment. As already noted, this issue is quite important if we think about the various designs in legal terms: when the researcher is involved with the delivery of the intervention, they can make certain declarations that researchers who analyze data retrospectively cannot. For example, if the research team reports that the response rate to a survey was 50%, or that the delivery of the intervention did not suffer from fidelity issues (eg Ariel et al, 2017a; Henstock and Ariel, 2017), we can rely on the researchers' affidavit about the implementation process. However, when the treatment has *already* been delivered by another party, we can no longer fully rely on the declaration of the researcher that the implementation occurred in the way in which it is described as they are counting on the reporting of a third party (eg Jennings et al, 2017). Similarly, the researcher is able to place certain controls and balances within the study when they conduct a prospective study in which they are involved in the administration of the treatment (eg Ready and Young, 2015). However, once the intervention and the outcomes have already happened, these factors can no longer be said to be applied by the researcher; rather, they have been applied by the organization of individuals with a vested interest in the success of the intervention.

At the same time, there are clear examples where retrospective studies are more appropriate given the realpolitik reasons of applied research. First, there are certain questions that cannot be dealt with prospectively because the exposure, outcomes, and categorization of cases have already happened. For example, testing the effect of the allocation of court cases to judges of a different ethnic background, with the view to measuring how different judges treat defendants of different backgrounds, is likely to be best studied as a "natural experiment": the allocation of cases, as well as the adjudication of the cases, have already happened (eg Gazal-Ayal and Sulitzeanu-Kenan, 2010). Such studies are still considered experiments because the distribution of cases to the various judges is done with a certain degree of randomness, that is, without a particularly noticeable pattern. Thus, the allocation of cases to the different judges is said to be exogenous, and we would therefore be able to falsify the null hypothesis of no differences between the groups of judges.

Next, we turn to quasi-experimental designs. These are designs that involve selecting groups upon which a variable is tested but without any random pre-selection processes. In other words, they look like true experiments but they lack the random allocation of units into treatment and control conditions. By employing statistical procedures of varying degrees of sophistication, quasi-experimental studies seek to exploit subgroups within the data that can serve as counterfactual conditions to the subgroup of cases that was exposed to the intervention of interest. In many respects, the "name of the game" in quasi-experimental designs is to convince the audience that the "treated" and "untreated" groups were as similar to one another as possible prior to exposure to the tested intervention. However, that the study convincingly maintained this "baseline equilibrium" is exactly the point of contention of many studies that use quasi-experimental designs: does the comparison group indeed represent a "like-with-like" comparison, which is often quite difficult to obtain? Selection biases, sufficiently large samples, historic events that effect the treatment and the comparison groups differently, differential maturity, varying follow-up periods, and a host of threats to the internal validity of the test exist that collectively interfere with the "cleanliness" of the assumption of baseline equilibrium (Shadish et al, 2002). If the two groups do not offer a like-with-like comparison at the pre-test baseline stage, then the quasi-experimental design will fail its purpose.

The struggle is real. Being able to state that the treatment group and control group are comparable at baseline implies that the researcher was able to control for (virtually) all extraneous and confounding variables in the statistical model. By accounting for the effect of as many as variables as possible, the disparities between the two groups can be minimized. However, the challenge is that many, if not most, variables are simply not collected or observed in the data, and cannot therefore be controlled for in the statistical model. This is the "specification error": having a model that is not specific enough in terms of the data that it represents (see, eg, Heckman, 1979). To create true counterfactual conditions, there is a need to control for a host of variables that may confound the direct causal link between the main IV and the outcome variable. Nevertheless, the assumption in these models is that they have access to all the relevant factors, which is not always the case (eg official records rarely include offenders' motivation to desist, or other "positive" protective factors that may help the offender stop offending). This leads to the "omitted variables" problem.

Despite the stated issues, we must acknowledge that "life" may simply not allow researchers the ability to conduct randomized controlled trials (RCTs), or prospective studies more broadly. EBP scholars from all fronts are likely to agree that, on paper, prospective experiments are the "gold standard" for impact evaluation research, but they should all equally agree that some research questions should be addressed with quasi-experimental designs. Ethical considerations should always be given the necessary attention when dealing with "human subjects" (see Mitchell and Lewis, 2017), access to data may not be available as a prospective approach, and budgetary constraints can also become formidable issues when addressing certain questions (see a discussion about and extension of these issues in Lum and Yang, 2005). Quasi-experimental designs are particularly helpful in answering questions about predictions that involve a wide range of options, for example, developing much-needed actuarial models (Berk et al, 2016), conducting path analyses (Cantor and Land, 1985), and multi-layered data approaches (Ulmer and Johnson, 2004) for EBP. To understand wider mechanisms, there are specific statistical models that are optimal (Holland, 1986).

On the other hand, if realpolitik concerns *can* be overcome, then prospective experiments should be considered as the viable option for impact evaluations. What proper experiments do best is to single out the effect of a particular intervention while keeping all other variables constant (Shadish et al, 2002). Prospective "experiments" represent a large family of designs; while the RCT is usually thought of when thinking about trials, it is one of several "experimental designs." As shown in Figure 6.2, we also have what methodologists refer to as pre-experimental designs, meaning that they are considered "pre-"—preparatory or prerequisite—to true experimental designs (Salkind, 2010), and at least two are noteworthy: the pre-test/post-test and the post-test only designs (see De Vaus, 2001). The pre-test/post-test design is basically the popular before-and-after methodology in which the studied group is observed once before its members are exposed to an intervention, and then again after the exposure has occurred. The researcher is able to illustrate change over time and is able to conclude, with a strong degree of validity, that exposure to the intervention and the outcome of interest are correlated with one another, as well as that there is a temporal sequence such that the intervention "appeared" prior to the measured outcome (see, eg, Carr et al, 2017; De Brito and Ariel, 2017). However, the design is unable to conclusively rule out alternative explanations for the appearance of the outcome measure because there are no control groups that are measured in parallel with the exposed study group. Without a comparison group, researchers will struggle to defend the argument that the internal validity of the test was not threatened. These studies are what Sherman (1997) referred to as Level 2 studies (on a scale of 1–5) on the Maryland Scale of Research Methods (see also Farrington et al, 2002).

Despite the criticism, before-and-after studies are particularly useful when the intervention is exceptionally potent. For example, if complaints against the police are reduced by more than 90% following the introduction of police body-worn cameras, across more than a dozen tests, it is difficult to argue that the treatment is caused by another intervention (Ariel et al, 2015, 2017b; for a review, see Maskaly et al, 2017). While there may be an interaction effect between the cameras and "something else," the fact remains that the series of independent tests have collectively shown a before-and-after reduction of a dramatic magnitude, which challenges the mind to find a rival explanation.

These types of before-and-after changes are, however, rare. The magnitude of differences between two study periods is usually characterized by small and moderate effect sizes, which then makes the assumption of internal validity more suspect. A purist approach might suggest that even with a dramatic before-and-after finding across several tests, it is still the case that alternative explanations for the outcome are possible. For this reason, studies should always try to establish a comparison group that "matured" in parallel with the exposed group. Such is the case with the post-test, after-only experiments. These are pre-experimental designs that look very much like the classic RCT design, with the random apportionment of a sample into treatment and control conditions; eligible cases are screened into the study and then a procedure of randomly allocating the units into those that would be exposed to the intervention and those that would not takes place. The comparison group is believed to be a true counterfactual of the treatment group due to the random assignment; therefore, any variations in the treated group are assumed to be a result of the treatment and not another factor.

Of course, there is an inherent assumption that the exposed and unexposed groups are similar at baseline in post-test experiments. The random allocation into the study conditions is *believed* to cause baseline equilibrium, so that we are comparing "like with like." However, achieving equivalence through random assignment is likely to occur when the overall sample size is "sufficiently large" (see Hertzog, 2008). In small(er) studies, achieving this baseline balance is problematic, not only in terms of extraneous variables, but even balance in terms of the very outcome variable at its pre-randomization values can be an issue if not enough participants are enrolled. The fact, however, is that the "small *n* problem" will continue to be an issue in EBP from both a statistical and practical angle. Large experiments can be very expensive. Managing a multisite experiment, with many units, is luxurious. Maintaining consistency over time can be daunting (eg Sherman and Weisburd, 1995). Yet, while this issue is not unique to our discipline (see Bruhn and McKenzie, 2009), from a statistical perspective, small sample sizes in experiments lead to designs that are "doomed to failure" since they are not large enough to detect small treatment effects.

Thus, saying that randomization leads to baseline equilibrium in a study is a declaration by itself. Practitioners as well as scholars should require researchers to be in a position to report on baseline factors, at least on the DV at its pre-test scores, in order to assume that the random assignment indeed created two or more groups that are similar to one another. (There is a debate in the statistical literature on whether significance testing is required in order to show baseline balance [eg Berger, 2005, 2009; Fayers and King, 2008]; however, we think that, at minimum, researchers should present these variables to the audience.) This is not always possible, especially if the experiment tests a novel intervention, if the data were not collected prior to random assignment, or if access to pre-test data is not feasible due to data-sharing constraints. Whenever such pre-test data are available, then the researcher is in a position to make an empirical declaration: the exposed and unexposed study groups are similar to one another. When this is the case, then the test can be called a true experimental design: an RCT.

Much has been said about the merits of the RCT design in answering questions of causality. EBP scholars seek the best methodological designs to provide them with the most reliable information on the possible benefits and costs of the intervention or policy under examination. There is an increasing agreement about the notion that the RCT is the most fitting for carrying out such examinations (Feder and Boruch, 2000; Weisburd and Taxman, 2000; Welsh and Farrington, 2001). In a "true experiment," the researcher has greater control over the design, and with the random sampling and random allocation of subjects into experimental groups and the administration of the studied manipulation under controlled conditions, the researcher can rule out alternative hypotheses and explanations (see White and McBurney, 2012: 222–3). At least in principle, only this method can "truly" allow the researcher to isolate the causal factor from alternative predicates through a design that is internally and externally valid (Sprinthall, 1994). Weisburd et al (2001: 3) concluded that "random allocation thus allows the researcher to assume that the only logical explanation for any systematic differences between the treatment and the comparison groups is found in the treatments or interventions applied." Therefore, this method is regarded as the most fit for contributing to the credibility of the results—more than any evaluation study (see discussion in Sherman, 2003).

Explicitly, there are several concerns that can be solved by using the RCT approach. First, randomized experiments can address the specification error encountered in observational models, as discussed earlier. Second, the random assignment of "one condition to half of a large population by a formula that makes it equally likely that each subject will receive one treatment or another" generates comparable distributions in each of the two groups of factors "that could affect results" (Sherman, 2013: 11). Third, the most effective way to study crime and crime-related policy is to intervene in a way that will permit the researcher to determine what effect, if any, the intervention has. Consequently, a decision-making process that relies on randomized experiments will result in more precise and reliable answers to questions about what works for decision-makers.

Given the advantages of experimental research, it is evident that there is a moral imperative for conducting randomized controlled experiments, an imperative rooted in researchers' obligation to furnish empirical evidence regarding criminal justice practices and policies. Moreover, there is an ethical obligation for the state to provide its citizens with programs that have been developed from empirical evidence and not based on ideo-political principles (Boruch et al, 2000).

At the same time, RCTs can be exposed to detrimental issues; if these cannot be overcome, then it might prove more cost-effective to resort to pre-experimental or even quasi-experimental designs instead. Perhaps more concerning than statistical power and sample size is the issue of treatment spillover effects. When spillover occurs, we can say that participants not offered the treatment will experience an indirect treatment effect from the program. While they were not allocated to the experimental group, they may experience a spillover effect from the treatment of other individuals that were assigned to a treatment group. In these situations, the spillover effect on the control participants is inadvertently to treat them despite being assigned to no-treatment conditions; subsequently, the intention to treat analysis suffers from crossover effects.

While all studies can suffer from the "bleeding" of treatment effects to no-intervention units, or even between the units (what is referred to as partial interference), RCTs lose their "purity" once we cannot assume that each unit of randomization is unaffected by the other units. In principle, we expect from RCTs that the outcome of one unit does not depend on the outcome of any other unit. When there is "interference," then we can assume that the treatment effect is either inflated or deflated, meaning that the true impact of the IV on the DV is masked to some degree, which depends on the level of contamination. This is referred to as the "spillover effect." Strictly speaking, spillover effects in randomized trials are said to contaminate the purity of the experimental design. The diffusion can take many forms; it can refer to the "bleeding" from the treatment to the control group, between treatment groups, within statistical blocks or clusters, or within individual treatment units (Campbell and Stanley, 1966; Shadish et al, 2002; Baird et al, 2016). For example, when the threat of spillover denotes an interference of the treatment group with the control group, it leads to "contaminated control conditions," and these conditions challenge the counterfactual contrast between units that were exposed to the intervention and units that were not. Rubin (1990; see also Cox, 1958) and others refer to this type of contamination as violation of the "stable unit treatment value assumption" (SUTVA); we assume that the effect of some intervention on a given individual is not related to the treatment assignments of other people (or observational units).

Purists might argue that their effects are detrimental to the internal validity of the test (see discussion in Sampson, 2010). In practice, however, many RCTs, especially field trials, encounter interference. It seems that, at least in "real-life sciences" such as criminology, these spillover effects are often unavoidable. Consequently, there are studies that deal directly with ways of minimizing the spillover problem. As summarized by Baird et al (2018: 1), the literature includes studies:

> that uncover network effects using experimental variation across treatment groups, leave some members of a group untreated, exploit plausibly exogenous variation in within-network treatments, or intersect an experiment with pre-existing networks. Further progress has been made by exploiting partial population experiments, in which clusters are assigned to treatment or control, and a subset of individuals are offered treatment within clusters assigned to treatment.

The conclusion from these studies is that interference is part and parcel of studies involving human beings, and that we need to "relax the assumption around interference between units" (Baird et al, 2018: 1).

Still, if these methodological issues can be addressed, scholars should then answer questions about impact using RCT methodologies. RCTs are increasingly recognized as the most fit design for policy evaluations, and we are seeing more and more of these over time (Braga et al, 2014). We suspect that their growing popularity in EBP will position them in the same position that they are given in medicine, pharmacy, engineering, and psychology: *the* research design for assessing causality. The EBP community is largely in agreement that RCTs form the premier methodology for these questions, but not all would agree about the ability of scholars to implement this design in criminology (Sampson, 2010; Greene, 2014). Experience suggests otherwise; EBP scholars have used RCTs to answer important questions in our profession about hot spots, restorative justice, technology in policing, and drug rehabilitation programs, to name a few. What is certain, however, is the growing usability of different evidence types in the formulation of policy—an aim shared by virtually all EBP scholars.

References

Antrobus, E., Thompson, I., and Ariel, B. (2018) "Procedural justice training for police recruits: results of a randomized controlled trial," *Journal of Experimental Criminology*, pp 1–25. Available at: https://doi.org/10.1007/s11292-018-9331-9.

Ariel, B., Farrar, W.A., and Sutherland, A. (2015) "The effect of police body-worn cameras on use of force and citizens' complaints against the police: a randomized controlled trial," *Journal of Quantitative Criminology*, 31(3): 509–535.

Ariel, B., Weinborn, C., and Sherman, L.W. (2016) "'Soft' policing at hot spots—do police community support officers work? A randomized controlled trial," *Journal of Experimental Criminology*, 12(3): 277–317.

Ariel, B., Bland, M., and Sutherland, A. (2017a) "Lowering the threshold of effective deterrence—testing the effect of private security agents in public spaces on crime: a randomized controlled trial in a mass transit system," *PLoS one*, 12(12): e0187392.

Ariel, B., Sutherland, A., Henstock, D., Young, J., Drover, P., Sykes, J., Megicks, S., and Henderson, R. (2017b) "Contagious accountability: a global multisite randomized controlled trial on the effect of police body-worn cameras on citizens' complaints against the police," *Criminal Justice and Behavior*, 44(2): 293–316.

Bachman, R. and Schutt, R.K. (2013) *The practice of research in criminology and criminal justice* (5th edn), Los Angeles: Sage.

Baird, S., Bohren, J.A., McIntosh, C. and Ozler, B. (2016) *Optimal design of experiments in the presence of interference*. PIER Working Paper No. 16-025. Available at: https://ssrn.com/abstract=2900967

Baird, S., Bohren, J.A., McIntosh, C. and Özler, B. (2018) "Optimal design of experiments in the presence of interference," *Review of Economics and Statistics*. Available at: https://doi.org/10.1162/REST_a_00716.

Barnham, L., Barnes, G.C., and Sherman, L.W. (2017) "Targeting escalation of intimate partner violence: evidence from 52,000 offenders," *Cambridge Journal of Evidence based Policing*, 1(2/3): 116–42.

Beebee, H., Hitchcock, C., and Menzies, P. (eds) (2009) *The Oxford handbook of causation*, New York, NY: Oxford University Press.

Berger, V.W. (2005) "The reverse propensity score to detect selection bias and correct for baseline imbalances," *Statistics in Medicine*, 24(18): 2777–2787.

Berger, V.W. (2009) "Do not test for baseline imbalances unless they are known to be present?" *Quality of Life Research*, 18(4): 399.

Berk, R.A., Sorenson, S.B., and Barnes, G. (2016) "Forecasting domestic violence: a machine learning approach to help inform arraignment decisions," *Journal of Empirical Legal Studies*, 13(1): 94–115.

Bland, M. and Ariel, B. (2015) "Targeting escalation in reported domestic abuse: evidence from 36,000 callouts," *International Criminal Justice Review*, 25(1): 30–53.

Boruch, R.F., Victor, T., and Cecil, J.S. (2000) "Resolving ethical and legal problems in randomized experiments," *NCCD News*, 46(3): 330–53.

Braga, A.A., Welsh, B.C., Papachristos, A.V., Schnell, C., and Grossman, L. (2014) "The growth of randomized experiments in policing: the vital few and the salience of mentoring," *Journal of Experimental Criminology*, 10(1): 1–28.

Bruhn, M. and McKenzie, D. (2009) "In pursuit of balance: randomization in practice in development field experiments," *American Economic Journal: Applied Economics*, 1(4): 200–32.

Bryman, A. (2015) *Social research methods* (5th edn), Oxford: Oxford University Press.

Burtless, G. (2002) "Randomized field trials for policy evaluation: why not in education," in F. Mosteller and R.F. Boruch (eds) *Evidence matters: Randomized trials in education research*, Washington, DC: Brookings Institution Press, pp 179–97.

Burton, D.L., Nesmith, A.A., and Badten, L. (1997) "Clinicians' views on sexually aggressive children and their families: a theoretical exploration," *Child Abuse & Neglect*, 21(2): 157–70.

Button, I.M., Angel, C., and Sherman, L.W. (2017) "Predicting domestic homicide and serious violence in Leicestershire with intelligence records of suicidal ideation or self-harm warnings: a retrospective analysis," *Cambridge Journal of Evidence based Policing*, 1(2/3): 105–15.

Campbell, D.T. and Stanley, J.C. (1966) *Experimental and quasi-experimental designs for research*, Chicago, IL: Rand McNally and Co.

Cantor, D. and Land, K.C. (1985) "Unemployment and crime rates in the post–World War II United States: a theoretical and empirical analysis," *American Sociological Review*, 50(3): 317–32.

Carr, R., Slothower, M., and Parkinson, J. (2017) "Do gang injunctions reduce violent crime? Four tests in Merseyside, UK," *Cambridge Journal of Evidence based Policing*, 1(4): 195–210.

Cartwright, W.S. (2000) "Cost–benefit analysis of drug treatment services: review of the literature," *The Journal of Mental Health Policy and Economics*, 3(1): 11–26.

Cox, D.R. (1958) *The planning of experiments*, New York: Wiley.

De Brito, C. and Ariel, B. (2017) "Does tracking and feedback boost patrol time in hot spots? Two tests," *Cambridge Journal of Evidence-Based Policing*, 1(4): 244–262.

De Vaus, D.A. (2001) *Research design in social research*, London: Sage.

Dudfield, G., Angel, C., Sherman, L.W., and Torrence, S. (2017) "The 'power curve' of victim harm: targeting the distribution of Crime Harm Index values across all victims and repeat victims over 1 year," *Cambridge Journal of Evidence-based Policing*, 1(1): 38–58.

Ethridge, D.E. (2004) *Research methodology in applied economics: organizing, planning, and conducting economic research*, Ames, IA: Blackwell Publishing.

Farrington, D.P., Petrosino, A., and Welsh, B.C. (2001) "Systematic reviews and cost–benefit analyses of correctional interventions," *The Prison Journal*, 81(3): 339–59.

Farrington, D.P., Gottfredson, D.C., Sherman, L.W., and Welsh, B.C. (2002) "The Maryland Scientific Methods Scale," in L.W. Sherman, D.P. Farrington, B.C. Welsh, and D.L. MacKenzie (eds) *Evidence based crime prevention*, London: Routledge, pp 13–21.

Fayers, P.M. and King, M. (2008) "A highly significant difference in baseline characteristics: the play of chance or evidence of a more selective game?" *Quality of Life Research*, 17(9): 1121–3.

Feder, L. and Boruch, R.F. (2000) "The need for experiments in criminal justice settings," *NCCD News*, 46(3): 291–4.

Fielding, N. and Schreier, M. (2001) "Introduction: on the compatibility between qualitative and quantitative research methods," *Forum Qualitative Sozialforschung/Forum: Qualitative Social Research*, 2(1). Available at: http://nbn-resolving.de/urn:nbn:de:0114-fqs010146

Fleiss, J.L., Levin, B., and Paik, M.C. (2013) *Statistical methods for rates and proportions*, New York, NY: John Wiley & Sons.

Gazal-Ayal, O. and Sulitzeanu-Kenan, R. (2010) "Let my people go: ethnic in-group bias in judicial decisions—evidence from a randomized natural experiment," *Journal of Empirical Legal Studies*, 7(3): 403–28.

Gibson, C., Slothower, M., and Sherman, L.W. (2017) "Sweet spots for hot spots? A cost-effectiveness comparison of two patrol strategies," *Cambridge Journal of Evidence based Policing*, 1(4): 225–43.

Gottfredson, M. and Hirschi, T. (1987) "The methodological adequacy of longitudinal research on crime," *Criminology*, 25(3): 581–614.

Greene, J.R. (2014) "New directions in policing: balancing prediction and meaning in police research," *Justice Quarterly*, 31(2): 193–228.

Grimes, D.A. and Schulz, K.F. (2002) "Bias and causal associations in observational research," *The Lancet*, 359(9302): 248–52.

Hagan, F.E. (2013) *Research methods in criminal justice and criminology* (9th edn), Needham Heights, MA: Pearson Higher Ed.

Hanges, P.J. and Wang, M. (2012) "Seeking the holy grail in organizational psychology: establishing causality through research design," in S.W.J. Kozlowski (ed) *The Oxford handbook of organizational psychology*, New York, NY: Oxford University Press, pp 79–116.

Haviland, A., Nagin, D.S., and Rosenbaum, P.R. (2007) "Combining propensity score matching and group-based trajectory analysis in an observational study," *Psychological Methods*, 12(3): 247.

Haynes, R.B. (2002) "What kind of evidence is it that evidence based medicine advocates want health care providers and consumers to pay attention to?" *BMC Health Services Research*, 2(1): 3.

Heckman, J.J. (1979) "Sample selection bias as a specification error," *Econometrica*, 47(1): 153.

Henstock, D. and Ariel, B. (2017) "Testing the effects of police body-worn cameras on use of force during arrests: a randomised controlled trial in a large British police force," *European Journal of Criminology*, 14(6): 720–750.

Hertzog, M.A. (2008) "Considerations in determining sample size for pilot studies," *Research in Nursing & Health*, 31(2): 180–91.

Hirschi, T. and Gottfredson, M. (1983) "Age and the explanation of crime," *American Journal of Sociology*, 89(3): 552–84.

Holland, P.W. (1986) "Statistics and causal inference," *Journal of the American Statistical Association*, 81(396): 945–60.

Jennings, W.G., Fridell, L.A., Lynch, M., Jetelina, K.K., and Reingle Gonzalez, J.M. (2017) "A quasi-experimental evaluation of the effects of police body-worn cameras (BWCs) on response-to-resistance in a large metropolitan police department," *Deviant Behavior*, 38(11): 1332–9.

Jupp, V.R. (1989) *Methods of criminological research*, London: Routledge.

Koper, C.S. (1995) "Just enough police presence: reducing crime and disorderly behavior by optimizing patrol time in crime hot spots," *Justice Quarterly*, 12(4): 649–72.

Lackner, N., Unterrainer, H.F., Skliris, D., Wood, G., Wallner-Liebmann, S.J., Neuper, C., and Gruzelier, J.H. (2016) "The effectiveness of visual short-time neurofeedback on brain activity and clinical characteristics in alcohol use disorders: practical issues and results," *Clinical EEG and Neuroscience*, 47(3): 188–95.

Laub, J.H. and Vaillant, G.E. (2000) "Delinquency and mortality: a 50-year follow-up study of 1,000 delinquent and nondelinquent boys," *American Journal of Psychiatry*, 157(1): 96–102.

Leon, A.C., Davis, L.L., and Kraemer, H.C. (2011) "The role and interpretation of pilot studies in clinical research," *Journal of Psychiatric Research*, 45(5): 626–9.

Lewis, D. (1974) "Causation," *The Journal of Philosophy*, 70(17): 556–67.

Lum, C. and Yang, S.M. (2005) "Why do evaluation researchers in crime and justice choose non-experimental methods?" *Journal of Experimental Criminology*, 1(2): 191–213.

Mann, C.J. (2003) "Observational research methods. Research design II: cohort, cross sectional, and case-control studies," *Emergency Medicine Journal*, 20(1): 54–60.

Marsh, C. (1979) "Problems with surveys: method or epistemology?" *Sociology*, 13(2): 293–305.

Maskaly, J., Donner, C., Jennings, W.G., Ariel, B., and Sutherland, A. (2017) "The effects of body-worn cameras (BWCs) on police and citizen outcomes: a state-of-the-art review," *Policing: An International Journal of Police Strategies & Management*, 40(4): 672–688.

McGue, M., Osler, M., and Christensen, K. (2010) "Causal inference and observational research: the utility of twins," *Perspectives on Psychological Science*, 5(5): 546–56.

Mitchell, R.J. (2017) "Frequency versus duration of police patrol visits for reducing crime in hot spots: non-experimental findings from the Sacramento hot spots experiment," *Cambridge Journal of Evidence based Policing*, 1(1): 1–16. Available at: https://doi.org/10.1007/s41887-017-0002-2

Mitchell, R.J. and Lewis, S. (2017) "Intention is not method, belief is not evidence, rank is not proof: ethical policing needs evidence based decision making," *International Journal of Emergency Services*, 6(3): 188–99.

Murphy, K. and Tyler, T.R. (2017) "Experimenting with procedural justice policing," *Journal of Experimental Criminology*, 13(3): 287–92.

Nagin, D.S. and Odgers, C.L. (2010) "Group-based trajectory modeling in clinical research," *Annual Review of Clinical Psychology*, 6: 109–38.

Nagin, D.S. and Telep, C.W. (2017) "Procedural justice and legal compliance," *Annual Review of Law and Social Science*, 13: 5–28.

Poyner, B. (1993) "What works in crime prevention: an overview of evaluations," *Crime Prevention Studies*, 1: 7–34.

Ready, J.T. and Young, J.T. (2015) "The impact of on-officer video cameras on police–citizen contacts: findings from a controlled experiment in Mesa, AZ," *Journal of Experimental Criminology*, 11(3): 445–58.

Rivera, A., Gago, B., Suárez-Boomgaard, D., Yoshitake, T., Roales-Buján, R., Valderrama-Carvajal, A., Bilbao, A., Medina-Luque, J., Diaz-Cabiale, Z., Van Craenenbroeck, K., Borroto-Escuela, D.O., Kehr, J., Rodríguez de Fonseca, F., Santín, L.J., de la Calle, A., and Fuxe, K. (2017) "Dopamine D4 receptor stimulation prevents nigrostriatal dopamine pathway activation by morphine: relevance for drug addiction," *Addiction Biology*, 22(5): 1232–45.

Rubin, D.B. (1990) "Formal mode of statistical inference for causal effects," *Journal of Statistical Planning and Inference*, 25(3): 279–292.

Salkind, N.J. (ed.) (2010) *Encyclopedia of research design*, Vol. 1. Thousand Oaks, CA: Sage.

Sampson, R.J. (2010) "Gold standard myths: observations on the experimental turn in quantitative criminology," *Journal of Quantitative Criminology*, 26(4): 489–500.

Shadish, W.R., Cook, T.D., and Campbell, D.T. (2002) *Experimental and quasi-experimental designs for generalized causal inference*, New York, NY: Houghton Mifflin Company.

Shaw, J.W. (1995) "Community policing against guns: public opinion of the Kansas City gun experiment," *Justice Quarterly*, 12(4): 695–710.

Sherman, L.W., Gottfredson, D.C., MacKenzie, D.L., Eck, J., Reuter, P., and Bushway, S.D. (1997) *Preventing crime: What works, what doesn't, what's promising: A report to the United States Congress*, Washington, DC: US Department of Justice, Office of Justice Programs.

Sherman, L.W. (1998) *Evidence based policing*, Ideas in American Policing, Washington, DC: The Police Foundation.

Sherman, L.W. (2003) "Misleading evidence and evidence-led policy: making social science more experimental," *The Annals of the American Academy of Political and Social Science*, 589(1): 6–19.

Sherman, L.W. (2009) "Evidence and liberty: the promise of experimental criminology," *Criminology & Criminal Justice*, 9(1): 5–28.

Sherman, L.W. (2010) "An introduction to experimental criminology," in A.R. Piquero and D. Weisburd (eds) *Handbook of quantitative criminology*, New York, NY: Springer, pp 399–436.

Sherman, L.W. (2013) "The rise of evidence based policing: targeting, testing, and tracking," *Crime and Justice*, 42(1): 377–451.

Sherman, L.W. and Rogan, D.P. (1995) "Effects of gun seizures on gun violence: 'hot spots' patrol in Kansas City," *Justice Quarterly*, 12(4): 673–93.

Sherman, L.W. and Weisburd, D. (1995) "General deterrent effects of police patrol in crime 'hot spots': a randomized, controlled trial," *Justice Quarterly*, 12(4): 625–48.

Sprinthall, N.A. (1994) "Counseling and social role taking: promoting moral and ego development," in J. Rest and D. Narváez (eds) *Moral development in the professions: Psychology and applied ethics*, Hillsdale, NJ: Lawrence Erlbaum Associates, pp 85–100

Stebbins, R.A. (2001) *Exploratory research in the social sciences*, Sage University Papers Series on Quantitative Methods, vol 48, Thousand Oaks, CA: Sage.

Sutherland, A. (2012) "Is parental socio-economic status related to the initiation of substance abuse by young people in an English city? An event history analysis," *Social Science & Medicine*, 74(7): 1053–61.

Sweeten, G., Piquero, A.R., and Steinberg, L. (2013) "Age and the explanation of crime, revisited," *Journal of Youth and Adolescence*, 42(6): 921–38.

Tankebe, J. (2009) "Public cooperation with the police in Ghana: does procedural fairness matter?" *Criminology*, 47(4): 1265–93.

Tankebe, J. and Ariel, B. (2016) "Cynicism towards change: the case of body-worn cameras among police officers." Available at: https://papers.ssrn.com/sol3/papers.cfm?abstract_id= 2850743

Tewksbury, R. (2009) "Qualitative versus quantitative methods: understanding why qualitative methods are superior for criminology and criminal justice," *Journal of Theoretical & Philosophical Criminology*, 1(1): 38–58.

Tyler, T.T. (2017) "Procedural justice and policing: a rush to judgment?" *Annual Review of Law and Social Science*, 13: 29–53.

Ulmer, J.T. and Johnson, B. (2004) "Sentencing in context: a multilevel analysis," *Criminology*, 42(1): 137–78.

Weisburd, D. and Taxman, F.S. (2000) "Developing a multicenter randomized trial in criminology: the case of HIDTA," *Journal of Quantitative Criminology*, 16(3): 315–40.

Weisburd, D., Lum, C.M., and Petrosino, A. (2001) "Does research design affect study outcomes in criminal justice?" *The Annals of the American Academy of Political and Social Science*, 578(1): 50–70.

Welsh, B.C. and Farrington, D.P. (2001) "Toward an evidence based approach to preventing crime," *The ANNALS of the American Academy of Political and Social Science*, 578(1): 158–173.

West, D.J., Farrington, D.P., and Cambridge Study in Delinquent Development (1973) *Who becomes delinquent? Second report of the Cambridge Study in Delinquent Development*, London: Heinemann Educational for the Cambridge Institute of Criminology.

White, T.L. and McBurney, D.H. (2012) *Research methods*, California, CA: Wadsworth Cengage Learning.

Wikström, P.O. (2008) "In search of causes and explanations of crime," in R. King and E. Wincup (eds) *Doing research on crime and justice*, Oxford: Oxford University Press, pp 117–40.

Wilcox, D.T., Richards, F., and O'Keeffe, Z.C. (2004) "Resilience and risk factors associated with experiencing childhood sexual abuse," *Child Abuse Review*, 13(5): 338–52.

7

Twitter: a new Tardis for policing?

Emma Williams

Canterbury Christ Church University

Ian Hesketh

Alliance Manchester Business School

Introduction

Social media and the data it offers can provide a gateway into the opinions, ideas, and feelings of entire communities of people. Furthermore, such insights offer police researchers an incredible opportunity to "study social and cultural processes and dynamics in new ways" (Manovich, 2012: 461). Police use of social media has attracted a huge amount of attention around the globe, both across the service and in the public arena (Goldsmith, 2015). However, it has primarily focused on the way in which forums such as Twitter and Facebook can facilitate communications with the public, as well as the inappropriate use of such media by both serving and retired police officers.

Using a case study of a relatively new online police discussion forum (@wecops), this chapter focuses on the potential use of social media within the field of police research. Hitherto, there has been much debate about the current perceptions among police officers regarding the presence of their voices within popular police research methodologies (Gundhus, 2012). The impact that this has on police officers' willingness to become involved in the implementation of the outputs driven by evidence based policing research (see Williams and Cockcroft, Chapter Ten) has also been regularly discussed. Sherman (2013) argues that research in policing can facilitate the transformation of the police into a more professional organization, and one that will also be considered more legitimate to the outside world. However, there are differing notions of what is meant by a "professional organization," as well as of "professional knowledge," which are worthy of further exploration within this narrative. Controversially, the professionalization of the UK police service is one of the highest priorities of the UK College of Policing.

Primarily, we are concerned with the use of social media as a forum to understand what Van Dijk et al (2015) refer to as "*what* matters," and just as importantly, we value what matters to who. We concede that much of the police research agenda is preoccupied with the "*what works, crime reduction*" agenda (Punch, 2015). The idea of "*what matters*" may link both to the wider wicked problems (Grint, 2010) that the police are now dealing with, and also to the impact that such complex demands have on officers' well-being and mental health (Hesketh and Cooper, 2017). This is analogous with the so-called "VUCA" world described by Casey (2014), where, like the military he refers to, the police deal with vulnerability, uncertainty, complexity, and ambiguity on an almost daily basis. As Punch (2015) posits, the "*pure*" applied science approach of police research does not always reveal the complexity of the variables involved, including the views of the practitioners working within the field. This position, arguably, also views the world as static and in denial of societal change (Young, 2004). Officers' voices are critical for furthering understanding about these complex changing issues. This is the world within which police officers and staff operate.

Evetts (2013) argues that an overreliance on pure statistics and prescriptive outputs can undermine an individual's sense of occupational professionalism, which recognizes the role of the craft skills being utilized in the highly complex situations that the police face. Indeed, this requires trusting officers to use their discretion and autonomy both effectively and ethically. This is in contrast to organizational professionalism, which sets to control, monitor, and standardize behavior, which may be consonant with arguments around discretionary activity and systems thinking philosophy.

In this chapter, we will focus on the merging of experiential knowledge and academic work, using social media as an innovative method to expand the evidence base for police research, and to capture the voice of the practitioner. The aim is to explore and report on what may deepen our understanding of what counts as valuable knowledge in this field. As new thinking emerges on social media use by the police, it is important to consider both opportunities and limitations.

As authors of this chapter, we contend that the research question being posed by the researcher should always define the methodology used. As Greene (2014) states, police research needs a range of methodologies that provide meaning to the sterility of the data provided in a purely quantitative, randomized controlled trial (RCT). While this method is considered, by some criminologists, as a dependable and reliable method to discover the truth (Hope, 2005: 290), the meanings and values of those actions need to be contextualized and understood given the complexity of police demand. Twitter can provide important and regular insights into this world that Greene (2014) refers to. Furthermore, such knowledge sharing could be a valuable method for attempting to reduce the perceived gap between academic researchers and police practitioners.

The meaning and value of knowledge

The use of social media as a method to identify "police knowledge" can offer original ways of assisting researchers both with the provision of information for research and for the purposes of involving practitioners in the development of research outputs. Indeed, as Lievrouw (2010) highlights, the options for sharing information on social media can have important consequences for scientific communication between researchers and users of their work. Therefore, it can transform the delivery of research "from a relatively straightforward process of gatekeeping, publishing and targeted search and retrieval, into a multi-layered, socialized arena for commentary, amendment, collaboration, critique, argumentation and recommendation" (Lievrouw, 2010: 221). There is potential for such involvement in the entire research process, from knowledge creation through to the development of outputs in order to drive a further commitment to the implementation of any research recommendations offered (Wood et al, 2008). Additionally, social media can help break down the "secret veil" of policing (Reiner, 2010) and offer real-time insights about issues affecting officers and what they might be doing in practice to deal with them.

Engaging practitioner groups in research is complicated for a number of reasons. These reasons may relate to a lack of access to academic journals, limited time to read what might be considered as irrelevant research reports, and a lack of opportunity to interact directly with researchers. This disconnect may be particularly exacerbated in the current climate, where officers are working in a period of austerity. As Dawson and Williams (2009) state, there has been a police perception of academics in "ivory towers" discussing theoretical concepts and rarely aligning their work to practical outputs. Schnitzler et al (2016) discuss this in the context of nursing research and argue that social media can offer researchers a new way of both engaging with practitioners for the purposes of research, and disseminating findings. They explored how Twitter could offer a way to engage with what they articulate as hard-to-reach audiences in the research process. Indeed, in the context of health care, they concluded that Twitter is an excellent forum to link practitioners into research that can help drive impact in practice. Our own observations go some way to supporting this in the context of UK policing (Hesketh and Williams, 2017).

The interchangeable notions of terms such as "evidence," "knowledge," and "research" are descriptions of what could theoretically amount to the same thing in this context. However, while they have differing meanings to both different researchers and practitioners, they are broadly used interchangeably to describe factors that influence practice. Briner et al (2009) suggest that there are four sources of evidence that inform management practice, practitioner expertise, organizational data, research findings, and stakeholder voice. Gibbons et al (1994) argue that in contemporary society, there is a need to consider a new mode of knowledge production that stretches beyond the work created in universities.

An online ethnographic research method ("netnography") is largely unrecognized and unused in policing (Kozinets, 2002). However, we consider that research approaches such as this can provide useful insight into the policing voice. The increase in what are commonly referred to as "pracademics" (practitioner-academics) is a further expansion of traditional research approaches, which are often so deeply rooted in philosophical methodology that practitioners report them as being problematic to operationalize. However, the professionalization agenda that we have mooted may be dependent on new thinking of this kind. Marketers have already moved quickly to test and report the usefulness of such research methods as netnography, for example, La Rocca et al (2014) discuss applying ethnography to web activity in order to establish buying and consumption patterns. It seems fair to consider a similar application in policing as potentially useful. As the policing service promotes academically rooted practice, or evidence based practice, as an approach to new policing, it is incumbent to consider how this is best achieved. We now discuss some of the challenges to these aspirations.

Despite the relationship between academia and police organizations improving, namely, through the growing number of academic–police consortiums and research collaborations, such perceptions are likely to risk the smooth embedding of this change in practice. Thacher (2008) highlights how a sustained body of knowledge can inhibit the normalization of research use in policing as it is viewed as supporting the needs of management as opposed to the front line. As Fleming and Wingrove (2017) argue, if officers consider evidence based policing as something that assists with promotion within the management ranks, the relationship will never be smooth. Initiatives such as Direct Entry, Fast Track, High Potential Development, and Talent Management introduced into UK policing are a good example and have been widely contested. The perception that managers implement new schemes and formally evaluate them based only on numerical data describes just part of the narrative. The perception that such schemes are "doomed to succeed" once again undermines the role of research. By not seeking the views of the officers delivering the work, the reality of the entire picture remains opaque. The barriers that have existed between police and researchers (Reiner, 2010) are compounded by some officers' perceptions of feeling ignored in the research process, and a sense that research is primarily aimed at developing policy over understanding their perspective as an active participant in that environment.

So, what about social media as a research tool?

The micro-blogging site Twitter was only launched in July 2006. Twitter claims to have the mission of giving everyone the power to create and share ideas and information instantly, without barriers (Twitter, 2016). There has been a move in public health research to use Twitter, both as a way of interacting with potential research participants, and to explore the forum for useful data about key issues (Schnitzler et al, 2016). In the context of policing, despite social media offering a unique and interactive, big data source for researchers, there has been little written, to date, about its use to provide research evidence.

Twitter, as social media, provides a huge opportunity for both researchers and practitioners. It is a wide forum with potential to be used as a site for research, innovation, knowledge exchange, advocacy, networking, and professional development, to name but a few (Geia et al, 2017). The space also offers a "cultural interface" (Geia et al, 2017: 281) between different groups and for decision-makers to hear a range of perspectives. While there are issues with the validity and reliability of the information gleaned from social media forums, we would still claim that the opportunity to use data from Twitter as a starting point is worthy of further consideration.

There have been a large number of police station closures in the UK over recent years and the trend continues throughout the country, initiated to a great extent by the *Comprehensive spending review* (Treasury, 2010). The ubiquitous "canteen culture" is often referred to in academic literature relating to policing (for extensive research, see, eg, Loftus, 2010; Reiner, 2010). This (canteen) environment provided a cultural home for researchers, in which they could garner significant and rich data about the police. These data was made up from storytelling and conversations that occurred within such police canteens in an informal manner. This is itself important for two reasons. First, as Waddington (1999) found in his research, canteen narratives can offer palliative care to officers for a number of reasons as they can relieve boredom and restore identities within a group setting. Police well-being is widely debated in the current environment, both within practitioner and researcher groups (Hesketh and Williams, 2017). Therefore, a reduction in this environment and its ability to provide this function may be detrimental to officers in this context. The value of defusing, as an approach to stress relief or for addressing anxiety or other worries about incidents that officers have dealt with, is widely known as a helpful therapeutic means of coping (see, eg, clinical supervision models in the National Health Service [NHS] or National Institute for Health and Care Excellence [NICE] guidelines in the UK).

Second, as Van Hulst (2013) postulates, police stories told here can offer a method to share vital knowledge about local criminals, tactics, environments, and events—so-called intelligence-gathering. Therefore, as an example, this can act as a stage for sharing information and craft knowledge with new recruits about what they might experience out in the field. This "informal" environment also offers researchers a space to observe officers in their natural setting, and, indeed, much of the scholarly and seminal work on policing has been driven from such ethnographic research arenas (Van Maanen, 1988). It is here perhaps that officers will reflect on their day and make personal and shared observations about what they delivered and what they might do differently should they experience a similar situation again, both positively and negatively.

Christopher (2015), in his analysis of reflective practice in policing, argues that officers construct and contribute relevant and grounded views to the local police debate, and that this can serve to promote their own approach to policing, as well as their sense of professionalism. It is in the canteen that this constructed narrative building featured. However, as Braga (2016) posited, it is rare that this information, and occupational knowledge and expertise, is systematically analyzed or considered next to other community or academic sources.

Arguably, along with the complex demands that officers now face (College of Policing, 2014), the limited environment for this exchange of reflections and narratives is decreasing, as are the environments and settings for researchers to access such storytelling. Therefore, social media might offer an alternative for both officers and researchers. This virtual environment allows for these discussions and for capturing information from these important learning debates in a more public arena. Van Zoonen et al (2016) found from their own analysis that employees' work-related messages posted on Twitter do provide an important depiction of work experiences. They can effectively assist with sharing knowledge and with internal socialization. The authors further argue that this can facilitate professional and organizational understanding, and can both foster internal communications across all levels of a workplace, and provide external communication for those interested in that occupation. This is worthwhile exploring in the context of both the police and police research.

The options for policing: @wecops

Considering the problematic nature of communication, and the transference of information about evidence based policing, it is worth mentioning here an example of an information sharing forum for police on social media. The online police discussion forum @wecops is an online bi-weekly debate focused on any given policing subject. Debates can be targeted at a particular, relevant audience when focused on something specific or they can be aimed at a more generic audience to gather views about wider policing issues. There has been relatively good take-up of the opportunity and the debates do provide a structured method to explore front-line officers' views on important subjects. The issues raised by officers through the @wecops debates concerning their ability to engage in social media are crucial to this chapter. They can reflect wider concerns about the general use of Twitter among police officers, and, in ways, this is also important to this chapter. The perceived opportunity to communicate across ranks and with other policing professionals is also important. Even cursory analysis indicates limited deference, which is helpful in facilitating open communication and engagement in such a traditionally hierarchical occupation. Officers who do use Twitter can be skeptical about anonymity, the disclosure of tactics used, and so on. However, perceptions about the positive role that social media can play in influencing open discussions and encouraging transparency among police leaders is vital at a time when officers feel disengaged from decision-making. The next section will explore one of these debates as an example.

Testing perceptions

During the "Policing under Stress" conference at Canterbury Christ Church University in June 2016, the use of social media came up frequently, particularly regarding Twitter being used as a forum for officers and staff to voice their thoughts on policing. As a result, the authors here suggested a Twitter debate, which they hosted in 2016. The debate posed three questions:

1. How do we gain evidence about policing practice through social media?
2. How do we put that evidence to good use?
3. What are the barriers to using social media for knowledge creation?

The extensive debate provided a useful narrative about both Twitter use and the broader policing field. It offered officers an opportunity to voice their opinion about using social media as a research tool and offered insight into the wider challenges around its effectiveness.

What the authors primarily wanted to explore concerned officers' thoughts on the provision of evidence from Twitter, and the debate revealed three main themes:

1. concern about officer anonymity and force inconsistency about the use of social media;
2. the importance of being discrete about what is disclosed regarding tactics and sensitive details, especially in relation to local communities; and
3. the role of social media in starting conversations about important issues, putting people in touch, and allowing leaders to be more transparent and explorative in their approach to the front line.

These points all relate to: negative communications and their sense of disengagement from leaders; perceptions of the poor decision-making around organizational change; understandings of research; and recent policy development and local decisions that impact on them and yet fail to consider their voices (Thacher, 2008; Hoggett et al, 2014). Considering this in the context of Twitter as a research tool, there is much evidence to suggest value in its use as a method of communicating with people about the issues affecting them and to understand the social reality of their experiences.

In relation to being careful with the practitioner description of the reality of policing to the outside world, this is indeed complicated. A recent example is the "Cuts have Consequences" campaign. This campaign sought to inform the UK public about the reality of resource cuts to policing, and to rebalance the expectations that they may have of the police. It was effectively a multifaceted protest about reduced officer numbers, increased budget constraints, and rising levels of criminality. Research is about seeking out the truth, leaning again on the ethics of *honesty, openness,* and *integrity* (College of Policing, 2014). This is exactly why Twitter is such a useful tool: it starts such investigative conversations for us; it raises new issues; it captures information that many currently in vogue methodologies can miss; and it provides real insight into those practitioners doing the job. Indeed, as described earlier, if it is the case that the police are now using this virtual arena to discuss work issues with other officers, it might be that this space is becoming the forum where police culture becomes reconstructed, and, likewise, officers' identities within that culture. Furthermore, it offers insight into the context of police actions in a new perhaps natural setting for practitioners (Bittner, 1978).

Many officers tweet under an anonymous account, as well as via a separate, formal work profile to provide information to the public. Interestingly, one thing that emerged from the @wecops debate was that the information is not useful purely for the research environment; it also provides an important insight for police leaders when considering the health of, and perceptions of, front-line staff. As @HelenKingMPS (2016) tweeted: "I see it as a way of keeping in touch—social media can lessen the barriers created by rank." Helen King was the Assistant Commissioner of the Metropolitan Police Service at the time.

Follow-up @wecops blogs offer vast amounts of information about a specific topic under enquiry. By trusting officers and allowing them the space to be honest, but in an informed and careful way, a range of audiences can surely use this information. A further point that emerged in discussions was police blogging, with blogs being another child of the Internet, originally "*web logs*," and the now-proud parents of micro-blogs, of which Twitter is one. Micro-blogs have a shortened format to that of their unruly and often lengthy parent activity. Academics have used officer blogs to expand student knowledge on a subject from a practitioner perspective. In some cases, this can be the quickest method to make research and theory feel real for police students, to bring it to life. For example, lecturers have referred to blogs in sessions, they have promoted presentations from police bloggers in conferences, and many papers are often widely published in police-related magazines, online publications, and journals. They were identified in the @wecops debate as excellent sources of information. This input is, indeed, evidence and it provides the context that other standalone, more sterile methods miss.

Considering this in the context of Twitter as a research and learning tool, there is much evidence to suggest value in its use as a method of communicating with people about the issues affecting them and to understand the social reality of their experiences. We are not suggesting that Twitter can offer the same environment as traditional research contexts, where researchers can build up trust with participants and immerse themselves in police life through ethnographic methods (Brown, 1996). Indeed, we acknowledge that, in some sense, the traditional canteen environment is far more invisible to leaders, the public, researchers, and other areas of the organization. Therefore, given the extent to which senior leaders are expected to evidence cultural change, Twitter as an open-source forum must, for many, feel very threatening (Hesketh and Williams, 2017). It is therefore unsurprising that officers can feel concern about the issues that they might discuss on Twitter. That said, there seems to be no reduction in the number of officers engaging actively in social media channels. It would, in our opinion at least, appear that the opposite is taking place.

There is a perception among the police that they are viewed as a simple resource whose personal knowledge and professionalism has been superseded by a more rational, objective knowledge that is provided by outsiders to the lived reality (Willis and Mastrofski, 2016). This is also important for academics as it appears in the current police research climate that the focus on the positive and the discovery of "what works" has negated the role of researchers and research as critical problem raisers over problem solvers (Christie, 1971). Indeed, research needs to focus on problem identification as well as the application of solutions. While this has, in the past, been viewed by practitioners as academics finding criticism with police practice, it can also mean developing an understanding of the issues that police officers themselves face in the current climate. Practitioners may argue that academics' obsession with long-term trials (eg RCTs) does little to resolve today's problems (as highlighted by "instant" social media coverage). Professional knowledge is about recognizing these individuals' expertise, listening to it, and identifying what meaning can be applied to it. It is not leaving the most important asset—the staff—feeling like a unit of production (Hesketh and Williams, 2017). Indeed, if academics fail to capture these voices, there is a risk that they will become further embroiled in a conformist, sociological agenda that has sought to politicize both criminological and sociological discourses (Narayanan, cited in Cockcroft, 2017: 2).

What good is it to the research community when conducting projects to hear an abundance of unreal false positivity when trying to create a picture of officer realities, what Collinson (2012) termed "Prozac leadership?" This is exactly why we think Twitter is such a useful tool: it begins conversations and brings new issues to the surface; it can capture information that many current methodologies can miss; and it provides real insight into the lives of the practitioners doing the job. Indeed, as described earlier, if it is the case that the police are now using the virtual environment to discuss issues with other officers, it might be that this space is becoming the forum where police culture becomes redefined (Hesketh and Williams, 2017). Furthermore, as Cockcroft (2017) highlights, police culture should not be continuously seen as negative and reduced down to a predicted set of behaviors that emerge from it. Notions of solidarity, support, and social isolation (Loftus, 2010) can perform a necessary and important role in reducing police stress, and rather than viewing it as an illegitimate concept, it may well be the opposite for those within it. It might be that a critical analysis of this new virtual space could provide a real insight into what Reiner (2010) identifies as the policing social world and officers' role within it.

For researchers interested in raising issues around the problematic nature of contemporary policing, both in relation to the issues officers face and those they experience themselves, Twitter may offer a window into the occupational culture that perhaps now pervades anonymously in a virtual world. This is not to say that methodologies and outputs grounded in what Young (2004) termed "administrative criminology" have not assisted the experience of those that both work in and experience the criminal justice system, but there is space for a wider understanding of policing from the voice of the practitioner. Furthermore, through focused debate and analysis, police leaders can learn significantly about the health of both their staff and their organization.

Contemporary policing environment

In an environment that is attempting to improve organizational well-being and the working environment (Hesketh et al, 2015), paying attention to the voices contributing to Twitter can contribute to this support. Interestingly, this was one of the first aims of @wecops. By trusting officers and allowing them the space to be honest, but in an informed and careful way, leaders can surely use and consider this while understanding the situation within their own teams or places of business. Invariably, for whatever reason, there is a particular narrative and audience that often, in the real world, can get lost as a result of issues with communication. In defense of the police community, academics have also been guilty of this in the past, and this is perhaps why research, despite its longevity in the police world, has been complex to embed, congruent with the points made by Fyfe and Wilson (2012).

Issues of anonymity, and concern about what you can and cannot communicate to the public, were expected. What was clear in the debate was the broad recognition of Twitter as a tool for better communications for leaders, the public, and the research community, for the police to link up with key people with similar interests and ideas, and for leaders to observe current feelings from those on the front line; it is undoubtedly a huge opportunity to grow a network, a critical mass, or "a movement," as described by Schillinger (2014). What was also clear in the debate was the current concern about reprisals for sharing certain "evidence" openly. Interestingly, for researchers, this is evidence in itself! It seems that the officers who use Twitter remain unclear about what they can share, with whom they can share it, and what will happen to them as a result. This may be an issue related to that word again: communication. Until this is clear, the research agenda has the potential to remain skewed by one-dimensional evidence that can ignore voice and context.

Twitter and social media should be welcomed as a way of helping to capture this, starting research conversations, questioning the current evidence base (or at least providing another view on it), and assisting with creating an environment that may be more conducive to sustaining and embedding the use of research in the practical world of policing in the longer term, and thus reducing the theory–practice gulf. Loftus (2010: 20) concluded from her research on police culture that the core characteristics that thread through the literature on this subject remain constant: "The timeless qualities of police culture endure because the basic pressures associated with the police role have not been removed." To truly understand this in context, the secretive veil needs opening further, and this may well be one of the ways to do so.

Conclusions

So, how do we work a virtual climate, which, as we have discussed, is volatile, uncertain, ambiguous, and extremely complex, into an evidence based practice approach? This being the crux, it is surely incumbent on those reporting on policing from whatever angle, whether ethnography or netnography, to use the best available evidence. The recent rise in the public using social media offers a plethora of public online data to researchers in the social sciences. Nonaka (1994) argues that any organization operating in and dealing with the consequences of a changing environment needs to not simply process and use knowledge, but also create it. The use of evidence garnered from social media conversations may well constitute the practitioner voice as part of this knowledge creation, and could be viewed in a similar way as other, more traditional, qualitative approaches for eliciting information from the police. Eliciting practitioner expertise and professional experience in this way may be wholly appropriate as a way of searching for knowledge available at that moment in time. It is feasible that there are multiple versions of that knowledge, or angles from which to view it; perhaps a philosophical description may be found in alethic pluralism. This issue seems deserving of further exploration and may have a number of positive consequences for the landscape of evidence based policing, practitioner involvement and participation in research, and the identification of creative and innovative practice in police work. In other sectors, for example, research shows that employee productivity and organizational survival are linked to innovation and creativity (Sigala and Chalkiti, 2015). Creativity and learning, the research argues, can be enhanced through the use of social media not only via the use of collecting new evidence and knowledge from academia and other practitioners, but also by co-creating it with them. Other research conducted in the financial industry by Leonardi (2014) concluded that internal social networks used for the purposes of sharing knowledge had a range of positive benefits. This confluence of ideas in the search for evidence included a growth in innovation, reduced work duplication, and increased trust between workers. The authors here suggest that exploring wider communication methods in the context of the policing world, both for academics and practitioners, is in need of further consideration. Moreover, there is perhaps added value in thinking about the further learning and knowledge that it can provide to officers themselves.

Experiential learning has traditionally developed via active face-to-face communications. However, if the canteen culture, discussed by so many, is diminishing (in the physical sense), then this virtual world might provide an environment for the creation of meta-knowledge via the process of vicarious learning (Ren and Argote, cited in Leonardi, 2014: 799), which can occur through the use of social media by officers and policing academics. We see a bottom-up movement of evidence creation; comparable with Minecraft, the world is added to by contributions from unknown and untested sources, yet it seems to make perfect sense and add value. The social movement described by Schillinger (2014) is most definitely in action on the web of things.

Furthermore, there is enough evidence available to highlight the importance of engagement with, and inclusion of, staff when attempting to change organizations and cultures (Bradford and Quinton, 2014). The use of social media for this seems like a healthy place to start. In the current climate of evidence based policing, could social media offer a new methodological approach that offers insight and knowledge of cultures, action, and human agency that some other methods miss? If there is reduced accessibility to physical locations for researchers to observe the police in a natural setting, could this new form and space for canteen culture be recreated in the virtual world of social media? Subsequently, could researchers be drawn into a world of virtual ethnography?

References

Bittner, E. (1978) "The functions of the police in modern society" in P. Manning and J. van Maanen (eds) *Policing: A view from the street*, Santa Monica, CA: Goodyear.

Bradford, B. and Quinton, P. (2014) "Self-legitimacy, police culture and support for democratic policing in an English constabulary," *British Journal of Criminology*, 54(6): 1023–46. ·

Braga, A. (2016) The value of "pracademics" in enhancing crime analysis in police departments. *Policing*, 10 (3): 308-314.

Briner, R. B., Denyer, D. and Rousseau, D. M. (2009) Evidence- based management: Concept clean-up time? *Academy of Management Perspectives*, 23(4): 19-32.

Brown, J. (1996) "Police research: some critical issues," in F. Leishman, B. Loveday, and S. Savage (eds) *Core issues in policing*, New York, NY: Longman.

Casey, G.W. (2014) "Leading in a VUCA world," *Fortune*, 169(5): 75.

Christie, N. (1971) "Scandinavian criminology facing the 1970s," *Scandinavian Studies in Criminology*, Vol. 43, 121–149.

Christopher, S. (2015) "The police service can be a critical reflective practice … if it wants," *Policing. A Journal of Policy and Practice*, 9(4): 326–339.

Cockcroft, T. (2017) "Police culture: histories, orthodoxies, and new horizons," *Policing: A Journal of Policy and Practice*, 11(3): 229–235.

College of Policing (2014) "Code of ethics." Available at: http://www.college. police.uk/What-we-do/Ethics/Documents/Code_of_Ethics_Summary.pdf

Collinson, D. (2012) "Prozac leadership and the limits of positive thinking," *Leadership*, 8(2): 87–107.

Dawson, P. and Williams, E. (2009) "Reflections from a police research unit," *Policing: A Journal of Policy and Practice*, 3(4): 373–80.

Evetts, J. (2013) "Professionalism: value and ideology," *Current Sociology*, 61(5/6): 778–96.

Fleming, J. and Wingrove, J. (2017) "'We would if we could…but not sure if we can': implementing evidence based practice," *Policing*, 11(2): 202–213.

Fyfe, N.R. and Wilson, P. (2012) "Knowledge exchange and police practice: broadening and deepening the debate around researcher–practitioner collaborations," *Police Practice and Research*, 13(4): 306–14.

Geia, L., Pearson, L. and Sweet, M. (2017) "Narratives of Twitter as a platform for professional development, innovation, and advocacy," *Australian Psychologist*, 52(4): 280–287.

Gibbons, M., Limoges, C., Nowotny, H., Schwartzman, S., Scott, P., and Trow, M. (1994) *The new production of knowledge: The dynamics of science and research in contemporary societies*, London: Sage.

Goldsmith, A. (2015) "Disgrace book policing: social media and the rise of police indiscretion," *Policing and Society*, 25(3): 249–267.

Greene, J.R. (2014) "New directions in policing: balancing prediction and meaning in police research," *Justice Quarterly*, 31(2): 193–228.

Grint, K. (2010) "Wicked problems and clumsy solutions: the role of leadership," in S. Brookes and K. Grint (eds) *The new public leadership challenge*, Basingstoke: Palgrave Macmillan, pp 169–86.

Gundhus, H. (2012) "Experience or knowledge? Perspectives on new knowledge regimes and control of police professionalism," *Policing*, 792: 178–94.

Hesketh, I. and Cooper, C. (2017) "Measuring the people fleet: general analysis, interventions and needs (GAIN)," *Strategic HR Review*, 16(1): 17–23.

Hesketh, I. and Williams, E. (2017) "A new canteen culture: social media as evidence in policing," *Policing: A Journal of Policy and Practice*, 11(3): 346–55.

Hesketh, I., Cooper, C., and Ivy, J. (2015) "Well-being, austerity and policing: is it worth investing in resilience training?" *The Police Journal: Theory, Practice and Principles*, 88(3): 220–30.

Hoggett, J., Redford, P., Toher, D., and White, P. (2014) "Challenge and change: police identity, morale and goodwill in an age of austerity," project report, University of the West of England, UK.

Hope, T. (2005) "Pretend it doesn't work: the anti-social bias in the Maryland Scientific Methods Scale," *European Journal of Criminal Policy and Research*, 11: 275–96.

Kozinets, R.V. (2002) "The field behind the screen: using netnography for marketing research in online communities," *Journal of Marketing Research*, 39(1): 61–72.

La Rocca, A., Mandelli, A., and Snehota, I. (2014) "Netnography approach as a tool for marketing research: the case of Dash-P&G/TTV," *Management Decision*, 52(4): 689–704.

Leonardi, P. (2014) "Social media, knowledge sharing and innovation: toward a theory of communication visibility," *Information Systems Research*, 25(4): 796–816.

Lievrouw, L.A. (2010) "Social media and the production of knowledge: a return to little science?" *Social Epistemology*, 24(3): 219–237, DOI: 10.1080/02691728.2010.499177

Loftus, B. (2010) "Police occupational culture: classic themes, altered times," *Policing and Society*, 20(1): 1–20.

Manovich, L. (2012) "Media after software," *Journal of Visual Culture*, 12(1): 30–7.

Nonaka, I. (1994) "A dynamic theory of organisational knowledge creation," *Organisation Science*, 5(1): 14–36.

Punch, M. (2015) "What really matters in policing?" *European Police Science Bulletin*, 13: 9–18.

Reiner, R. (2010) *The politics of the police* (4th edn), Oxford: Oxford University Press.

Schillinger, C. (2014) "Forget social networks, think social impact." Available at: http://weneedsocial.com/blog/2014/10/2/forget-social-networks-think-social-impact

Schnitzler, K., Davies, N., Ross, F. and Harris, R. (2016) "Using Twitter™ to drive research impact: a discussion of strategies, opportunities and challenges," *International Journal of Nursing Studies*, 59 (July): 15–26.

Sherman, L. (2013) "The rise of evidence based policing: targeting, testing, and tracking," *Crime and Justice*, 42(1): 377–451.

Sigala, M. and Chalkiti, K. (2015) "Knowledge management, social media and employee creativity," *International Journal of Hospitality Management*, Vol 45, 44–58.

Thacher, D. (2008) "Research for the front lines," *Policing and Society*, 18(1): 46–59.

Treasury, H. (2010) *Comprehensive spending review 2012–2013*, London: HM Treasury.

Van Dijk, A., Hoogewoning, F., and Punch, M. (2015) *What matters in policing: Change values and leadership in turbulent times*, Bristol: The Policy Press.

Van Hulst, M. (2013) "Storytelling at the police station: the canteen culture revisited," *The British Journal of Criminology*, 53(4): 624–642. Available at: https://doi.org/10.1093/bjc/azt014

Van Maanen, J. (1988) *Tales of the field: On writing ethnograph*, Chicago, IL: University of Chicago Press.

Van Zoonen, W., Joost, W. and Vilegenthart, V. (2016) "How employees use Twitter to talk about work: a typology of work-related tweets," *Human Behaviour*, 55 (February): 329–339.

Waddington, P.A.J. (1999) "Police (canteen) sub-culture: an appreciation," *British Journal of Criminology*, 39(2): 287–309.

Willis, J. and Mastrofski, S. (2016) "Improving policing by integrating craft and science: what can patrol officers teach us about good police work?" *Policing and Society*, 28(1). Available at: http://www.tandfonline.com/doi/full/10.1080/10439463.2015.1135921

Wood, J., Fleming, J., and Marks, M. (2008) "Building the capacity of police change agents: the nexus policing project," *Policing and Society: An International Journal of Research and Policy*, 18(1): 72–87.

Young, J. (2004) "Voodoo criminology and the numbers game," in J. Ferrell, K. Hayward, W. Morrison, and M. Presdee (eds) *Cultural criminology unleashed*, London: Glasshouse Press, pp 13–28.

8

Systematic reviews: "better evidence for a better world"[1]

Peter Neyroud

University of Cambridge

Introduction

Systematic reviews have a surprisingly long history in the field of criminal justice. However, they have been both controversial and crucial right from the start. One of the earliest—Barbara Wootton's (1959) research on anti-social behavior in her seminal work *Social science and social pathology*—cut a swathe through prior research. Through her systematic review of 50 years of studies on "social deviation," she demonstrated that earlier research was largely unreliable. It was also incapable of performing what Oakley (2017) has argued to be the key role for systematic reviews: the guidance of policy and practice.

The capacity for evidence to influence policy and practice is central to evidence based policing. As Sherman emphasized in his seminal definition, evidenced based policing is the "use of the best available research on the outcomes of police work to implement guidelines and evaluate agencies, units and officers" (Sherman, 1998: 3). This chapter will argue that systematic reviews provide the most rigorous and reliable form of "best available research" with which to guide policy and practice. The chapter will start by explaining the systematic review process. Drawing on the Campbell Collaboration library of systematic reviews, the second part will set out and analyze the published reviews on policing and the lessons that they provide for an evidence based strategy.

The systematic review process

A systematic review is not to be confused with a literature review (Farrington and Petrosino, 2000). Literature reviews tend to be one-off exercises, usually confined to a single national literature, and frequently not focused on a tight set of pre-published criteria. In contrast, a Campbell Collaboration systematic review must follow a set of transparent international standards (Campbell Collaboration, 2017), which require peer-reviewed agreement of the title and the protocol, a clear description of the scope of the searches and components of the agreed topic to be covered, and the criteria for assessing the intervention under review. Critically, when the reader—whether policymaker or practitioner—approaches a systematic review, they should be able to see the process laid out clearly and, therefore, be able to assess the weight and significance of the conclusions with confidence.

The comparison set out in Table 8.1 shows the contrast between a largely unsystematic and subjective literature review and the systematic review process. While there are conventions for the former, which are laid out in methods texts (eg Ridley, 2012), they are principles for guidance that fall far short of the very tight requirements of guidelines like the "Methodological Expectations of Campbell Collaboration Intervention Reviews" (MECCIR) standards for Campbell reviews (Campbell Collaboration, 2017).

As Table 8.1 suggests, there are a number of key steps in the systematic review process. Drawing on the Campbell Collaboration standards, the most important are:

- *Title registration:* title registration requires a clear rationale for addressing the problem, a clear and specific question to be addressed, the relevant outcome variables that are intended to be measured, the relevant target populations of interest, and the relevant interventions that will be included in the review. This clarity becomes all the more important when the review is intended to cover a wide-ranging and diverse topic such as "community policing." Figure 8.1 shows the objective set out by Weisburd et al (2011) in their title registration for the National Policing Improvement Agency (NPIA)-funded review of community policing.

- *Protocol:* the protocol builds on the initial title registration by expanding on a number of key areas: the criteria for inclusion and exclusion of studies in the review; the search strategy for the identification of relevant studies; the description of methods used in the component studies; the criteria for the determination of independent findings; the details of study coding categories; the statistical procedures and conventions for meta-analysis; and the treatment of qualitative research. The protocol for the community policing review (Gill et al, 2011) identified around 80 databases, websites, and journal sources for their search. In the subsequent search (see

Table 8.1: Narrative reviews versus systematic reviews

	Narrative reviews	Systematic reviews
Authors	One or more authors who are usually experts in the topic	Two or more authors with expertise both in the topic and in systematic reviews
Study protocol	No study protocol	Written study protocol including details of the title, scope, and methods, which must be approved by peer review
Research question	Broad to specific questions and often no hypothesis stated	A specific question, clear justification, and clearly stated hypothesis
Search strategy	No detailed search strategy or a keyword search	A detailed and comprehensive search strategy, including search terms, literature sources, and languages agreed and specified
Sources of literature	Not usually stated but likely to be readily accessible journals and databases. Problems of publication bias	List of databases and sources agreed and grey literature covered. Careful attention to problems of publication bias
Selection criteria	No specific selection criteria	Specified inclusion and exclusion criteria, with emphasis on high-quality studies with lower risk of bias
Critical appraisal	Variable and subjective evaluation of the material	Rigorous and structured appraisal of the quality of studies
Synthesis	Qualitative analysis	Narrative, qualitative, and quantitative analysis
Conclusions	Tendency for these to be subjective	Required to be evidence based
Replication	Unlikely to be capable of replication	Documentation of the method required to enable replication and updating
Update	Unable to update	Required to be updated as new material is published

Source: Rother (2007) and Campbell Collaboration (2017).

Figure 8.1: Objective from the title registration for a systematic review of community policing

> The objective of this systematic review is to synthesize the extant empirical evidence (published and unpublished) on the effectiveness of the various strategies and policies collectively termed "community-oriented policing." Specifically, this review seeks to answer the following questions:
>
> 1. To what extent do community-oriented policing strategies reduce crime, disorder, and residents' fear of crime in the target neighborhoods?
> 2. To what extent do community-oriented policing strategies improve citizen engagement and satisfaction, perceived legitimacy of the police, and cooperation between neighborhood residents and the police?
> 3. Do the effects of community-oriented policing vary according to the particular strategy/combination of strategies used?
> 4. Do the effects of community-oriented policing vary by crime type or neighborhood characteristics?

Source: Weisburd et al (2011)

Figure 8.2), Gill et al distilled 35,000 hits from the initial search terms down to 25 eligible studies that met the protocol standards for quality and risk of bias. Such a dramatic thinning out of the available research before analysis is typical of the systematic review process. Even though there has been a significant increase in research in policing, the number of randomized controlled trials (RCTs) and quasi-experimental studies remains relatively small when compared to fields such as medicine and education (Neyroud, 2017). However, although experimental designs are likely to form the core of any systematic review analysis, the wider literature remains important for the interpretation and context of the results.

- *Synthesis and analysis:* once the search process is complete, the synthesis and analysis of the eligible studies must conform to the MECCIR standards, which are designed to ensure that the review process is transparent, robust, and replicable. A key part of this is the meta-analysis of the outcomes of the studies against the parameters set out in the protocol. Gill et al (2014) conducted a series of meta-analyses of the eligible studies: the impact on crime; the effect on citizen perceptions of disorder and fear of crime; and the effect on perceptions of police legitimacy. Figure 8.3 reproduces Gill et al's forest plot of the last of these: perceptions of legitimacy. The analysis shows that of the 10 eligible studies that included a measure for legitimacy, a significant majority showed a positive impact, and the overall effect—represented by the diamond at the bottom of the plot and showing an overall odds ratio of greater than 1—was in favor of community policing having a positive effect on police legitimacy.

- *Report:* given that the process of conducting a systematic review is such a structured process, it is unsurprising that the demands on the reviewers when they come to report the review are also stringent. The requirements are aimed at several different audiences: the academic community in order to ensure transparency and potential replication; the policy community in

Figure 8.2: Systematic search results from a systematic review of community policing

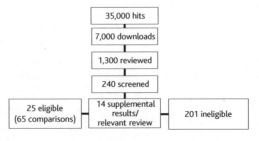

Source: Gill et al (2014)

Figure 8.3: Community policing effects on the legitimacy of the police

Study name	Comparison	Outcome	Statistics for each study				Odds ratio and 95% CI
			Odds ratio	Lower limit	Upper limit	p-Value	
Tuffin et al. 2006 Burghfield	Legitimacy	Confidence in police	3.342	1.884	5.928	0.000	
Tuffin et al. 2006 E. Wickham	Legitimacy	Confidence in police	1.828	1.036	3.224	0.037	
Tuffin et al. 2006 Failsworth West	Legitimacy	Confidence in police	1.736	0.965	3.124	0.066	
Tuffin et al. 2006 Ingol	Legitimacy	Confidence in police	1.651	0.930	2.930	0.087	
Bond & Gow 1995	Legitimacy	Treating people politely	1.628	1.078	2.460	0.021	
Weisburd et al. 2008	Legitimacy	Procedural justice	1.244	1.083	1.429	0.002	
Tuffin et al. 2006 Ash Wharf	Legitimacy	Confidence in police	1.027	0.584	1.805	0.927	
Wycoff & Skogan 1993	Legitimacy	Police are fair	1.013	0.778	1.319	0.925	
Tuffin et al. 2006 New Parks	Legitimacy	Confidence in police	0.895	0.492	1.627	0.716	
Sabath & Carter 1998	Legitimacy	Trust in police	0.440	0.280	0.693	0.000	
			1.276	0.974	1.672	0.077	

0.1　0.2　0.5　1　2　5　10

Favors control　　Favors treatment

Source: Gill et al (2014: 417)

order to demonstrate the robustness of the reported outcomes; and the practice community in order to encourage dissemination. One key product that is designed to support this last aim is the plain language summary (PLS). Divorced of forest plots and statistics, the aim of the PLS is identify and explain the key messages from the review. Figure 8.4 shows an excerpt from the PLS of the Campbell Collaboration systematic review on hot spots policing (Braga et al, 2012).

The subject of Braga et al's hot spot policing review also illustrates one of the key areas for criticism of systematic reviews. Cowen et al (2017) have argued that systematic reviews can suffer from the same shortcomings as RCTs: the problem of external validity or the extent to which findings from systematic reviews can be generalized to a variety of different contexts. In the case of Braga

Figure 8.4: Excerpt from the PLS on "Hotspots policing is effective at reducing crime"

> Focusing police efforts at high crime locations ('hot spots') is effective in reducing crime. Hot spot policing does not displace crime to nearby areas. Rather, the benefits of reduced crime diffuse into the areas immediately surrounding the targeted locations. A problem-oriented approach has a larger effect than a traditional policing approach.

Source: Campbell Collaboration (2015)

et al's hot spot policing review, it would be fair to say that at the time they conducted their search, the overwhelming majority of the studies were from the US. It would have been reasonable to question whether results based on urban America would generalize to European or developing-country contexts. As Cowen et al (2017) suggest, context matters. Given that most of the first 40 years of RCTs in policing were conducted in North America (Neyroud, 2017), this limitation—an overreliance on generalizing from findings in a specific national context—was a potential limitation on the utility of police systematic reviews.

However, this limitation is gradually being overcome by two factors: the expansion in RCTs outside North America (Neyroud, 2017); and the requirement for systematic reviews to be updated at regular intervals, particularly when significant new research has been published. Braga et al's review has been updated (Braga, 2017), and since the original review, the number of eligible studies has been expanded significantly, as has the range of contexts in which the intervention has been tested. Not only does this re-emphasize the importance of the wide-ranging, multilingual searching strategies, but it also highlights the importance of systematic review authors paying close attention to both the context and the theories underpinning interventions in order to provide their audience with the broadest understanding of the findings, the mechanisms by which the intervention operates to achieve its effect, and the situations in which it is most likely to be successful.

Systematic reviews of policing

In the second part of this chapter, we turn to look at the systematic reviews in the Campbell Collaboration library that have been completed on topics relevant to policing. A significant proportion of these were funded by the NPIA in the UK as part of a deliberate, evidence based strategy (Telep and Weisburd, 2014). There are 22 reviews, which have been listed in Table 8.2 by author(s), topic, and a short summary of the key findings.

Telep and Weisburd (2012, 2014, 2016) have demonstrated that it is valuable to explore more general conclusions from looking across the systematic reviews in policing. First, they undertook an analysis of the lessons for the police-led reduction of crime and disorder (Telep and Weisburd, 2012). Subsequently, they explored the learning from the NPIA-funded reviews (Telep and Weisburd, 2014) and, most recently, from a wider sample of police reviews (Telep and Weisburd, 2016). Drawing these lessons together, with the addition of a number of more recent reviews, there are a number of key themes that stand out.

Table 8.2: Police-related Campbell Collaboration systematic reviews by author(s), topics, and summary findings

Author(s)	Topic	Key findings
Lum et al (2006)	Terrorism prevention	Little evidence of effective strategies and a paucity of good-quality research
Mazerolle et al (2007)	Drug law enforcement	Third-party policing approaches provide a promising approach to preventing street-level drug crime
Welsh and Farrington (2008)	Closed-circuit television (CCTV)	CCTV has a modest impact on crime. Effectiveness varies across settings. Surveillance is more effective at preventing crime in car parks, and less effective in city and town centers, public housing, and public transport
Bennett et al (2008)	Neighborhood watch	Neighborhood watch was effective in reducing crime
Weisburd et al (2008)	Problem-oriented policing	Problem-oriented policing has a statistically significant impact on reducing crime and disorder
Davis and Weisburd (2008)	Second responder visits to domestic violence victims	The second response intervention does not affect the likelihood of new incidents of family violence, but slightly increases victims' willingness to report incidents to the police, possibly as a result of greater confidence in the police
Petrosino et al (2010)	Formal processing of juveniles in court	Juvenile-system processing appears to not have a crime control effect, and across all measures—prevalence, incidence, severity, and self-report—appears to increase delinquency
Bowers et al (2011)	Micro-displacement of crime	Displacement is far from inevitable as a result of focused police operations; rather, the opposite, a diffusion of crime control benefits appears to be the more likely consequence
Wilson et al (2011)	DNA for police investigations	DNA testing has value when used to investigate a broad range of crime types
Van der Laan et al (2011)	Prevention of human trafficking	As a result of the lack of high-quality studies, no conclusions could be drawn on the effectiveness of intervention strategies for preventing and reducing sexual exploitation
Patterson et al (2012)	Stress management	Stress management interventions had no significant effect on psychological, behavioral, or physiological outcomes
Braga and Weisburd (2012)	Effects of "Pulling Levers"-focused deterrence on crime	"Pulling Levers"-focused deterrence strategies seem to be effective in reducing crime

(continued)

Table 8.2: Police-related Campbell Collaboration systematic reviews by author(s), topics, and summary findings (continued)

Author(s)	Topic	Key findings
Braga et al (2012)	Hot spots policing	The research provides fairly robust evidence that hot spots policing is an effective crime prevention strategy
Koper and Mayo-Wilson (2012)	Prevention of illegal gun carrying	Directed patrols focused on illegal gun carrying prevent gun crimes
Meissner et al (2012)	Interrogation techniques	The research supports the effectiveness of an information-gathering style of interviewing suspects
Telep et al (2014)	Macro-displacement of crime	The most likely outcome from meso-/macro-level studies is neither displacement nor a diffusion of benefits, although diffusion may be somewhat more likely than displacement
Gill et al (2014)	Community policing	Community-oriented policing has a small positive impact on property-focused crime and feelings of safety, and stronger benefits for violence-focused crime and citizen-based outcomes of perceived disorder, satisfaction, trust, and confidence in the police
Strang et al (2013)	Restorative justice conferencing (RJC)	RJCs delivered in the manner tested by the 10 eligible tests in this review appear likely to reduce future detected crimes among the kinds of offenders who are willing to consent to RJCs, and whose victims are also willing to consent
Mazerolle et al (2013)	Interventions to increase police legitimacy	Police can achieve positive changes in citizen attitudes to police through adopting procedural justice dialogue as a component part of any type of police intervention
Toon and Gurusamy (2014)	Forensic examination in rape and sexual assault	Forensic nurse examiners seem to be statistically significantly better in the provision of clinical care and are able to provide a cheaper service than that led by physicians
Wilson et al (2016)	Juvenile curfews	Juvenile curfews are ineffective at reducing crime or victimization
Wilson et al (2018)	Pre-court diversion managed by the police	Police-led diversion reduces the future delinquent behavior of low-risk youth relative to traditional processing

Proactive policing of people and places

The police can be effective at reducing crime and disorder by focusing on "high activity people and places" (Telep and Weisburd, 2016: 164). This "proactive" approach is most effective when targeting micro-places (hot spots) or when deploying strategies, such as "focused deterrence," which are aimed at specific groups of high-harm offenders. In the National Academies of Science report on *Proactive policing*, Weisburd and Majmundar (2017) have added the caveat that most of the studies of these strategies were themselves focused. As such, they do not necessarily provide a clear guide on the extent to which such proactive policing can be sustained across a whole jurisdiction, or the potential impact of such an agency-wide approach. However, the evidence that crime and disorder is not usually displaced (Bowers et al, 2011; Telep et al, 2014) suggests that a targeted, intelligence-led crackdown approach on the "power few" locations and offenders might well be effective, and particularly if tracked effectively (Sherman, 2013).

Problem-solving

Proactivity should not be confined to targeting places and people. Goldstein's (1990) original model of problem-solving was a proactive one, in contrast to the reactive, response-driven model of policing that still prevails in most police agencies. Problem-oriented policing and the use of partnership-based problem-solving approaches to issues such as street drug crime are both supported by systematic reviews. There are undoubted challenges to the effective implementation of such approaches (Maguire et al, 2015), but they emphasize the importance of the police thinking beyond emergency response and law enforcement tactics, such as arrest and prosecution.

Diversion

The reviews of formal processing (Petrosino et al, 2010) and diversion (Wilson et al, 2018) reinforce this lesson. A simple reliance on formal processing and prosecution is not supported by the reviews, particularly in the case of young offenders. Police-led diversion schemes compare favorably with prosecution. The reviews are not clear as to whether diversion with conditions should be preferred. Some more recent studies, such as Operation Turning Point, suggest that if the police can overcome the problems with the consistency of treatment delivery that beset such interventions (Neyroud, 2017), deferred prosecution with conditions to support and encourage desistance is a promising approach (Sherman et al, 2017).

Engagement and legitimacy

A further key thread running through the reviews is the importance of strategies to support and enhance the legitimacy of the police. Mazerolle et al's (2013) review on police legitimacy emphasized the potential benefits for police from paying attention to procedural justice in their routine transactions with citizens. Gill et al (2014) found that community policing had a significant benefit in enhancing police legitimacy.

Indeed, overall, the dominant lesson of the reviews is that police can improve both their performance and their perception by the public by adopting strategies that reach beyond the three "R's": rapid response, random patrol, and reactive investigation. This almost certainly also applies to some of the areas that have, until recently, had limited high-quality research, for example, the prevention of terrorism and tackling organized crimes, such as people trafficking.

Conclusions

Systematic reviews provide an important source for evidence based strategies in policing. There are, as yet, a limited number of reviews in policing and some important gaps: there is only one review on terrorism and one on serious and organized crime. These gaps are largely a result of the relative paucity of controlled design studies in these areas. However, there are other areas—domestic violence, body-worn video, and the electronic monitoring of offenders—where there are studies but no systematic reviews. These gaps are primarily the result of funding priorities. Until there were sufficient systematic reviews in the field, it was difficult for potential funders, policymakers, and practitioners to see the benefits of investing time and effort in this type of research product. However, systematic reviews not only provide an authoritative statement on the impact of important interventions in policing, but can also help to identify the gaps in primary studies and research agendas for the future.

Note
1 "Better evidence for a better world" is the vision statement of the Campbell Collaboration, see: https://www.campbellcollaboration.org/about-campbell/vision-mission-and-principle.html

References
Bennett, T., Farrington, D.P., and Holloway, K. (2008) "The effectiveness of neighbourhood watch," Campbell Collaboration systematic review. Available at: https://www.campbellcollaboration.org/library/effectiveness-of-neighbourhood-watch.html

Bowers, K., Johnson, S., Guerette, R., Somers, L., and Poynton, S. (2011) "Spatial displacement and diffusion of benefits among geographically focused policing initiatives," Campbell Collaboration systematic review. Available at: https://www.campbellcollaboration.org/library/geographically-focused-policing.html

Braga, A.A. (2017) "Proactive policing impacts on crime and disorder," in D.W. Weisburd (ed) *Proactive policing: Effects on crime and communities*, Washington, DC: National Academy of Sciences.

Braga, A.A. and Weisburd, D.W. (2012) "The effects of 'Pulling Levers' focused deterrence strategies on crime," Campbell Collaboration systematic review. Available at: https://www.campbellcollaboration.org/library/pulling-levers-focused-deterrence-strategies-effects-on-crime.html

Braga, A.A., Papachristos, A., and Hureau, D. (2012) "The effects of hotspot policing on crime," Campbell Collaboration systematic review. Available at: https://www.campbellcollaboration.org/library/effects-of-hot-spots-policing-on-crime.html

Campbell Collaboration (2015) "Hotspots policing is effective at reducing crime. Plain language summary for the Campbell Collaboration." Available at: https://www.campbellcollaboration.org/media/k2/attachments/CC_PLS_Hot_spot_PRODUCTION.pdf

Campbell Collaboration (2017) "Methodological Expectations of Campbell Collaboration Intervention Reviews (MECCIR)." Available at: https://www.campbellcollaboration.org/mec2ir.html

Cowen, N., Virk, B., Mascarenhas-Keyes, S., and Cartwright, N. (2017) "Randomized controlled trials: how can we know 'what works'?" *Critical Review*, 29(3): 265–92.

Davis, R. and Weisburd, D.W. (2008) "Effect of second responder programs on repeat incidents of family abuse," Campbell Collaboration systematic review. Available at: https://www.campbellcollaboration.org/library/family-abuse-repeat-incidents-effects-of-2nd-responder-programmes.html

Farrington, D.P. and Petrosino, A. (2000) "Systematic reviews of criminological interventions: the Campbell Collaboration and crime and justice groups," *International Annals of Criminology*, 38: 49–66.

Gill, C., Weisburd, D.W., Telep, C., Vitter, Z., and Bennett, T. (2011) "Community-oriented policing to reduce crime, disorder, and fear and improve legitimacy and satisfaction with police: a systematic review," protocol for Campbell Collaboration systematic review. Available at: https://www.campbellcollaboration.org/media/k2/attachments/0129_CJCG_Gill_Protocol.pdf

Gill, C., Weisburd, D.W., Telep, C., Vitter, Z., and Bennett, T. (2014) "Community-oriented policing to reduce crime, disorder and fear and increase satisfaction and legitimacy among citizens: a systematic review," *Journal of Experimental Criminology*, 10: 399–428.

Goldstein, H. (1990) *Problem-oriented policing*, New York, NY: McGraw-Hill.

Koper, C. and Mayo-Wilson, E. (2012) "Police strategies for reducing illegal possession and carrying of firearms," Campbell Collaboration systematic review. Available at: https://www.campbellcollaboration.org/library/police-strategies-for-reducing-illegal-firearms.html

Lum, C., Kennedy, L.W., and Sherley, A.J. (2006) "The effectiveness of counter-terrorism strategies," Campbell Collaboration systematic review. Available at: https://www.campbellcollaboration.org/library/effectiveness-of-counter-terrorism-strategies.html

Maguire, E.R., Uchida, C.D., and Hassell, K.D. (2015) "Problem-oriented policing in Colorado Springs: a content analysis of 753 cases," *Crime and Delinquency*, 61(1): 71–95.

Mazerolle, L., Soole, D.W., and Rombouts, S. (2007) "Street-level drug law enforcement: a meta-analytic review," Campbell Collaboration systematic review. Available at: https://www.campbellcollaboration.org/library/meta-analytic-review-street-level-drug-law-enforcement.html

Mazerolle, L., Bennett, S., Davis, J., Sargeant, E., and Manning, M. (2013) "Legitimacy in policing," Campbell Collaboration systematic review. Available at: https://www.campbellcollaboration.org/library/legitimacy-in-policing-a-systematic-review.html

Meissner, C., Redlich, A., Bhatt, S., and Brandon, S. (2012) "Interview and interrogation methods and their effects on investigative outcomes," Campbell Collaboration systematic review. Available at: https://www.campbellcollaboration.org/library/interview-interrogation-effects-on-investigations.html

Neyroud, P.W. (2017) "Learning to field test in policing: using an analysis of completed randomised controlled trials involving the police to develop a grounded theory on the factors contributing to high levels of treatment integrity in Police Field Experiments," unpublished PhD dissertation, Institute of Criminology, University of Cambridge.

Oakley, A. (2017) "Foreword," in D. Gough, S. Oliver, and J. Thomas (eds) *An introduction to systematic reviews*, London: Sage.

Patterson, G., Chung, I., and Swan, P.G. (2012) "The effects of stress management interventions among police officers and recruits," Campbell Collaboration systematic review. Available at: https://www.campbellcollaboration.org/library/stress-management-police-officers-and-recruits.html

Petrosino, A., Guckenburg, S., and Turpin-Petrosino, C. (2010) "Formal system processing of juveniles: effects on delinquency," Campbell Collaboration systematic review. Available at: https://www.campbellcollaboration.org/library/formal-system-processing-of-juveniles-effects-on-delinquency.html

Ridley, D. (2012) *The literature review: A step-by-step guide for students*, London: Sage.

Rother, E.T. (2007) "Revisão sistemática X revisão narrativa" ["Systematic literature review v narrative review"]. Available at: http://www.scielo.br/scielo.php?script=sci_arttext&pid=S0103-21002007000200001&lng=en

Sherman, L.W. (2013) "The rise of evidence based policing: targeting, testing and tracking," *Crime and Justice*, 42(1): 377–451.

Sherman, L.W., Neyroud, P.W., and Slothower, M.P. (2017) "Operation Turning Point," presentation to the American Society of Criminology 2017 Conference in Philadelphia, November 15.

Strang, H.S., Sherman, L.W., Mayo-Wilson, E., Woods, D., and Ariel, B. (2013) "Restorative justice conferencing (RJC) using face-to-face meetings of offenders and victims: effects on offender recidivism and victim satisfaction," Campbell Collaboration systematic review. Available at: https://www.campbellcollaboration.org/library/restorative-justice-conferencing-recidivism-victim-satisfaction.html (accessed December 20, 2017).

Telep, C. and Weisburd, D.W. (2012) "What is known about the effectiveness of police practices in reducing crime and disorder," *Police Quarterly*, 15: 331–57.

Telep, C. and Weisburd, D.W. (2014) "Generating knowledge: a case study of the National Policing Improvement Agency program on systematic reviews in policing," *Journal of Experimental Criminology*, 10: 371–98.

Telep, C. and Weisburd, D.W. (2016) "Policing," in D.W. Weisburd, D.P. Farrington, and C. Gill (eds) *What works in crime prevention and rehabilitation*, New York, NY: Springer.

Telep, C.W., Weisburd, D., Gill, C.E., Vitter, Z., and Teichman, D. (2014) "Displacement of crime and diffusion of crime control benefits in large-scale geographic areas: a systematic review," *Journal of Experimental Criminology*, 10(4): 515–48.

Toon, C. and Gurusamy, K. (2014) "Forensic nurse examiners vs doctors for the forensic examination of rape and sexual assault complainants," Campbell Collaboration systematic review. Available at: https://www.campbellcollaboration.org/library/forensic-nurse-examiners-vs-doctors-for-rape-sexual-assault.html (accessed December 19, 2017).

Van der Laan, P., Smit, M., Busschers, I., and Aarten, P. (2011) "Cross-border trafficking in human beings: prevention and intervention strategies for reducing sexual exploitation," Campbell Collaboration systematic review. Available at: https://www.campbellcollaboration.org/library/trafficking-strategies-for-reducing-sexual-exploitation.html

Weisburd, D.W. and Majmundar, M.K. (2017) *Proactive policing: Effects on crime and communities*, Washington, DC: National Academies Press.

Weisburd, D.W., Eck, J.E., Hinkle, J.C., and Telep, C. (2008) "The effects of problem-oriented policing on crime and disorder," Campbell Collaboration systematic review. Available at: https://www.campbellcollaboration.org/library/effects-of-problem-oriented-policing-on-crime-and-disorder.html

Weisburd, D.W., Gill, C., and Telep, C. (2011) "Title registration for a review proposal: community-oriented policing to reduce crime, disorder and fear and increase legitimacy and citizen satisfaction in neighbourhoods." Available at: https://www.campbellcollaboration.org/media/k2/attachments/Weisburd_Community_Policing_title.pdf

Welsh, B. and Farrington, D.P. (2008) "Effects of closed circuit television surveillance on crime," Campbell Collaboration systematic review. Available at: https://www.campbellcollaboration.org/library/effects-of-closed-circuit-television-surveillance-on-crime.html

Wilson, D., Weisburd, D.W., and McClure, D. (2011) "The use of DNA testing in police investigative work for increasing offender identification, arrest, conviction and case clearance," Campbell Collaboration systematic review. Available at: https://www.campbellcollaboration.org/library/dna-testing-police-for-identification-arrest-conviction-case-clearance.html

Wilson, D., Gill, C., Olaghere, A., and McClure, D. (2016) "Juvenile curfew effects on criminal behaviour and victimization," Campbell Collaboration systematic review. Available at: https://www.campbellcollaboration.org/library/juvenile-curfew-effects-on-behaviour.html

Wilson, D., Brennan, I., Olaghere, A., and Kimbrell, C.S. (2018) "Police initiated diversion for youth to prevent future delinquent behaviour," Campbell Collaboration Systematic review. Available at: https://www.campbellcollaboration.org/library/police-initiated-diversion-to-prevent-future-delinquent-behaviour.html

Wootton, B. (1959) *Social science and social pathology*, London: George Allen and Unwin.

9

The case for open police research

Craig Bennell
Carleton University

Brittany Blaskovits
Carleton University

Evidence based policing

E vidence based policing (EBP) advocates believe that research has a
role to play in developing effective and efficient policing practices,
programs, and/or policies (Sherman, 2013). For the benefits of EBP
to be realized, policing research must meet standards of methodological
rigor (regardless of what specific methodology is relied on to conduct the
research), and the research must be able to be transferred to the real world
of policing in a meaningful way. Those who promote EBP believe that
this kind of "actionable" research usually results from a blending of police
experience with academic research skills (Huey and Ricciardelli, 2016); in
other words, *true collaboration* between practitioners and researchers. This
chapter will focus on two aspects of EBP that are acknowledged by EBP
advocates as being important for moving the field forward, but are often
implicit in discussions of EBP: the wide-scale accessibility of police research
findings, and the replicability of such research. We believe that a more
detailed, explicit examination of these issues is required. In this chapter,
we highlight why these two issues are so important for the field of EBP
and we provide recommendations that should allow research accessibility
and research replicability to be improved. These recommendations relate
specifically to open science practices.

The problem of accessibility

As argued earlier, for research to positively impact decisions about police practices, programs, and/or policies, that research must be available to relevant end users (eg rank-and-file officers, crime analysts, police executives, etc). We believe that, currently, this is often not the case. One of the major reasons why policing research remains largely inaccessible to police professionals relates to the choices being made by academic researchers about where they publish their research. While academic researchers are, of course, not the only ones conducting police research (we collaborate with several researchers who work *within* police agencies), much of the research in this area is conducted in academic settings, and most of that research is published in peer-reviewed journals. A variety of factors likely influence where academic researchers decide to publish their studies (eg a journal's reputation, impact factors, the databases where a journal is abstracted, a journal's relevance to the research topic, the likelihood of acceptance) (eg Knight and Steinbach, 2008; Sandesh and Wahrekar, 2017). Rarely, however, in our experience, are these decisions based primarily on whether the chosen outlet will be read by police professionals. On the one hand, this makes complete sense: the incentive structure in place at many universities is based on publishing in high-impact, peer-reviewed journals (we are aware of some university departments that will not even consider publications for tenure and promotion decisions unless they appear in journals with a certain impact factor). On the other hand, publication decisions based on such factors decrease the likelihood that police professionals will ever know about the research being conducted.

Research has clearly indicated that police professionals (in North America at least) rarely access peer-reviewed journals. For example, Lum, Telep, Koper, and Grieco (2012) surveyed 523 officers from the Sacramento Police Department about their receptivity to research. They asked survey respondents which academic journals or trade magazines they had accessed in the previous six months. Seven well-known journals and magazines were included in the list and the vast majority of respondents ($n = 402$; 76.9%) had not read any of the publications. The most accessed resource was the *FBI Law Enforcement Bulletin* ($n = 32$; 6.1%). None of the academic journals were widely accessed (eg *Criminology*, 0.8%; *Police Quarterly*, 0.8%; *Justice Quarterly*, 0.4%). Similar results were recently found when police professionals from seven municipal police agencies in Canada were surveyed (Blaskovits et al, forthcoming). In this survey, the only two resources that were accessed by a reasonable number of respondents were Canada's national law enforcement magazine, *Blue Line Magazine* ($n = 347$; 58%), and policeone.com ($n = 137$; 22.9%), which is well-known for its police-related content. Neither of the peer-reviewed academic journals listed in the Canadian survey (*Criminology* and *Canadian Journal of Criminology and Criminal Justice*) were accessed by more than 10% of respondents.

Unfortunately, these survey results do not shed light on *why* police professionals do not access the sorts of journals where academic researchers regularly publish their work. It may be that these individuals cannot access these journals, but if they could, they would. We suspect that this is not the case, at least not in North America. In Canada, for example, the Canadian Police College has an impressive catalogue of e-journals that most Canadian police professionals could likely access if they wanted to; they simply do not. More likely explanations are that police professionals are unaware of the many peer-reviewed journals where we publish our research, or they do not access them, either because they are too busy given the demands of their job or because they do not expect that published research will be of value to them. Anecdotally, when we have discussed this issue with police colleagues, they often assume that academic research will be irrelevant to "real-world" policing issues (eg the research is unable to be applied *on the street*) or they assume that academic research will be impenetrable, couched in academic jargon and complicated statistics that are difficult to understand.[1] Whatever the reason, if the primary goal of EBP advocates is to have a positive impact on policing through the research they conduct, using academic journals as the sole outlet for their research is unlikely to accomplish this objective.

The problem of replicability

Unlike some academic disciplines where research is primarily conducted for its own sake (ie to expand knowledge about a particular topic), a primary goal for many police researchers is to have a positive impact on policing (eg shaping how policing is developed and practiced). For any academic discipline, it is important for the research being conducted to be replicable (OSC, 2015), but for an applied field where the hope is that research will be used to inform decisions that have consequences, the need to demonstrate replicability is even more important. By replicability, we mean that researchers should be able to show that research findings can be repeated (eg by other researchers using other methodologies) (Asendorpf et al, 2013), and ideally under diverse conditions (at which point one could say that the research is not only replicable, but also generalizable) (Asendorpf et al, 2013).[2] Ideally, research should be replicated before it is applied in any setting. If police research cannot be replicated, but is still used to inform decisions that are being made, the grounds upon which those decisions are based is shaky at best. We would go so far as to say that for police research to have its intended impact, replicability and generalizability must be cornerstones of EBP.

This discussion begs the question: is police research that is currently being conducted replicable? Unfortunately, the answer to that question at present is: we do not yet know. Historically, like in other fields (eg biology, psychology, medicine), little attention has been paid to the replicability question in the field of policing research and, with some notable exceptions, few replication attempts have been published.[3] In the field of criminology more generally, McNeeley and Warner (2015: 581) revealed that "replication studies constitute just over 2 percent of the [criminology] articles published between 2006 and 2010." With respect to policing research specifically, Huey and Bennell (2017) found that out of the 218 policing studies they coded (studies conducted by Canadian police researchers between 2000 and 2015), approximately 8% of the papers met the criteria for being a replication attempt (and many of these studies came from one specific lab).[4] This suggests to us that if existing academic research is being used by police professionals to inform their practices, programs, and/or policies, these professionals are likely relying on an inadequate base of evidence to justify their decisions.

These concerns are further heightened by the fact that in fields where attempts have been made to determine rates of replicability, the results are not promising. For example, a large international team of psychologists has recently attempted to determine the reproducibility of psychological science (OSC, 2015). They identified 100 psychology experiments published in 2008 across three top-tier psychology journals and attempted to replicate the results of the studies. Using a variety of different metrics to establish replicability, the results suggested that relatively few of the original studies could be replicated. For example, the mean effect size for the replication attempts was half the magnitude of the mean effect size in the original studies, and while 97% of the original studies reported significant p-values ($p < .05$), only 36% of the replicated studies had significant p-values. Similar large-scale projects are being conducted in other fields at present (eg cancer biology), with initial results also suggesting that researchers (and practitioners that depend on the research) should be concerned (eg Begley and Ellis, 2012).

Complementing these sorts of large-scale replication efforts are researcher surveys, which raise similar concerns. For example, in one survey of approximately 1,500 scientists across various disciplines, over 70% of respondents (on average across disciplines) claim to have tried and failed in a replication attempt of someone else's work, and over 50% of respondents (on average across disciplines) claim to have tried and failed in a replication of their own work (Baker, 2016). If similar results apply to the policing field, and research within this field is informing police practices, programs, and/or policies, then these decisions could be based on research findings that may be mere flukes (ie unable to be reproduced, replicated, or generalized).

Enhancing accessibility and replicability: the role of open science

To summarize, we believe that for research to have a positive impact on policing, this research must be more accessible to end users and it must be empirically demonstrated that the research upon which the real-world decisions are being based is replicable (and generalizable to whatever situation the research is being applied to). There are multiple ways to enhance accessibility to policing research and to improve the degree to which that research is able to be replicated. In our view, a reliance on open science practices is one obvious option.

Open access publishing

One important aspect of open science is open access publishing. Formally, open access literature is defined as being digital, free of charge (for the reader), and free of most copyright restrictions (see: https://www.plos.org). There are multiple options for open access publishing, the two most common being *open access peer-reviewed journals* and (non-peer-reviewed) *open access repositories*. In both cases, the goal is to make research findings more widely available, particularly to the public (including police professionals), who ultimately fund much of the research being conducted by academic researchers. While there are always barriers that will limit how accessible open access literature is (eg lack of access to the Internet), open access publishing practices will, at the very least, allow police researchers to *increase* the degree to which their research is accessible to a wider group of people beyond other academics who are interested in their work.

There is certainly no shortage of open access publishing options. For example, the Directory of Open Access Journals (available at: https://doaj.org) currently lists about 10,000 open access journals, although only a small fraction of these are relevant to the police researcher. The nature of these journals varies, with some being completely open access, others being hybrid journals (where certain articles in the journal are open access), and still others being best characterized as delayed open access (where articles are open access after a delay). Quality (as measured by impact factors) also naturally varies across open access journals, just as quality varies across journals that do not have open access policies. The business models associated with these journals also varies, with some being fee-based (authors must pay to have their article published) and others being free.

Likewise, there is no shortage of open access repositories where research can be archived and made available to the masses. The features of these also vary. Many academic institutions host their own open access repositories (eg our university maintains the Carleton University Repository Virtual Environment, available at: https://library.carleton.ca/services/curve). Other open access repositories are discipline-specific, such as PSYArXiv, a repository for pre-prints in the field of psychology maintained by the Society for the Improvement of Psychological Science (available at: https://psyarxiv.com).

We believe that such open access publishing options need to be considered more seriously by police researchers if we are to collectively get our research into the hands of the professionals we want to impact. We also urge police researchers to go beyond these formal open access options, to think of other ways in which we can enhance accessibility to our research. Formal open access publishing channels may not adequately deal with the resistance that some end users may show toward accessing academic research outlets, but other options might address these issues: in addition to publishing peer-reviewed articles, we can publish our work in trade magazines or newsletters that are distributed to policing organizations; instead of focusing solely on presentations at academic conferences, we can consider presenting our research at professional conferences and meetings as well; and we can harness the power of the Internet to greater effect, as some of our colleagues have done, and spread the word about our research through Twitter, blogs, and website posts (eg on policeone.com). Of course, it would be remiss if we did not stress that while exploiting all these channels to make our research more accessible, we also need to pay much more attention to making our writing more accessible (reducing our use of academic jargon, presenting our results in a more meaningful fashion, and describing the practical implications of our research).

Open science practices

Beyond focusing on making policing research more accessible by leveraging non-traditional, underutilized outlets to distribute academic research (in addition to traditional, peer-reviewed channels), the value of EBP will grow considerably, in our view, if police researchers begin to follow open science practices more generally. Open science practices are a collection of actions designed to make scientific processes more transparent and "to build a more replicable and robust science" (Spellman et al, 2017: 1). Open science practices entail recording and publicly sharing data, research materials, statistical analysis scripts, relevant hypotheses, and design and analysis choices, typically before one conducts a study. Making pre-prints of manuscripts publicly available before formally submitting them to journals is also a growing practice. Numerous sharing websites exist for this purpose; the one we are most familiar with is the Open Science Framework (available at: https://osf.io).

While some concerns have been raised about these practices (eg that the public might not understand much of the science that is made public) (Pew Research Centre, 2015), there are many potential benefits associated with open science. Here, we will focus specifically on one potential benefit: how open science practices may enhance the replicability of policing research, thus producing, over the long term, a more solid base of research upon which police professionals can base decisions.

One of the key advantages of open science practices is that they increase the degree to which others will know what researchers have actually done in their studies because that information is made explicit and available to other researchers (on sites like the Open Science Framework). If researchers do not have access to important information in published (or unpublished) papers, including a full description of hypotheses, methods, procedures, and results, it is difficult, if not impossible, to replicate the studies reported in those papers.[5] For a variety of reasons, such pertinent details are often not included in published papers.[6] Editors, for example, often ask authors to remove material from their papers due to page limit restrictions in their journals, and authors themselves are often selective in what they report in their papers in order to enhance readability and increase the likelihood that their papers will be accepted (eg non-significant results may be removed from the paper if authors believe that their inclusion will increase the chance of rejection). Open science practices can help remedy this situation by making all of this important information more readily available to researchers wanting to carry out replications.

Related to this point is the fact that open science practices can likely increase the replicability of policing research by reducing the degree to which researchers rely on questionable research practices (QRPs). There seems to be a growing consensus that the sorts of practices outlined in Table 9.1 are not only commonly practiced by researchers across many disciplines, including in our own discipline of psychology (eg John et al, 2012; Agnoli et al, 2017), but "bias the scientific literature and undermine the credibility and reproducibility of research findings" (Agnoli et al, 2017: para 1). Such practices are thought to result from a combination of factors, but two of the primary causes appear to be the increasing pressure for academics to publish their research (ie "publish

Table 9.1: Commonly practiced, but questionable, research practices

1.	Failing to report all of a study's dependent measures
2.	Deciding whether to collect more data after looking to see whether the results were significant (a practice referred to as p-hacking)
3.	Failing to report all of a study's conditions
4.	Stopping data collection earlier than planned because one found the result that one had been looking for
5.	Rounding off a p-value (reporting a p of .054 as $p < .05$)
6.	Selectively reporting studies that worked
7.	Deciding whether to exclude data after looking at the impact of doing so on the results
8.	Reporting an unexpected finding as having been predicted from the start (a practice referred to as HARKing, or hypothesizing after the results are known)
9.	Claiming that results are unaffected by demographic variables when one is actually unsure (or knows that they do)
10.	Falsifying data

Source: Agnoli et al (2017)

or perish") and the view that journal editors and reviewers are more likely to accept papers that report significant results (something that appears to be supported by empirical analysis of publication trends [see, eg, Fanelli, 2012]).

It should not be surprising when a published study in the policing field cannot be replicated if the author(s) of the to-be-replicated study relied on some or all of these QRPs (because these questionable practices "produce research findings when they should not be produced" [Ioannidis, 2005: para 5]). Moreover, it may be argued that if studies relying on QRPs are used as the basis for decisions in real-world policing contexts, then this could be problematic. To the extent that open science practices can minimize the use of QRPs by making all hypotheses and research plans explicit and publicly accessible before studies are conducted, not only are replication attempts more likely to be successful, but the scientific rigor associated with primary research studies will also increase.[7]

Challenges for open science in policing

From our perspective, there are at least two sets of challenges associated with the idea of conducing open science in the policing field: academic challenges and policing challenges.

Challenges from an academic perspective

As indicated at the outset of this chapter, many of the researchers conducting police research work in academic settings, and various challenges associated with conducting open science in academic settings have been raised. Perhaps most common among these challenges is the view, held by at least some academics, that practicing open science may present a risk to career advancement (McKiernan et al, 2016). This fear seems to be related to other concerns associated with open science, such as "the rigor of peer review at open access journals, risks to funding ... and forfeiture of author rights" (McKiernan et al, 2016: para 2). Essentially, some academics appear to believe that practicing open science will put them in a compromising position by making their research (and research record) appear less impressive when compared to their counterparts who do not adopt such practices.

Thankfully, these challenges appear to be largely unfounded. For example, contrary to the view that open science may decrease the impact of one's research, researchers who practice open science appear to be having a larger impact than their colleagues, as measured by traditional metrics of research impact. Indeed, numerous (but not all) studies have shown that open access publications are often cited at a higher rate (citation counts are frequently considered in tenure, promotion, and funding decisions) than those published in traditional peer-reviewed journals (eg Eysenbach, 2006), with some studies putting the advantage at 36%–172% additional citations (Hajjem et al, 2006). In addition, peer-reviewed journals are increasingly pushing researchers to adopt open science practices. For example, in the social sciences, many journals now reward authors for adopting such practices (eg the top-tier psychology journal, *Psychological Science*, now offers electronic "badges" for open data, open materials, and pre-registration of studies to signal that open science practices were followed by the published authors). Funding bodies are also urging researchers to practice open science, for example, research funding agencies in Canada (and elsewhere) are not only encouraging authors to publish in open access outlets as a way of facilitating knowledge mobilization, but also providing the financial means to do so (ie costs associated with open access publishing are now considered "eligible" grant expenses).

In contrast to the concerns expressed by some academic researchers toward open science practices, we personally believe that the opposite is true. Given the fast pace with which open science practices are being adopted by researchers around the world, and the rate at which journals and funding agencies are getting on board to encourage and reward such practices, it seems that researchers who resist such practices will soon be in the minority, at least in the social sciences. We also believe that resisting such practices is not good for science, particularly the sort of science that EBP advocates conduct (where we want our research to have a positive, evidence based impact on the field of policing).

Challenges from a policing perspective

Beyond the academic challenges that may serve as obstacles to the practice of open science, we also perceive that certain challenges may exist from a policing perspective. Two challenges in particular have been raised anecdotally in conversations with colleagues. The first, which we feel is less valid than the second, is that police agencies may fear open science practices because they see research as risky. Essentially, police agencies may not want research made available for public scrutiny until they can confirm what the research results actually "say" (presumably, so that they can ensure that the research does not paint the agency in a negative light and/or that the results are consistent with internal "agendas"). While we understand the caution exhibited by such agencies—to the extent that it does actually exist[8]—and appreciate the position that open science practices may put police agencies in, we hope that the long-term value of adopting such practices is recognized by police organizations. Ultimately, open science will likely produce higher-quality research that is more likely to be replicable. This, in turn, will provide police organizations with a more solid evidence base to rely on to make informed decisions about police practices, policies, and/or programs.

The second challenge we see in the policing field relates to the sensitivity of some police data and/or research topics. Unlike other fields where researchers examine data and phenomena that may not be sensitive at all, there are likely to be certain research topics within policing that are too sensitive to share openly (eg research findings, if accessible by the public, may compromise operational effectiveness and put police officers, and the public they serve, at increased risk). We reluctantly accept this view. When this is the case, appropriate decisions need to be made regarding access and openness. Given that peer review cannot take place under such circumstances, we would also urge researchers working on these types of projects to be extra vigilant about the research practices they adopt, so that the use of QRPs is kept in check and the research is of sufficient quality that it can and should be acted upon.

To conclude this section, we would like to point out that many police organizations do appear to see value in being open and transparent, even in relation to topics that are highly sensitive (eg police use of force). For example, most police researchers will know of the National Archive of Criminal Justice Data, an initiative that has involved the archiving and dissemination of police data since 1978.[9] Much of the data stored in this archive comes from publicly funded research with police agencies in the US. We have also recently seen exciting new initiatives coming out of the Dallas Police Department (DPD), where they have made the decision to make their data on officer-involved shootings (OISs) publicly available.[10] The Stanford Open Police Project is also an important program. This project makes traffic stop data from police agencies across the US available for public scrutiny and research.[11] While the primary driving force behind some of these initiatives may not be the facilitation of open science (eg the DPD initiative appears to have increased transparency to improve police–community relations as its primary goal), these initiatives are consistent with the spirit of open science and they facilitate the sharing of sensitive police data for research purposes—data that would be difficult to come by otherwise.

Conclusion

Ultimately, the goal of EBP is to develop a rigorous evidence base that can be used by police professionals to develop more efficient and effective police practices, policies, and/or programs. We believe two major obstacles may prevent EBP researchers from accomplishing this goal: (1) the fact that police professionals do not access much of the research being conducted that is published in peer-reviewed journals; and (2) the current lack of focus on research replications in the policing field. In this chapter, we have proposed that open science practices (including open access publishing) can be adopted by researchers to help overcome these obstacles. Adopting these approaches will not only produce high-quality police research that is easier for police professionals to access, but will also help EBP advocates accomplish their primary goal of encouraging the police profession to become more evidence based.

Notes

[1] Based on our reading of the academic literature, including our own research, both assumptions appear to be valid in many cases.

[2] We would also argue that for research to be *replicable* and *generalizable*, it must also be *reproducible*, meaning that it is possible to obtain the exact same results produced by another researcher when applying the original methodology to the original data (Asendorpf et al, 2013).

[3] It is important to point out that, as we are preparing this chapter, a special issue in the *Journal of Contemporary Criminal Justice* is being put together that will publish replication attempts from the field of criminology.

[4] As is the case with academic publishing practices, the low rate of replication attempts reported in these studies is not particularly surprising given that academic incentive structures (eg the policies of peer-reviewed journals and grant-funding agencies) have historically rewarded novelty over replication (Nosek et al, 2012).

[5] Any researcher who has attempted to conduct a meta-analysis, whereby the results from previous research are combined to estimate overall effects, will have experienced the frustration of not having access to all necessary information (procedural, methodological, and/or statistical) in the primary studies.

[6] The papers themselves may also not even be accessible to many researchers if open access publishing is not relied on.

[7] For a review of research practices that are likely to increase the replicability of policing research, readers should consult Asendorpf et al (2013).

[8] For the record, we have been very fortunate in our collaborations with police organizations and have found them open to publishing research, even when it does relate to "sensitive" topics.

[9] See: http://www.icpsr.umich.edu/icpsrweb/content/NACJD/index.html

[10] See: https://www.dallasopendata.com/Public-Safety/Dallas-Police-Officer-Involved-Shootings/4gmt-jyx2

[11] See: https://openpolicing.stanford.edu

References

Agnoli, F., Wicherts, J.M., Veldkamp, C.L., Albiero, P., and Cubelli, R. (2017) "Questionable research practices among Italian research psychologists," *PLOS ONE*, 12(3): e0172792.

Asendorpf, J.B., Conner, M., De Fruyt, F., De Houwer, J., Denissen, J.J., Fiedler, K., Fiedler, S., Funder, D.C., Kliegl, R., Nosek, B.A., Perugini, M., Roberts, B.W., Schmitt, M., van Aken, M., Weber, H., and Wicherts, J. (2013) "Recommendations for increasing replicability in psychology," *European Journal of Personality*, 27(2): 108–19.

Baker, M. (2016) "1,500 scientists lift the lid on reproducibility," *Nature News*, 533(7604): 452–4.

Begley, C.G. and Ellis, L.M. (2012) "Drug development: raise standards for preclinical cancer research," *Nature*, 483(7391): 531–3.

Blaskovits, B., Bennell, C., Huey, L., Kalyal, H., Walker, T., and Jalava, S. (forthcoming) "A Canadian replication of Telep and Lum's (2014) examination of police officers' receptivity to empirical research," *Canadian Journal of Criminology and Criminal Justice*.

Eysenbach, G. (2006) "Citation advantage of open access articles," *PLOS Biology*, 4(5): e157.

Fanelli, D. (2012) "Negative results are disappearing from most disciplines and countries," *Scientometrics*, 90(3): 891–904.

Hajjem, C., Harnad, S., and Gingras, Y. (2006) "Ten-year cross-disciplinary comparison of the growth of open access and how it increases research citation impact," *IEEE Data Engineering Bulletin*, 28(4): 39–47.

Huey, L. and Bennell, C. (2017) "Replication and reproduction in Canadian policing research: a note," *Canadian Journal of Criminology and Criminal Justice*, 59(1): 123–38.

Huey, L. and Ricciardelli, R. (2016) "From seeds to orchards: using evidence based policing to address Canada's policing research needs," *Canadian Journal of Criminology and Criminal Justice*, 58(1): 119–31.

Ioannidis, J.P. (2005) "Why most published research findings are false," *PLOS Medicine*, 2(8): e124.

John, L.K., Loewenstein, G., and Prelec, D. (2012) "Measuring the prevalence of questionable research practices with incentives for truth telling," *Psychological Science*, 23(5): 524–32.

Knight, L.V. and Steinbach, T.A. (2008) "Selecting an appropriate publication outlet: a comprehensive model of journal selection criteria for researchers in a broad range of academic disciplines," *International Journal of Doctoral Studies*, 3: 59–79.

Lum, C., Telep, C.W., Koper, C.S., and Grieco, J. (2012) "Receptivity to research in policing," *Justice Research and Policy*, 14(1): 61–95.

McKiernan, E.C., Bourne, P.E., Brown, T., Buck, S., Kenall, A., Lin, J., McDougall, D., Nosek, B.A., Ram, K., Soderberg, C.K., Spies, J.R., Thaney, K., Updegrove, A., Woo, K.H., and Yarkoni, T. (2016) "Point of view: how open science helps researchers succeed," *eLIFE*, July 7. Available at: https://elifesciences.org/articles/16800

McNeeley, S. and Warner, J.J. (2015) "Replication in criminology: a necessary practice," *European Journal of Criminology*, 12(5): 581–97.

Nosek, B.A., Spies, J.R., and Motyl, M. (2012) "Scientific utopia: II. Restructuring incentives and practices to promote truth over publishability," *Perspectives on Psychological Science*, 7(6): 615–31.

OSC (Open Science Collaboration) (2015) "Estimating the reproducibility of psychological science," *Science*, 349(6251): aac4716-1–aac4716-8.

Pew Research Center (2015) "Public and scientists' views on science and society," January 29. Available at: http://www.pewinternet.org/files/2015/01/PI_ScienceandSociety_Report_012915.pdf

Sandesh, N. and Wahrekar, S. (2017) "Choosing the scientific journal for publishing research work: perceptions of medical and dental researchers," *Clujul Medical*, 90(2): 196–202.

Sherman, L.W. (2013) "The rise of evidence based policing: targeting, testing, and tracking," *Crime and Justice*, 42(1): 1–75.

Spellman, B., Gilbert, E.A., and Corker, K.S. (2017) "Open science: what, why, and how," *PsyArXiv Preprints*, pp 1–84. Available at: https://doi.org/10.31234/osf.io/ak6jr

10

Knowledge wars: professionalization, organizational justice, and competing knowledge paradigms in British policing

Emma Williams

Canterbury Christ Church University

Tom Cockcroft

Leeds Beckett University

Introduction

The professionalization agenda in British policing is being driven by the College of Policing. While there are a number of definitions of professionalism (Sklansky, 2014), the basic tenets of a professional organization are that the employees follow a code of ethics, there is a commitment to use expert knowledge, and there is an element of self-regulation. Within the professionalization agenda for the British police, there are a number of strands. These include the implementation of a police code of ethics, the development of a police education qualification framework (PEQF), and wide support for police and academic collaborations to ensure police practice becomes increasingly evidence based. This chapter focuses on the latter strand of work—evidence based policing (EBP)—particularly as there has been extensive debate in both the academic and policing fields about the extent to which police officers are both supportive and understanding of this concept and the extent to which they feel involved in EBP at all stages of the process (Fleming and Wingrove, 2017). In doing so, the chapter will

131

seek to explore some of the potential issues that arise in respect of EBP by using the theory and principles of organizational justice. This will be used to explore the changing conceptualization of knowledge within police organizations and the link this has with the professionalization of policing. We will attempt to do this, first, by exploring the concept and principles of organizational justice and applying this to the context of policing, EBP, and knowledge work. Second, we will explore what we mean by knowledge in a police context and, third, we will examine the potential to apply the concept of organizational justice to current views on the constitution of knowledge and knowledge outputs in the modern policing milieu.

What constitutes knowledge in the context of policing?

The application of ideas of procedural knowledge have become increasingly common to policing, not least in respect of our understanding of how the public perceive and respond to interactions with police officers (see, eg, Bradford, 2014), which are grounded in procedural elements of the police role. These have been especially helpful in developing our understanding of how police organizations can seek to enhance their legitimacy in respect of external public audiences. Allied to the concept of procedural justice, which highlights the perceived fairness of procedures, is that of distributive justice, which instead focuses on the fairness of outputs (Moorman, 1991). Taken together, these allied concepts constitute the concept of "organizational justice," a subject that has been applied to numerous occupational contexts by organizational scientists. Drawing from Adams's equity theory (1963), organizational justice focuses, at its basic level, on the idea that perceptions of justice are a fundamental expectation within an organization that expects to both function effectively and ensure an appropriate level of expectation among those employed by that organization (Greenberg, 1990). Myhill and Bradford (2013) have applied ideas of organizational justice to the policing environment and argue that identification with the police organization is stronger when officers feel a sense of procedural fairness from both their direct supervisors and the organization as a whole. Procedural justice, therefore, is attributed to a sense of involvement and of being listened to by organizations and their leaders. Such perceptions of organizational and procedural justice tend to promote a sense of empowerment, a willingness to put in discretionary effort, and a commitment to new organizational goals and priorities.

This broad concept provides a means of understanding the dynamics of a wide range of organizational contexts. However, there is scope, we believe, to expand on the work of Myhill and Bradford (2013) and to relate these ideas to current applications of evidence based practice within the policing environment, and particularly the concept of police knowledge. A primary justification for this can be the idea that the advent of late modernity has fundamentally changed the role of the police, not least in how they approach their fundamental role of enforcing order. The result has been to increasingly embed actuarialism and rationality within the role of the police, and this is evidenced by the "paper burden" of police officers (Ericson and Haggerty, 1997: 296) working in roles that are increasingly characterized by large administrative workloads. This is but one of the recent substantive developments that led Ericson and Haggerty to characterize modern police work as "knowledge work," where officers "generate, analyse and present various forms of knowledge within ever-changing formats" (Cockcroft, 2009: 23). The work of Thompson and Heron (2005) is of interest here as it explores the ways in which organizational justice relates to workers whose roles might be termed "knowledge work." In doing so, they provide a fitting lens through which to understand police officer experiences by focusing not so much on the context of their work (public sector) as on the *type* of work they did. The central tenet of their argument is that "In knowledge-intensive firms that rely primarily on the problem-solving capabilities of their employees for long-term success, the quality of internal relationships becomes central to organisational strategies to achieve knowledge creation and appropriation" (Thompson and Heron, 2005: 383).

To Thompson and Heron, therefore, high levels of commitment to the organization led to more effective knowledge sharing, as did heightened perceptions of a supportive and safe working environment. At one level, therefore, we can show how organizational environments, and the relationships within them, can shape workers' feelings of institutional fairness in terms of both the procedures by which they are treated and the resultant outcomes that they experience. For those engaged in knowledge work, perceived levels of organizational justice will impact on the extent to which those working environments will be characterized by effective knowledge sharing. This is pertinent to the concept of what counts as knowledge in the current police debates about EBP. We will return to this later in this chapter.

The preceding brief discussion has hopefully encouraged us to consider the nature of knowledge in a policing context. In particular, it has focused on the relationship between the police and knowledge in respect of the police role and how that role is increasingly characterized by what has become known as knowledge work. Recent years have also seen practitioners, academics, and policymakers address the ways in which understanding of knowledge is embedded into policing in ways other than those pertaining to the roles and processes of police *work*. In particular, some debate and discussion has fallen upon the issue of "*What constitutes knowledge in policing?*" At one level, it is helpful to present this argument in terms of a binary between cultural and, what Eraut (2000) would term, "codified" knowledge. Cultural knowledge represents those forms of knowledge that arise informally. In respect of policing, it is easy to see how the pragmatic nature of the role, the propensity for an infinite array of potential scenarios, the legal basis of much police work, and the inherently discretionary nature of policing mean that much day-to-day knowledge of police work is generated experientially and outside of any prescribed formal academic knowledge framework. The organizational sociologist John Van Maanen (1978), in a classic piece entitled "Observations on the making of policemen," quotes a recruit talking about what his expectations for learning were while enrolled at the police academy:

> I want them to tell me what police work is all about. I could care less about the outside speakers or the guys they bring out here from upstairs who haven't been on the street for the last twenty years. What I want is for somebody who's gonna level with us and really give the lowdown on how we're supposed to survive out there. (Van Maanen, 1978: 297)

Indeed, more recent work by Chan (1997) in Australia found that much taught knowledge imparted to new officers in a classroom environment was considered as secondary to the narratives provided by their more established and experienced colleagues. Such accounts, which very much recall traditional depictions of the police occupational culture, highlight the historic assertion that police knowledge is largely viewed, by its practitioners at least, in experiential terms. Over the years, however, academics such as Tong, Bryant, and Horvath (2009) have noted that police knowledge is portrayed in many arenas, rather ambiguously, as an amalgam of science, craft, and art. Increasingly, this view has begun to lose traction as policing has sought to reshape itself in terms of a profession. This move towards professionalization, especially in respect of "new" professions, can serve a number of functions. As Evetts (2013) notes, it can operate positively as a means of enforcing regulation on key societal functions or it can operate negatively by creating market closure through occupational monopolies. Similarly, Fournier (1999) notes that these moves toward professionalization (among previously non–professionalized occupations) often result not in the empowerment of members, but in power being exercised *upon* members. Notwithstanding such discussions about the positives or negatives associated with professionalization, there are undoubted benefits. As Sklansky (2014) notes, professionalization allows for audiences to assume greater efficiency, push reformist agendas, and enhance their status through association with specialized forms of knowledge.

The latter, in particular, raises some interesting dynamics. While we noted earlier that one can detect a changing trajectory of what constitutes police knowledge over the years, it is probably the case that we are currently witnessing the most defined era yet in respect of a formalized knowledge agenda in policing. The EBP agenda, as Wood et al (forthcoming) acknowledge, represents a largely welcome development in policing as it draws us away from the overly experiential knowledge base described by Van Maanen (1978). We would argue that such a concept is not new in terms of the use of research and analysis in police work. Indeed, the intelligence-led policing focus of the early 2000s was based on the collection, and rational analysis, of police data. However, Cope (2003) found that officers were reluctant to follow the deployment options specified by the analytical outputs, and a preference for the use of experiential and learnt policing knowledge remained.

Where does this fit with evidence based policing?

Eraut (2000) helpfully distinguished between "personal" and "codified" knowledge, where the former refers to "tacit" or informal knowledge and the latter refers to knowledge that has been derived by formal means, which "includes propositions about skilled behaviour, but not skills or 'knowing how'" (Eraut, 2000: 114). The EBP agenda very strongly resembles "codified" or formal knowledge in that it seeks to develop a corpus of accepted knowledge that those accepted into the profession will draw upon. In respect of every strategy regarding an evidence base, the question, of course, emerges of which forms of evidence are acceptable and which are not. The EBP agenda, suggest Wood et al (forthcoming: 9), is "shaped by epistemological assumptions and a police science discourse favouring scientifically tested informed policy directives." They go on to conclude that the EBP agenda actually appears to promote a view of police work that negates the importance of police officer discretion. Lest we forget, discretionary decision-making (facilitated by informal knowledge) has, according to many of the classic works in police culture, been instrumental in delivering policing on the streets of our communities. Would such a knowledge base as proposed under EBP reduce the need for officers to utilize discretion or would it merely mean that discretionary decision-making was informed by a different form of knowledge? These are moot points. However, one important consideration, drawing on the work of Fournier (1999) again, is the potential for this professionalizing form of knowledge to control rather than empower those in the office of constable. In the context of officers having that sense of organizational justice, this is worthy of further exploration. At the same time, what status would remain for those elements of police knowledge that held value among practitioners at the cultural level for such a long period of time? There is very real concern that tried and tested cultural knowledge or "common sense" policing would be rendered inappropriate under a paradigm that favors the randomized controlled trial (RCT) over human experience.

The College of Policing in the UK recently published a definition of EBP. Partly, this was a response to the criticism that certain supporters of this concept place increased value on certain types of knowledge as the "gold standard" and negate the importance of human voice within the research agenda (Punch, 2015). This has resulted in a common perception that quantifiable data and a positivist, scientific approach are superior in police research, and that qualitative methodologies are unreliable and anecdotal (Hesketh and Williams, 2017). Those that are more skeptical of pure, quantitative research methods suggest that the constant focus on "what works" and crime prevention is motivated by political agendas and ignores the voice of the practitioner. Moreover, particularly during a time when demand for police services is becoming so complex, such research can ignore "what matters" (Punch, 2015).

The recent publication of the College of Policing's definition of EBP recognizes the importance of a range of methodologies and sources of knowledge, including the experience of the practitioner. However, the current perception among some police officers is that EBP ignores critical context and views the world as static (Greene, 2014). Furthermore, there is a sense that practical outputs from research can undermine officers' professionalism and serve the needs of management rather than the front line (Thacher, 2008). Relating this back to the concept of organizational justice, we feel that there is value in thinking about both the hierarchy of knowledge within the EBP arena and the purpose of the outputs created in the context of organizational justice. Officer knowledge can only be accessed for the purposes of research if police researchers listen and involve practitioners at every stage of the process. Fleming and Wingrove (2017) describe how reform and change is often considered to be driven by and imposed by outside influences without explanation of any of the aims or reasoning for the reform. They suggest that this "may have led to a sense of obligation to protect their [officers'] practices where they perceive their experience/craft knowledge justifies it" (Fleming and Wingrove, 2017: 210). Therefore, we argue that there is scope to consider this in the context of officers' involvement in EBP as one of the most recent reforms in policing (Willis and Mastrofski, 2016).

First, we would like to consider the issue of police knowledge. As previously stated, listening to and engaging with practitioners can drive an increased commitment to change and a sense of empowerment (Myhill and Bradford, 2013). During a period of public sector austerity, and one within which EBP has been so strongly supported, there is a precedence for research to be focused on crime prevention and "what works." This has inevitably resulted in the use of primarily scientific methods to objectively measure whether something is having the correct impact. As Sparrow (2016) claims, this form of research can appeal to senior leaders as it relates to cost effectiveness and management decisions. Indeed, it can be the favored method in terms of what research is funded, which is also problematic for the academic community. However, many officers believe that this minimizes their experience of implementing such initiatives and impairs their understanding of the problems that might have arisen or, conversely, the facilitating factors that might have driven a successful outcome. As Pease and Roach (2017) argue, evaluations are not seen to derive from the experience of police officers and they do not capture the choices that officers have to routinely make as part of their daily business.

There is an additional exclusionary factor in the current EBP discourse that relates to language and accessibility. The application of scientific language drawn from medical and criminological terminology is not translated for the wider population of police officers. Indeed, resistance to the implementation of research recommendations can be exacerbated by the language currently used by some academics involved in the application of science to police work. The application of a "treatment" and ensuring the correct "dosage" assumes a level of understanding that, first, is not generic across all officers and, second, ignores the fact that policing is always dependent on the context and circumstances within which it is being delivered (Pease and Roach, 2017). It is this knowledge, experience, and judgment that officers hold in their heads and such "evidence" that can provide a far deeper level of understanding to any quantifiable evaluation. Moreover, as Van de Ven and Schomaker (2002) argue, the absence of this can devalue this critical part of police knowledge. By exploring this in the context of organizational justice, the links are evident. Engagement, inclusion, and participation are critical when attempting to encourage staff commitment to a reform program. However, reviewing this evidence of officers' perceptions of involvement, it is clear what might be driving some of the negativity concerning the implementation of and drive for EBP in policing. Sklansky (2008) argues that given concerns about the subsequent negative effect on officers who perceive reform to be top–down and irrelevant to their lived experiences, the impact that these perceptions have on their willingness to support research outputs should not be of surprise. Currently, they feel that they have made a limited contribution, if at all, to outputs. This moves us on to the second issue that we would like to discuss here.

Notions of professionalism

Gundhus (2012) explores the notion of professionalization in the context of policing and suggests that it can condone certain forms of legitimate knowledge that arguably results in the creation of new professional guidance about methods of operational practice. What results is the reliance on a more systematic and measurable type of knowledge that can simplify methods of management and performance. However, this can undermine the craft or occupational professional knowledge that officers hold (Willis and Mastrofski, 2016). Understanding officers' reluctance to buy into the concept of EBP and its outputs needs to be considered in the context of personal professional identities. Professionalism at the individual and organizational levels needs to be congruent and balanced. Occupational professional experience gives officers a knowledge set that guides their working day. However, the new notion of organizational professionalism (Gundhus, 2012) can be experienced by officers as a method of controlling practitioner behavior through prescriptive outputs based on objective, and abstracted, knowledge. Hence, when applying the notion of organizational justice, we would argue that officers' sense of professionalism is impacted in two ways. First, their own working professionalism is largely absent from many purist forms of EBP and is therefore believed by officers to not be considered as legitimate. Second, this results in the creation of operational directives that aim to produce a corporate form of behavior to control its staff. Moreover, it ultimately creates a more simplistic frame for police managers to monitor behavior and operate a command-and-control structure within the organization. This makes the use of discretion and officers' independent decision-making more regulated (Petersson, cited in Fleming and Wingrove, 2017) and can result in what Sklansky (2008) has termed "the turning of artisans into robots." Understanding this in more detail is critical in the current climate of police professionalism developments and against the wider context of increased support for knowledge-driven activity within the policing world. It seems that any process that results in particular types of knowledge not being considered legitimate leads to a delegitimization of the process being implemented—in this case, EBP.

Fleming and Wingrove (2017) argue that if we want the police to incorporate knowledge from research into their daily business, there has to be a climate that is ready for this change. They suggest that the police need to be "enabled and empowered to push back, bottom up, for the organisational structures and resources which they need to implement an EBP approach" (Fleming and Wingrove, 2017: 186). Applying the principles of organizational justice to officers' active involvement in and support for EBP provides a framework with which to understand the current resistance among some officers.

Concluding remarks

Given that good communication and participatory styles of leadership can result in support for change, we would argue that similar issues need to be addressed in the process of research. Gundhus (2012) describes the distinction between "thin" and "thick" professionalism. The former relies more on a standardized approach to create standards, a scientific approach, and an objective truth. Conversely, thick professionalism captures the gut feeling and intuition held by officers when decision-making in the field. The merger of these two would incorporate the voice of the practitioner at the start of the process, produce contextual knowledge that could be more responsive to the diverse environment within which the police operate, and, according to organizational justice theory, influence officers to buy into the outputs. The perception of the highly skilled officer, as articulated by Bittner (1983), would be recognized through this methodology, and it would also secure the capture of the "rarely codified" (Flanigin, cited in Willis and Mastrofski, 2016: 4) tacit knowledge that is generally only experienced via police narratives. It is this knowledge that provides situational and local understanding and recognizes such craft as professional knowledge. As Thacher (2008) argues, we cannot underestimate the ability of officers to identify, categorize, and apply previous experience to their working encounters, and we argue that it is this that needs further exploration if we want officers to support this reform.

Returning to the definition of professionalism, the notion of organizational justice can explain some of the wider problems around the fundamental characteristics of a profession, particularly in this chapter, those relating to a reliance on expert knowledge and self-regulation. Officers describe the need to understand the context of their force area and yet the application of this local knowledge and expertise is rarely systematically analyzed or considered next to other community or academic sources (Braga, 2016). This professional knowledge must count in this conversation. It seems to us that there needs to be more understanding of how to reduce this gap between what is considered expert knowledge in a generic, external sense and the expertise of the individual officer. Indeed, it is only with this further link that a culture of learning will be established within, and through, EBP. Additionally, in order for officers to effectively self-regulate, a trust-based environment is vital to ensuring that police officers both act professionally and identify as "professionals." However, research suggests that the perception of many practitioners is that they are over-regulated by EBP outputs, unable to make professional operational decisions without making reference to a toolkit, and at risk of reprimand if they do not refer to the abstract expertise that negates their craft knowledge (Willis and Mastrofski, 2016). Paradoxically, it would appear that academic ignorance of the residual tacit professional knowledge inside the organization serves to destabilize the very agenda of professionalization that the academy is advocating.

References

Adams, J.S. (1963) "Towards an understanding of inequity," *The Journal of Abnormal and Social Psychology*, 67(5): 422–36.

Bittner, E. (1983) "Legality and workmanship: introduction to control in the police organisation," in M. Punch (ed.) *Control in the police organisation*, Cambridge MA: MIY Press.

Bradford, B. (2014) "Policing and social identity: procedural justice, inclusion and cooperation between police and public," *Policing and Society*, 24(1): 22–43.

Braga, A. (2016) "The value of 'pracademics' in enhancing crime analysis in police departments," *Policing*, 10(3): 308–14.

Chan, J. (1997) *Changing police culture: Policing in a multicultural society*, Cambridge: Cambridge University Press.

Cockcroft, T. (2009) "Late modernity, risk and the construction of fear of crime," in G. Mesko, T. Cockcroft, A. Crawford, and A. Lemaitre (eds) *Crime, media and fear of crime*, Ljubljana: Tipografia, pp 15–26.

Cope, N. (2003) "Crime analysis principles and practice," in T. Newburn (ed.) *Handbook of policing*, Devon: Willan Publishing.

Eraut, M. (2000) "Non-formal learning and tacit knowledge in professional work," *British Journal of Educational Psychology*, 70(1): 113–36.

Ericson R.V. and Haggerty K.D. (1997) *Policing the risk society*, Toronto: University of Toronto Press.

Evetts, J. (2013) "Professionalism: value and ideology," *Current Sociology*, 61(5/6): 778–96.

Fleming, J. and Wingrove, J. (2017) "'We would if we could … but not sure if we can': implementing evidence based practice," *Policing*, 11(2): 202–13.

Fournier, V. (1999) "The appeal to 'professionalism' as a disciplinary mechanism," *The Sociological Review*, 47(2): 280–307.

Greenberg, J. (1990) "Organizational justice: yesterday, today, and tomorrow," *Journal of Management*, 16(2): 399–432.

Greene, J.R. (2014) "New directions in policing: balancing prediction and meaning in police research," *Justice Quarterly*, 31(2): 193–228.

Gundhus, H. (2012) "Experience or knowledge? Perspectives on new knowledge regimes and control of police professionalism," *Policing*, 792: 178–94.

Hesketh, I. and Williams, E. (2017) "A new canteen culture: the potential to use social media as evidence in policing." Available at: https://academic.oup.com/policing/article/doi/10.1093/police/pax025/3745171/A-New-Canteen-Culture-The-Potential-to-Use-Social

Moorman, R.H. (1991) "Relationship between organizational justice and organizational citizenship behaviors: do fairness perceptions influence employee citizenship?" *Journal of Applied Psychology*, 76(6): 845–55.

Myhill, A. and Bradford, B. (2013) "Overcoming cop culture? Organizational justice and police officers' attitudes toward the public," *Policing: An International Journal of Police Strategies and Management*, 36(2): 338–56.

Pease, K. and Roach, J. (2017) "How to morph experience into evidence," in J. Knuttson and L. Thompson (eds) *Advances in evidence based policing*, London: Routledge.

Punch, M. (2015) "What really matters in policing?" *European Police Science Bulletin*, 13: 9–18.

Sklansky, D. (2008) *Democracy and the police*, Stanford, CA: Stanford University Press.

Sklansky, D. (2014) "The promise and perils of police professionalism," in J. Brown (ed) *The future of policing*, London: Routledge, pp 343–54.

Sparrow, M. (2016) *Handcuffed. What holds policing back and the keys to reform*, Washington, DC: The Brookings Institute.

Thacher, D. (2008) "Research for the front lines," *Policing and Society*, 18(1): 46–59.

Thompson, M. and Heron, P. (2005) "The difference a manager can make: organizational justice and knowledge worker commitment," *The International Journal of Human Resource Management*, 16(3): 383–404.

Tong, S., Bryant, R., and Horvath, M. (2009) *Understanding criminal investigation*, London: John Wiley & Sons.

Van de Ven, A. and Schomaker, M. (2002) "Commentary: the rhetoric of evidence based medicine," *Health Care Review*, 27(3): 89–91.

Van Maanen, J. (1978) "Observations on the making of policemen," in P.K. Manning and J. Van Maanen (eds) *Policing: A view from the street*, Santa Monica, CA: Goodyear, pp 292–308.

Willis, J. and Mastrofski, S. (2016) "Improving policing by integrating craft and science: what can patrol officers teach us about good police work?" *Policing and Society*. Available at: http://www.tandfonline.com/doi/full/10.1080/10439463.2015.1135921

Wood, D., Cockcroft, T., Tong, S., and Bryant, R. (forthcoming) "The importance of context and cognitive agency in developing police knowledge: going beyond the police science discourse," *The Police Journal: Theory, Practice and Principles*. Available at: https://create.canterbury.ac.uk/15612/1/15612.pdf (accessed July 31, 2017).

SECTION III:
Current and emerging research areas

11

The trials and tribulations of evidence based procedural justice

Sarah Bennett

The University of Queensland

Lorraine Mazerolle

The University of Queensland

Emma Antrobus

The University of Queensland

Peter Martin

Queensland Corrective Services

Lorelei Hine

The University of Queensland

Introduction

The relationship that police build with the public can affect a range of crime control outcomes. The President's Task Force on 21st Century Policing is a landmark report offering insight as to how "policing practices can promote effective crime reduction while building public trust" (President's Task Force on 21st Century Policing, 2015: 1). The report organizes recommendations around six topic areas or "pillars." Pillar One is "Building Trust and Legitimacy," and it is the foundational principle for the Task Force to foster "strong, collaborative relationships between local law enforcement and the communities they protect" (President's Task Force on 21st Century Policing, 2015: 5). Police depend on the consent and cooperation of the communities they serve to maintain general order.

To effectively claim authority to enforce the law, the way in which police engage with communities must be seen as procedurally just (Tyler, 1990).

The Queensland Community Engagement Trial (QCET) was the first experimental study to implement the four key components of procedural justice in an operational dialogue. Specifically, QCET sought to test whether police could influence perceptions of legitimacy by operationalizing the ingredients of procedural justice—dignity and respect, trust/trustworthy motives, neutral decision-making, and open communication—in a routine traffic encounter with the Australian public. The survey results from this trial demonstrated that police did increase public satisfaction with the encounter, confidence in police, and willingness to comply with police directives (Mazerolle et al, 2012). Formatively, the operationalization of procedural justice increased perceptions of police legitimacy (Mazerolle et al, 2013a).

However, replications of the Queensland trial by researcher–police partners in the US, Scotland, England, and Turkey show mixed results, leading some to query if the police really can operationalize procedural justice to foster legal compliance and legitimacy (Lum et al, 2016; Nagin and Telep, 2017). In this chapter, we explore the challenges of operationalizing research evidence through the several trials and reported tribulations of a small corpus of procedural justice experiments.

This chapter starts with a brief review of the literature on procedural justice policing. We then introduce the Queensland trial and the significant role of replication for building evidence based practice. We then explore QCET replications, with a focus on how procedural justice has been operationalized, to identify whether different outcomes may relate to challenges of research translation. Our method and data include a systematic analysis of the replications of QCET, our own critical reflections as developers of QCET, and reflections by those responsible for replications.

Evidence based procedural justice

The term "procedural justice" refers to decision-making processes and procedures that are perceived to be fair and transparent (Thibaut and Walker, 1975), and it is widely believed to consist of four key components: neutrality, voice, respect, and trust/trustworthiness (Tyler, 2004). The first two components relate to the quality of decision-making procedures, where police resolve events in a neutral, unbiased manner, and where there is an opportunity for people to "have their say" (Murphy et al, 2013). The second two components relate to the quality of treatment, where people assess that they have been treated respectfully and that decisions are made with the intention to help or to do what is best for those involved (Murphy et al, 2013).

Communication is a critical vehicle in the relationship between procedural justice and legitimacy. Perceptions of procedural justice can impact views of legitimacy and willing compliance in written communication (Murphy, 2005) and verbally. Bottoms and Tankebe (2012: 141) emphasize the "dialogic" importance of procedural justice during encounters, arguing that authorities "must derive their authority from, and act within, the shared beliefs and values of a given society." They suggest that when police interact with members of the public, their communication and dialogue convey their shared beliefs. Therefore, the approach (eg dialogue) and manner (eg procedural justice) with which police communicate with the public can facilitate legitimacy.

Research consistently suggests that when police apply procedural justice in their encounters with the public, they are more likely to be viewed as legitimate authorities, with people more willing to comply and cooperate with police instructions, and ultimately being more satisfied with the interaction and/or outcome (eg fine or sentence) (eg Tyler, 2004). A systematic review and meta-analysis of 40 evaluations by Mazerolle and colleagues (2013b: 246) found that using a dialogue that incorporates at least one of the principles of procedural justice as part of a police response (eg routine police activity or defined crime control program) is an "important precursor for improving the capacity of police to prevent and control crime." This review also found that no experiments existed that tested whether the police could directly influence perceptions of police legitimacy by explicitly communicating the four ingredients of procedural justice.

Operationalising procedural justice in QCET

The first randomized controlled trial to explore the operationalisation of procedural justice during a routine police–citizen encounter was QCET. In Australia, random breath testing (RBT) is a consistent and highly visible policing response to minimize drink-driving and related road accidents and fatalities. In Queensland, police conduct an average of one RBT per licensed driver (eg 3 million RBTs at the time of the trial) (Watson and Freeman, 2007), which means that people are more likely to encounter police during RBTs than for any other circumstance (Bates, 2014). During RBT operations, police follow a prescribed procedure that lasts 20–30 seconds (where no excess alcohol is detected) with minimal police–driver engagement. The combination of a highly consistent, observable/monitorable, and high-volume police encounter with the public made RBTs an attractive opportunity to conduct a first operationalization of procedural justice.

QCET was conducted in three Metropolitan policing districts. The trial, conducted between 2009 and 2010, involved 60 RBT operations randomly assigned to either business-as-usual control or procedurally just experimental conditions, involving over 21,000 police–driver encounters. Queensland Police Service (QPS) officers who conducted the routine RBTs in the control condition communicated the mandated message to provide a specimen of breath by blowing through a disposable tube into the alcoholmeter, an encounter that lasted for about 25 seconds. Officers in the experimental condition completed the required breath test with drivers but within a longer structured conversation (lasting on average 99.11 seconds), which was guided by a series of procedural justice prompts. Police handed drivers a survey and reply-paid envelope at the end of all trial encounters.

The operationalization of procedural justice dialogue and prompts required considerable attention. The first key challenge was to ensure that the officers' conversations with intercepted drivers in experimental RBTs consistently and appropriately included all elements of procedural justice. The second challenge was to enable officers to naturally converse with drivers using their own preferred style of delivery. This gave the effect of keeping the strategy tight but gave some flexibility in the execution. Flexibility also allowed the officer to deliver the script or conversation in an authentic manner.

QCET benefitted from the perspectives of both researchers and police coming together not only in the facilitation stage of the experiment, but also in the design phase. Priority was given to operationalizing the theoretical constructs of procedural justice. Together, researchers and police co-produced an example script and operational prompts on a postcard-sized card to guide the dialogue that officers had with drivers during their RBT encounters, which included each of the components of procedural justice (see Table 11.1).

In terms of *neutrality*, we wanted to demonstrate to drivers that they were not singled out for attention based upon discriminatory constructs. Police explained to drivers that RBT interceptions were random and the purpose of the interception was to test for alcohol use. The second component—*trustworthy motives*—challenged police to explain to drivers why they were undertaking RBT operations. Linking the RBT strategy to the quantum of deaths on the road was one part of this message, but a second crucial component was for officers to convey how they are personally impacted by road trauma and motivated to positively influence this situation. The third procedural justice prompt was *voice* or citizen participation, where police provided drivers with crime prevention information and asked them if they had any specific concerns. The fourth and last component—*dignity and respect*—was operationalized by officers respectfully acknowledging the drivers' time and ending the encounter on a positive note.

The conversational prompts sought to meld the theory of procedural justice into a dialogue that could easily be operationalized by police. While police officers were asked to address each of the prompts to ensure procedural justice "dosage" (eg all components were delivered as intended), they were also encouraged to flexibly adjust and adapt their dialogue to suit their communication style.

Table 11.1: Operationalizing procedural justice script and prompts in QCET

Theoretical construct	Operationalization scripting	Prompts
Neutrality	Have you ever taken part in a random breath test before? We are pulling cars over today at random. That means that you were not specifically singled out for this test. We are randomly testing drivers for alcohol use so that we can reduce the number of alcohol related traffic crashes on our Queensland roads.	• Hello, • We are pulling cars over today at random. • You were not specifically singled out for this test.
Trustworthy motives	In Queensland alone there were 354 deaths in 2009. One of the hardest parts of our job is to tell a person that their loved one has died or has been seriously injured in a traffic crash. Can you please help us to reduce these accidents by continually driving carefully and responsibly?	• 354 deaths in 2009. • Hardest parts of our job … • Can you please continually help?
Citizen participation	Here is a police bulletin that has additional crime prevention tips. It also tells you about what's going on in this community and gives you some important numbers if you want to get in contact with us for any event that is not life threatening. Please be aware that thieves are targeting money, satellite navigation systems and mobile phones that are left in people's cars. Please make sure you remove all valuables when you leave your car. Do you have any questions about this?	• Here is a police bulletin that has additional crime prevention tips • Thieves are targeting money, sat navs and mobile phones left in cars … • Do you have any questions about this?
Dignity and respect	I just want to finish off by thanking you for … [say something positive to the driver … e.g. child being buckled up in a car seat/well maintained car/seat belt use for passenger or driver etc…]. Thank you for taking part in this Random breath test, I appreciate your time and attention.	• I just want to finish off by thanking you for [positive thing that driver had done] • *If over the RBT limit …* process as usual.

Source: Adapted from Mazerolle et al (2012)

How operationalizing procedural justice in encounters impacted driver perceptions

To date, results from QCET have been presented in numerous publications, including journal articles, briefs, and industry reports. Survey analysis found that drivers in the experimental condition were significantly more satisfied with their RBT encounter and reported significantly greater perceptions of fairness, respectful treatment, and compliance with and confidence in police than the business–as–usual RBTs (Mazerolle et al, 2012). Drivers were more likely to report that their views on drink-driving had changed and that the way that they think about police had changed as a result of the experimental encounters. Drivers in the procedurally just condition also reported greater perceptions of trust, confidence, and compliance, and significantly higher levels of satisfaction, generalized trust, and fairness (Mazerolle et al, 2013a). The length of the encounter affected these results; a longer procedurally just dialogue increased confidence and compliance in police, but not trust in police (Mazerolle et al, 2015). Murphy (2017) confirmed that trust is a critical ingredient for fostering compliance, showing that lower levels of trust during RBT encounters related to lower obligations to obey police. The main experimental findings of QCET were robust and not influenced by bias due to non-responders (Antrobus et al, 2014).

Operational challenges

QCET was not without its challenges. Before the trial started, a group of officers argued that the longer procedural justice dialogue conflicted with the primary operational aim of RBTs to process a large volume of drivers in order to detect those over the alcohol limit (Mazerolle et al, 2014). As a standard RBT can take as little as 20 seconds, the extended QCET conversation with drivers meant that officers could not process as many drivers as normal during their shift. These officers took their complaint to their union, but a legal challenge was overruled and the trial continued.

Some officers expressed embarrassment at having to "lecture" motorists in the context of the RBTs and hold drivers longer than absolutely necessary (Mazerolle et al, 2014). Officers also complained that the procedural justice dialogue was more physically demanding—whole shifts of leaning over and talking to drivers through their window. Finally, given the 1:1 RBT target for Queensland, officers were asked to make up missing breath tests outside of the trial hours. These challenges were managed through a strong commitment to the trial by senior QPS executives. Additionally, both a dedicated QPS inspector *and* research staff were present at every RBT operation to monitor that officers were doing what they were meant to do.

Replicating QCET

Replications of trials are especially valuable when the original research question is considered to be particularly important or when the findings have implications for policy or practice; indeed, "innovation points out paths that are possible; replication points out paths that are likely; progress relies on both" (Open Science Collaboration, 2015: 943). Replications ensure that findings are unbiased, reliable, and generalizable by other researchers in other places and for other participants. There is no doubt that replication is at the core of the scientific method (Schmidt, 2009).

In direct replications, researchers aim to use the same methods as the original study but with another sample of participants/places/events in order to test the stability of findings (Schmidt, 2009). However, direct replications are challenging to achieve outside of highly controlled laboratory settings. Consequently, researchers more commonly conduct conceptual replications. Conceptual replications aim to reproduce the theoretical underpinnings and experimental result but within a modified study design (Schmidt, 2009).

Replications often find weaker evidence than original findings, even where replicators use original trial materials (Open Science Collaboration, 2015). Such results can unsettle policymakers trying to use research findings to inform their policies (Garner and Maxwell, 2000). Michie and colleagues (2009) suggest that publishing the challenges encountered in the original study may prevent similar challenges from reoccurring in replications. Additionally, knowing the theoretical "dosage" (eg the amount of specific components) may not be fully developed or understood in early results and/or until studies are replicated with different samples.

Methods for identifying replications

To identify replications of QCET, all published works on QCET were collated and a forward citation search was conducted in Google Scholar and Web of Science. As QCET developers, we had consulted with a number of replication teams on the details of the QCET operationalization. Through this process, four studies were identified as conceptual replications of QCET: the South Carolina sobriety checkpoint study, USA (Antrobus et al, 2015); the Scottish Community Engagement Trial (ScotCET) (MacQueen and Bradford, 2014); the Adana randomized controlled trial, Turkey (Sahin, 2014); and the Birmingham procedural justice in airport security settings experiment, UK (Langley, 2014). Table 11.2 provides a summary of the details of the studies.

We reviewed the publications for all studies to identify and code details on the operationalization of procedural justice. We focused our data collection on two themes: "operational requirements" and "challenges." For operational requirements, we captured descriptive text relating to the procedures and materials that the authors reported were necessary for the trial to take place. Examples include descriptions of officer training/briefing, aide memoires, and supervision. For challenges we collected descriptions of anything that the authors identified as hindrances to the successful implementation of the trial (in both planning and implementation stages).

Table 11.2: QCET and replication trial summaries

Place	Year(s)	Population	Intervention summary	Comparison	Outcome
Queensland, Australia	2009/10	n=1,649	Procedural justice script at Random Breath Test (RBT) locations. Script contained neutrality, trustworthy motives, participation (or 'voice'), and dignity/respect	Routine stops for RBT	Citizen perceptions of procedural justice were increased in the intervention condition.
South Carolina, USA	2012	n=321	Officers at sobriety checkpoints used scripted procedural justice dialogue.	Routine traffic stops	No significant difference between intervention and comparison conditions. The procedural justice script had no effect.
Scotland	2013/14	n=816	Police roadside stops. Delivered series of key messages which contained procedural justice elements.	Routine traffic stops	Citizen perceptions of procedural justice decreased in the intervention condition.
Adana, Turkey	2013	n=702	Drivers who were stopped for exceeding the speed limit received a scripted procedural justice message (neutrality, trust, participation, dignity/respect) from police.	Routine stop for exceeding speed limits	The experimental condition had a statistically significant effect on views of police in the specific encounter with police.
Birmingham, United Kingdom	2013	n=781	Two treatment groups – Treatment A was a procedural justice checklist at airport embarkment/disembarkment points. Treatment B was experienced utility – i.e. offering complimentary offers (fast track security lane voucher and luggage trolley token), or offering a personal escort to an embarkation gate.	No control group	Public willingness to cooperate with police and police legitimacy were both increased when the procedural justice checklist was utilized. The PJ treatment was statistically significantly more effective than Treatment B.

South Carolina sobriety checkpoint study (2012)

- *Summary citations:* Antrobus, Alpert, and Rojek (2015).

- *About:* The replication in South Carolina followed the same principles as QCET, with drivers at sobriety checkpoints assigned to an experimental or control condition. Officers in the experimental condition received information on procedural justice and delivered a community bulletin on safety tips, while officers in the control condition continued business-as-usual procedures. Drivers in both conditions completed surveys about their perceptions of procedural justice and the encounter.

- *Operational requirements:* The researchers provided training in the experiment and procedural justice to police supervisors, who then conducted practice and training sessions with the officers. This approach resulted in less researcher oversight and collaboration with front-line police. Experimental officers were asked to utilize a procedural justice script that incorporated both the specific components of procedural justice and the rationale behind the study.

- *Results:* There were no significant differences between the experimental or control conditions for perceptions of procedural justice, satisfaction, compliance within the specific encounter, or general perceptions of the procedural justice of the police in South Carolina. Further, no significant effects of the condition emerged for whether the encounter changed drivers' views about drink-driving or police.

- *Replication challenges:* A key challenge was that there was no police champion for the trial. While researchers conducted some training with the supervisors, a lack of police buy-in was noted (personal communication with Alpert, 2017). Further, the researchers were unable to monitor the sobriety checkpoints to ensure that there was consistency across encounters and that the intervention was implemented as planned. Some officers reverted to business-as-usual practices when they were supposed to be delivering the procedural justice intervention. There were thus concerns that the study did not fully follow the intervention protocol.

The Scotland Community Engagement Trial (ScotCET) (2013/14)

- *Summary citations:* MacQueen and Bradford (2014), MacQueen and Bradford (2015a), MacQueen and Bradford (2015b), and MacQueen and Bradford (2016).

- *About:* ScotCET was conducted in Scotland during the National Festive Road Safety Campaign and involved all road policing units. The purpose of the safety campaign was to deter drink-driving and encourage safe driving in winter conditions. Routine encounters during this campaign mostly involved "mass vehicle stops" like Queensland RBTs. However, because RBTs are not permitted in Scotland without reasonable belief that the driver has consumed alcohol, the purpose of the vehicle stops was to ascertain whether police needed to request an RBT and to perform safety checks on the vehicle. ScotCET utilized a pre–post matched design. In the pre-condition, all matched and paired sites operated business-as-usual during encounters, distributing the study questionnaire at the end of each encounter. In the post-condition, each pair was randomly assigned to either continue business-as-usual or to the experimental group, where police were encouraged to include all elements of procedural justice in the encounter.

- *Operational requirements:* The research team and Police Scotland undertook several meetings in the development phase of the experiment, and actively engaged operational officers in the design. Rather than enforcing a procedural justice script, officers were asked to incorporate a list of "key messages" into their delivery during the routine traffic stops. Experimental officers received some training on the concept/theory of procedural justice and the research team verbally briefed experimental units on their part in the study. Further, a written briefing was developed by the researchers and road police management and sent to all experimental officers. This briefing detailed the study aims, objectives, and instructions for implementation of the experimental condition. An aide memoire was also provided to officers to carry with them on shift. This approach was chosen to allow them to maintain a level of flexibility during the experiment. A leaflet was also provided to drivers that aimed to reinforce procedural justice messages.

- *Results:* Overall, driver perceptions of police encounters were very positive. No significant difference between the control and the experimental condition on measures of trust emerged. However, drivers in the *control* condition reported that police were more procedurally just and were more satisfied with the encounter than drivers in the experimental condition, suggesting that the experimental conditional had a detrimental effect on driver impressions of and satisfaction with the encounter.

- *Replication challenges:* First, policing in Scotland had recently undergone a restructure to form one entity (Police Scotland). The issues surrounding this may have hindered buy-in and made some police suspicious as to the intention of the trial. Additionally, many officers felt that they had already informally adopted procedural justice elements into their practice. The authors hypothesize that this weakened the experimental intervention as it did not largely differ from business-as-usual. Further, while the researchers obtained buy-in from higher-level officers, they did not provide formal training to experimental officers and relied on the supervisors for information to trickle down to front-line police. Consequently, researchers were not sure if/how much training occurred or whether there was officer buy-in. The researchers were unable to monitor traffic stops in order to ensure that implementation was being carried out, and supervisors were often not present at stops as they were conducted in single two-officer units.

The Adana randomized controlled trial (2013)

- *Summary citations:* Sahin (2014), and Sahin, Braga, Apel, and Brunson (2017).

- *About:* In this experiment, police randomly assigned (on the spot) drivers stopped for speeding to either business-as-usual or the experimental condition, where police operationalized a scripted procedural justice message and longer dialogues with drivers before issuing a ticket. Drivers completed an on-site survey conducted by researchers.

- *Operational requirements:* Several strategies were utilized for successful operationalization of this study. First, the researcher briefed all officers involved in the research and provided officers assigned to the experimental condition with extensive training in procedural justice. Senior officers monitored the experimental condition and researchers observed most traffic stops in order to ensure that the intervention was correctly delivered. Officers in the experimental condition were asked to memorize a procedural justice script and were provided with an aide memoire that contained the full text of the script with key points highlighted.

- *Results:* The overall perceptions of police were very positive and while there were no significant differences between the experimental and control conditions on procedural justice and trust, drivers in the experimental condition reported that they were more satisfied with the encounter. The study also highlighted an important finding: police who believed in the advantages of procedural justice may have been more procedurally just.

- *Replication challenges:* One of the biggest challenges identified by the researchers was that buy-in from officers may have been lacking at certain points. Before the trial began, officers were worried that the procedural justice script would put an extra burden on them if it became normal practice. Officers were also suspicious of the intention of the trial, voicing fear that it was a covert investigation. More information was provided to officers by the researchers to ease these concerns. Other difficulties arose with individual officers who were observed not following the study protocols during the implementation of the trial.

Birmingham procedural justice and legitimacy—an airport security setting (2013)

- *Summary citation:* Langley (2014).

- *About:* The experiment in Birmingham, UK focused specifically on border security at the international Birmingham Airport. This study was guided by Schedule 7 of the Terrorism Act 2000, which is used at ports and borders in the UK to enable officers (police/immigration/customs) to stop, question, search, and detain persons in order to determine whether they are involved in terrorism. During the trial period, ports officers employed either a procedural justice or experienced utility treatment to Schedule 7 passengers at Birmingham Airport upon embarkation/disembarkation. The experienced utility treatment involved an offer of complimentary vouchers for fast-tracking through airport security, luggage trolleys, and an escort to the embarkation gate. Officers used a checklist in the procedural justice condition. There was no control group.

- *Operational requirements:* Researchers and ports officers in this study held workshops to modify the procedural justice script used in QCET, and consulted with the airport and relevant officers. This was to encourage cultural buy-in and ensure that the checklist was appropriate for the trial. The checklist was then made into an aide memoire that officers were asked to carry. Ports supervision oversaw over 90% of interactions in both conditions.

- *Results:* Telephone surveys were conducted post-implementation. The authors found a direct causal relationship between the procedural justice checklist and greater levels of public willingness to cooperate with police in counterterrorism activities. Passengers felt that the experienced utility (ie complimentary vouchers) compensated them more, especially at disembarkation.

- *Replication challenges:* The Birmingham study compared two interventions (eg no control group). The same group of officers delivered both treatments, meaning that there was a concern that the lines of the intervention had been blurred and procedural justice seeped into the experienced utility condition.

Discussion and conclusions

The prevailing international research finds that police can foster positive perceptions of police legitimacy when their communication and behavior toward citizens is perceived to be procedurally just. Research also shows that positive perceptions of police legitimacy can lead to a range of social benefits, including greater law-abiding behavior. With such potential for police to increase their capacity to prevent and control crime, there is clearly a lot of interest in whether police can operationally apply procedural justice to build trust and legitimacy. While QCET demonstrated that a routine procedurally just encounter with citizens could impact perceptions of police legitimacy, the replications of QCET produced mixed results. Our analysis of the replication trials shows some commonalities across the operational requirements and experienced challenges.

First, all of the trials described the importance of meetings/briefings and the training of supervising officers and/or officers involved in the implementation of the trial as critical operational requirements. In both ScotCET and the South Carolina study, the lack of formal training to front-line police officers may have hindered their buy-in and the delivery of the study. Greater emphasis may be needed on fostering the *legitimacy* of operationalizing all the components of procedural justice among the involved "rank and file." Such efforts are likely to facilitate willing compliance from officers and ownership in the outcomes of employing procedural justice in a manner that will move officers beyond the "we do that already" response and feeling that their practice is being questioned.

Second, all replications operationalized procedural justice in a manner that was "natural" and suitable to the specific enforcement context. This was achieved through the careful crafting of scripts (Queensland, South Carolina), prompts (Queensland, Adana, and Birmingham), or key messages (Scotland).

Third, in Scotland and South Carolina, the monitoring of officers was not possible and thus led the researchers to question the fidelity of some of the treatment components. By contrast, in Queensland, Adana, and Birmingham, monitoring was possible, leading researchers to be more confident regarding their findings. Strategies that effectively monitor the use of a procedural justice dialogue that are achievable through consultation with and agreement from the officers conducting the intervention are needed so that officers are not "suspicious" and disempowered.

Finally, in Queensland and Adana, officers raised concern that the longer procedural justice dialogue would adversely impact their ability to complete other duties (eg RBTs). Operationalizing procedural justice in a longer dialogue needs senior police support and an organizational emphasis on targets that align with procedural justice outcomes.

Understanding "what works" is foundational to evidence based policing (Sherman, 2013), and so, too, is a clear understanding of "what makes it work" operationally. Evidence based policing will benefit from understanding operational requirements and challenges when considering findings, as well as better detail requirements and challenges, in order to avoid replicating tribulations in future research.

References

Antrobus, E., Elffers, H., White, G., and Mazerolle, L. (2014) "Non-response bias in randomized controlled experiments in criminology: putting the Queensland Community Engagement Trial (QCET) under a microscope," *Evaluation Review*, 37(3/4): 197–212.

Antrobus, E., Alpert, G., and Rojek, J. (2015) "Replicating experiments in criminology: lessons learned from Richland," unpublished short report.

Bates, L. (2014) "Procedural justice and road policing: is it important?" *Proceedings of the 2014 Australasian Road Safety Research, Policing & Education Conference*, 12–14 November, Melbourne, Australia.

Bottoms, A. and Tankebe, J. (2012) "Beyond procedural justice: a dialogic approach to legitimacy in criminal justice," *Journal of Criminal Law and Criminology*, 102(1): 119–70.

Garner, J.H. and Maxwell, C.D. (2000) "What are the lessons of the police arrest studies?" *Journal of Aggression, Maltreatment & Trauma*, 4(1): 83–114.

Langley, B. (2014) "A randomised control trial comparing the effects of procedural justice to experienced utility theories in airport security stops," master's thesis, University of Cambridge, UK.

Lum, C., Koper, C.S., Gill, C., Hibdon, J., Telep, C., and Robinson, L. (2016) *An evidence-assessment of the recommendations of the President's Task Force on 21st Century Policing —Implementation and research priorities*, Virginia: Center for Evidence based Crime Policy, George Mason University, and International Association of Chiefs of Police.

MacQueen, S. and Bradford, B. (2014) *The Scottish Community Engagement Trial (ScotCET)*, Scotland: The Scottish Institute for Policing Research.

MacQueen, S. and Bradford, B. (2015a) "Enhancing public trust and police legitimacy during road traffic encounters: results from a randomised controlled trial in Scotland," *Journal of Experimental Criminology*, 11(3): 419–43.

MacQueen, S. and Bradford, B. (2015b) "Procedural justice in practice: findings from the Scottish Community Engagement Trial (ScotCET)," *Scottish Justice Matters*, 3(2): 11–12.

MacQueen, S. and Bradford, B. (2016) "Where did it all go wrong? Implementation failure—and more—in a field experiment of procedural justice policing," *Journal of Experimental Criminology*, 13(3): 1–25.

Mazerolle, L., Bennett, S., Antrobus, E., and Eggins, E. (2012) "Procedural justice, routine encounters and citizen perceptions of police: main findings from the Queensland Community Engagement Trial (QCET)," *Journal of Experimental Criminology*, 8(4): 343–67.

Mazerolle, L., Antrobus, A., Bennett, S., and Tyler, T. (2013a) "Shaping citizen perceptions of police legitimacy: a randomized field trial of procedural justice," *Criminology*, 51(1): 33–64.

Mazerolle, L., Bennett, S., Davis, J., Sargeant, E., and Manning, M. (2013b) "Legitimacy in policing: a systematic review," *The Campbell Collaboration Library of Systematic Reviews*, (9)1: 1–147.

Mazerolle, L., Sargeant, E., Cherney, A., Bennett, S., Murphy, K., Antrobus, E., and Martin, P. (2014) *Procedural justice and legitimacy in policing*, Switzerland: Springer Briefs.

Mazerolle, L., Bates, L., Bennett, S., White, G., Ferris, J., and Antrobus, E. (2015) "Optimising the length of random breath tests: results from the Queensland Community Engagement Trial," *Australian and New Zealand Journal of Criminology*, 48(2): 256–76.

Michie, S., Fixsen, D., Grimshaw, J.M., and Eccles, M.P. (2009) "Specifying and reporting complex behaviour change interventions: the need for a scientific method," *Implementation Science*, 4(40): 1–6.

Murphy, K. (2005) "Regulating more effectively: the relationship between procedural justice, legitimacy, and tax non-compliance," *Journal of Law and Society*, 32(4): 562–89.

Murphy, K. (2017) "Challenging the 'invariance' thesis: procedural justice policing and the moderating influence of trust on citizens' obligation to obey police," *Journal of Experimental Criminology*, 13: 429–37.

Murphy, K., Mazerolle, L., and Bennett, S. (2013) "Promoting trust in police: findings from a randomized experimental field trial of procedural justice policing," *Policing and Society: An International Journal of Research and Policy*, 24(4): 405–24.

Nagin, D.S. and Telep, C.W. (2017) "Procedural justice and legal compliance," *Annual Review of Law and Social Science*, 13: 5–28.

Open Science Collaboration (2015) "Estimating the reproducibility of psychological science," *Science*, 349(6251): Acc4716.

President's Task Force on 21st Century Policing (2015) *Final report of the President's Task Force on 21st Century Policing*, Washington, DC: Office for Community Oriented Policing Services.

Sahin, N. (2014) "Legitimacy, procedural justice, and police–citizen encounters: a randomized controlled trial of the impact of procedural justice on citizen perceptions of the police during traffic stops in Turkey," PhD thesis, Rutgers University, Newark.

Sahin, N., Braga, A.A., Apel, R., and Brunson, R.K. (2017) "The impact of procedurally-just policing on citizen perceptions of police during traffic stops: the Adana randomized controlled trial," *Journal of Quantitative Criminology*, 33(4): 701–26.

Schmidt, S. (2009) "Shall we really do it again? The powerful concept of replication is neglected in the social sciences," *Review of General Psychology*, 13(2): 90–100.

Sherman, L.W. (2013) "The rise of evidence based policing: targeting, testing and tracking," *Crime and Justice*, 42(1): 377–451.

Thibaut, J. and Walker, L. (1975) *Procedural justice: A psychological analysis*, Hillsdale, NJ: Erlnaum.

Tyler, T.R. (1990) *Why people obey the law*, New Haven, CT: Yale University Press.

Tyler, T.R. (2004) "Enhancing police legitimacy," *The Annals of the American Academy of Political and Social Science*, 593(1): 84–99.

Watson, B. and Freeman, J. (2007) "Perceptions and experiences of random breath testing in Queensland and the self-reported deterrent impact on drunk driving," *Traffic Injury Prevention*, 8(1): 11–19.

12

Hot spots policing made easy

Renée J. Mitchell

American Society of Evidence-Based Policing

Introduction

Over the past few years, police agencies have increasingly embraced hot spot policing as a strategy for addressing violent and other crimes (PERF, 2008). Despite growing popularity, there is no consensus as to what "hot spotting" should look like, that is, what police activity should take place in the hot spot, the size of the hot spot, and/or what crimes to target in the hot spot. This lack of consensus can make hot spotting seem complicated to a novice crime analyst or area commander. Police managers may end up unsure about whether to saturate hot spots with high-visibility policing, use a problem-oriented policing (POP) approach, or have officers engage in specific self-initiated proactivity.

Despite the lack of a unified approach, the research literature on hot spot policing demonstrates that the overall strategy of hot spotting has one of the strongest foundations of evidence for police effectiveness (National Research Council, 2004: 250). Furthermore, this evidence base continues to grow: from 25 studies (Braga et al, 2014) to over 60 in the last four years (Braga et al, 2017). What does this body of research tell us? In short, that hot spot policing reduces crime and calls for service without creating negative reactions from the community (Braga et al, 2014). A strategy that reduces crime without reducing police legitimacy is necessary in today's policing environment.[1]

Hot spot policing appears to be a simple approach when applied superficially. For example, errors can occur in hot spot policing when one or two weeks of data determine a hot spot area. Reliance on such little data produces ineffective results for two reasons: (1) crime is stable (3–4% of a city's street segments make up 50% of the crime)—chasing crime's ghost of weeks past does not prevent future crime; and (2) sending officers to patrol the area may not be the most effective response to the type of crime occurring. As crime is stable, hot spot policing should be a proactive strategy rather than a reactive one, and this requires a more analytical and thoughtful approach. Applying hot spot policing superficially is efficient but ineffective. By taking the time to understand where, when, and how often hot spots occur and what to do about them, a hot spot strategy can be used in a more effective and efficient manner. In this chapter, I use my experience of designing and implementing two randomized controlled trials to demonstrate the best use of a hot spot policing strategy for a police department. The art and science of hot spot policing frames this chapter, giving guidance and advice for the novice.

Applying hot spot research to the field

Applying a field practice to conform to a research protocol is different from applying a field practice to achieve crime and calls for service reductions. Research protocols require conformity. Field protocols require flexibility. Research, especially a randomized controlled trial, tests a specific intervention to answer specific questions. In the field, the intervention conforms to the crime problem. This chapter uses the hot spot research as a framework to inform the hot spot field approach outlined here. The hot spot model I espouse is intended to reduce crime and calls for service while creating the least harm possible—although, if precisely applied, and in a procedurally just manner, hot spot policing should not create any unintended negative consequences in the community or push crime to the neighboring area (Weisburd et al, 2011; Kochel et al, 2015). Moreover, hot spot policing has even shown a diffusion of benefits to the immediate areas around the hot spot (Weisburd et al, 2006). The overarching goal of the hot spot approach outlined here is crime reduction.

The reduction of crime and calls for service is the heart of the Evidence based Policing Matrix, a formal translational tool created to help practitioners locate relevant crime-reduction studies within an easily understood matrix (Lum et al, 2011). The Matrix visually lays out 138 scientifically moderate to rigorous policing studies[2] that have been conducted in policing. The Matrix visually reveals the "realms of effectiveness" in studies that applied focused, place-based (specific), highly proactive (focused) interventions (Center for Evidence-based Crime Policy, n.d.). In the next section, I apply the Lum et al (2011) suggestion that to reduce crime and calls for service, the police intervention in the hot spot must be specific, focused, and tailored. The specific approach focuses on analyzing the hot spot—determining where the hot spots are located, the time of day the spots are "hot," the underlying causes of the problem, and how often the problem occurs—and then applying solutions once the hot spot problem has been thoroughly defined.

Where, when, what, and how often?

Where is the crime occurring?

Crime maps allow an agency to visually observe where problems occur in a city or county (Santos, 2016). Crime mapping is "the process of using geographic information to conduct spatial analysis of crime problems and other police related issues" (Santos, 2016). Maps come in a variety of forms: single-symbol mapping depicts an individual symbol indicating one crime or call for service; buffer maps display crime in the 500 or 1,000-foot area around a specific area, like a bar or a park; graduated maps display different gradations of crime according to the numbers; and density maps show the concentration of crime in particular areas, with the center of the crime being darker than the area outside of the crime (Santos, 2016). All crime maps have pros and cons. Single-symbol mapping can become too busy when mapping more than a week's worth of data for a large agency. Graduated maps show the variance in crime in different areas but do not show any specificity. Density maps also lack specificity. Density maps show where the largest amounts of crime are occurring in a city, condensing in the center, but do not show where the individual crimes occur. Street segment maps show where crime occurred by individual streets (intersection to intersection), which follows Lum et al's (2011) advocacy for police interventions to be specific.

Street segment maps can display exactly where crime is occurring and at what rate. Street segments are large enough areas to avoid the crime coding errors that occur when using specific addresses, but they are small enough to show the variation of crime within neighborhoods (Weisburd et al, 2004). Street segment maps show where crime concentrates, and it does concentrate; a small percentage of street segments make up 50% of crime (Sherman et al, 1989; Sherman and Weisburd, 1995; Telep et al, 2014). Street segment maps can highlight the concentration, allowing police commanders to allocate resources more efficiently and effectively. If 100% of a city's crime occurs in little over half of a city's street segments, then resources should not be wasted sending officers to crime-free street segments (Weisburd et al, 2004). Translating this finding, police agencies do not need to police 40% of their city's street segments (Sherman et al, 1989). Street segment maps delineate where to send officers.

Creating street maps for a city is not an easy undertaking. It requires out-thinking the ArcGIS mapping system by forcing the system to bring the center point of the geographic information system (GIS) indicator from the middle of a parcel of land to the center of the street. Police departments in Sacramento, California, and Austin, Texas, are two agencies that have developed street segment maps. Centering the crime or call for service to the street segment rather than a land parcel gives command staff the ability to identify which areas of the city require police interventions to reduce crime. A crime analyst can also display the number of crimes occurring on street segments over a time period. Figure 12.1 (created by Sarah Davis of the Austin Police Department) demonstrates the streets of the City of Austin, Texas, by color—no crime (gray), 1–6 crimes (blue), 7–20 crimes (teal), 21–51 crimes (green), 52–109 (yellow), and 110–318 crimes (red)—over a three-month period. A street segment map clearly demonstrates where crime is occurring in a city. Furthermore, it shows exactly how much crime is occurring. Notice the very limited amount of red and yellow occurring throughout the city. Figure 12.1 visually demonstrates the theory of crime concentration. This type of map should lead an agency to patrol on the specific streets where the majority of crime is occurring rather than wasting resources patrolling where little to no crime exists.

Street segment maps can also demonstrate the stability of crime. A common misconception of hot spot policing is that police need to respond rapidly to hot areas where crime materializes. This happens when agencies look at weekly, bi-monthly, or monthly crime counts on a map rather than a longer period of historical data. Chasing short periods of data leads to reactive policing rather than proactive policing strategies, and the greatest crime reductions come from focused, specific, and tailored approaches (Lum et al, 2011). Unless there is an immediate problem, such as a crime series or pattern (a robbery spree with similar modus operandi or a burglary series in a specific area), there is no need to chase two weeks of crime statistics by sending officers to patrol an area. Stable factors and chance influence crime. This means that crime counts will fluctuate over time around an average. Looking at short temporal periods of crime will only reflect natural fluctuations in crime and is not meaningful data. When crime exceeds its natural mean because of the influence of chance factors, the crime count will innately fall back toward its natural mean—called regression to the mean (Morton and Torgerson, 2005). Sending officers to immediate spikes in crime is inefficient; most likely, crime would have regressed to the mean and fallen back to average levels anyway without police intervention.

Crime concentrates *and* is relatively stable over longer temporal periods. This is an important point. If crime concentrates *and* is stable, then police *can* approach crime reduction more effectively and efficiently. Bi-monthly maps can tell you if there are crime series or patterns, but they cannot show where the chronic crime problems are located. Crime maps for the City of Seattle, Washington, showed that crime remained relatively stable over a 14-year period (Weisburd et al, 2004). The Seattle maps color-code the crime trajectories (the change over the 14 years). The street segments fell into three groups: stable, increasing, and decreasing trajectories. There were 18 trajectories in total:

Figure 12.1: Map of the City of Austin, Texas

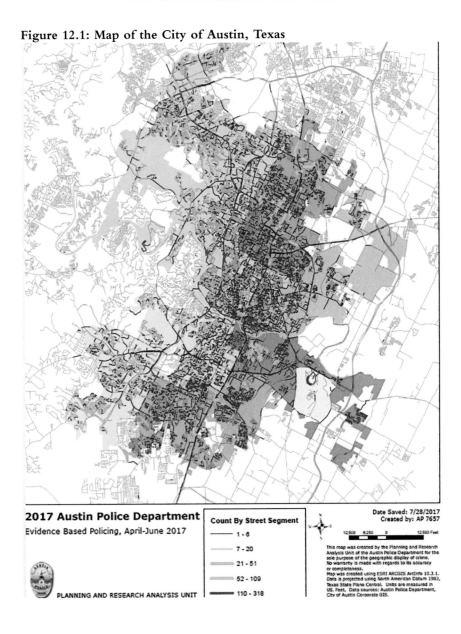

2017 Austin Police Department
Evidence Based Policing, April-June 2017

PLANNING AND RESEARCH ANALYSIS UNIT

Count By Street Segment

——— 1 - 6

——— 7 - 20

═══ 21 - 51

═══ 52 - 109

━━━ 110 - 318

Date Saved: 7/28/2017
Created by: AP 7657

12500   6250   0   12500 Feet

This map was created by the Planning and Research
Analysis Unit of the Austin Police Department for the
sole purpose of the geographic display of crime.
No warranty is made with regards to its accuracy
or completeness.
Map was created using ESRI ARCGIS ArcInfo 10.3.1.
Data is projected using North American Datum 1983,
Texas State Plane Central. Units are measured in
US. Feet. Data sources: Austin Police Department,
City of Austin Corporate GIS.

eight of the 18 were stable, three were increasing, and seven were decreasing. Overall, the highest-rate trajectories remained high over the 14-year period and the lowest-rate trajectories remained low. By analyzing crime data by street segment and for a longer historical period, the City of Seattle was able to determine which street segments contributed to the overall increases and decreases in crime. This type of analysis is vital to policing hot spots more efficiently and effectively.

When is the crime occurring?

Crime occurs during different times of the day depending on the offender and the type of crime. Hot spot policing is about analyzing the crime data. Once the where of the hot spots is established, the when needs to be sorted. Every hot spot is different. For example, one hot spot may have a school located on the street segment, which would translate to calls for service occurring before or after school. There would be no reason to send officers to the school during the middle of the school day if this street segment did not generate calls during that time. Another hot spot may have a bar or pub located on the street segment, generating calls at 0100–0300 hours in the morning. Reviewing the crime and calls for service data of each individual street segment should reveal a narrower period in which to send officers to the hot spot, rather than sending them all day, every day. This should reduce the amount of time officers patrol a hot spot.

How often is the crime occurring?

How "hot" is the hot spot? The literature suggests that effective hot spot interventions only occur when a threshold of crime or calls for service has been met. Hot spots may need to be "hot" hot spots to generate reductions. Ratcliffe et al (2011) suggested that the pre-treatment incidents may have to meet a certain "tipping point" before the effects of the treatment can be observed (Tittle and Rowe, 1974). Ratcliffe et al (2011) found the top 40% of baseline violent crime to be an indicator that the hot spots were "hot" enough to see the effects of an intervention. Deterrence may only be taking place if there is enough crime in the area for officers to convey a risk of apprehension. There may need to be a baseline before a hot spot is "hot" enough to detect the effects of an intervention. Reaching 30 calls for service in the previous 90 days was the threshold needed to reduce crime in 77.3% of the hot spots in the Sacramento Hot Spot Experiment (Mitchell, 2017b). If policing a "warm" hot spot is ineffective no matter the level of police presence, dosage, or proactivity, then police managers should not waste resources sending officers to that area.

What problems are occurring in the hot spot?

The type of problem occurring in the hot spot should drive the type of police activity directed at the hot spot. Individual hot spot data should be broken down into type of crime and call for service, this determines how many of each type of crime or call for service are occurring in the hot spot. Ranking type from high to low gives an overall picture of what is occurring in the hot spot. Once the top three call types have been determined, a literature review should be conducted to evaluate what evidence based approach works best for that particular crime or call for service. Hot spot research shows a variety of police activity works to reduced crime and calls for service. Hot spot research has shown that: increasing officers' presence in hot spots, on average, reduces calls for service (Sherman and Weisburd, 1995); engaging in POP, on average, can reduce drug calls and violent crimes (Mazerolle et al, 2000; Weisburd and Green, 1995; Taylor et al, 2011); and offender-focused patrols and foot patrols can reduce violent crime (Ratcliffe et al, 2011; Groff et al, 2015). Taylor et al (2011) also demonstrated that a POP strategy had effects that lasted 90 days after the initial intervention. Mitchell (2017b) showed that hot spot interventions were more effective in commercial areas that sold alcohol as opposed to residential areas. Police proactivity research not limited to hot spot policing showed that specific activity can reduce specific types of crime. For example, Sampson and Cohen (1988) showed that an increase in traffic stops reduced robberies in the area. The top three types of problems occurring in the hot spot should direct the intervention.

What to do in the hot spot?

Once the officers know where and when they should go to a hot spot, what should they do when they get there, how often should they go, and how long should they stay? A typical police response to any type of uptick in crime or call for service activity is increasing the amount of police presence in the area. The officers are instructed to be proactive but without any parameters of how often, how long, or what type of proactivity to engage in. Creating precise interventions with less impact on the community requires instructing officers about specific evidence based methods on what to do in the hot spot. The evidence based instructions should be specific to the problem in the hot spot. Once a specific type of proactivity has been designated for the hot spot, then the number of daily visits and the time spent in the hot spot should be defined.

The optimal frequency and length of police patrol visits in a hot spot for maximum crime and calls for service reductions has yet to be established. Sherman et al (2014: 105) proposed that "the more frequent the visits of uniformed police to each hot spot, other things being equal (ceteris paribus), the more initial and residual deterrence each hot spot will experience." In the Minneapolis hot spot experiment, officers drove through the area, stopped sometimes for hours at a time, or stayed for mere minutes (Sherman and Weisburd, 1995). Both frequency and length of patrol visits are likely to vary from hot spot to hot spot, and time of day and year, because crime is dynamic. Crime hot spots are rarely "hot" all day. For example, the area around a local high school can witness an increase in assaults, vehicle burglaries, and vandalism before or after school, when kids are either walking to school or walking home, respectively. It would not benefit a police department to direct an officer to patrol the perimeter of that high school all day long. An intermittent schedule of "hot spotting" (police patrols of hot spots, as they are described by police themselves) could be more effective.

Several studies support the idea of the increased frequency, rather than duration, of visits to hot spots for crime and calls for service reductions. The Sacramento Hot Spots Experiment showed that 15-minute high-visibility patrols could reduce crime and calls for service when visits to the hot spots were approximately every two hours and averaged three to four visits a day (Telep et al, 2014). In a follow-up analysis, Mitchell (2017b) demonstrated that the computer aided dispatch (CAD)-measured duration of patrols showed a weaker correlation to crime and calls for service reductions than the CAD-measured frequency of visits. This examination of the Sacramento Hot Spots Experiment supports Ariel et al's (2016) work, which demonstrated that the number of visits had more influence on crime reduction than the number of minutes of patrol by Police Community Support Officers (PCSOs). Shorter but more frequent visits may have a greater influence on reducing crime and calls for service than lengthier visits (Mitchell, 2017a). The key is finding the patrol "sweet spot," or the right amount of frequency and duration for the individual hot spots (Gibson et al, 2017). Although frequency and duration are a concern if proactive patrols are the hot spot protocol, this is not the case if a POP approach is employed.

There is support for POP approaches reducing crime in hot spots (Weisburd and Green, 1995; Mazerolle et al, 1998) and continuing to work even when the intervention ends (Taylor et al, 2011). A POP approach requires more in-depth analysis as to the root causes of the crime in the hot spot. This approach is recommended if a hot spot has been chronically hot over multiple years. Chronic "hotness" indicates that there are locational conditions that generate crime, and these conditions should be identified before solutions are applied (Nagin et al, 2015). This chronic "hotness" could be due to social cues or "signals" occurring in the hot spot that create the call for service threshold (Bottoms, 2007). When analyzing chronic hot spots, an analyst should determine what opportunities the hot spots offer to offenders and whether the opportunities can be reduced through environmental design or improved guardianship (Cohen and Felson, 1979).

Creating a hot spot strategy for patrol

Applying and evaluating a hot spot strategy, although not simple, is straightforward. The steps listed below can be followed, implemented, and evaluated with the assistance of a good crime analyst and an area commander:

1. Map crime and calls for service separately by street segment for the following periods:
   a. 30/60/90 days—this allows for visually observing emerging patterns;
   b. one year; and
   c. three years.
2. Using a street segment map, identify street segments that have had over 30 calls for service in the last 90 days—these street segments are the "hot" hot spots.
3. Rank the crime and calls for service in the "hot" hot spots by type.
4. Review the research to determine what police proactivity is the most effective approach to the top three crime types identified in the hot spot.
5. For a simple patrol intervention, use high-visibility, 15-minute patrols every two hours during the period of day in which the crimes are occurring.
6. Evaluate the effectiveness of the intervention by using an A–B–A application of the intervention, meaning 30 days of intervention–30 days of no intervention–30 days of intervention, and so on. Then use a time-series analysis to compare the crime and calls for service in the intervention periods to those in the no intervention periods.

Mapping crime over different time periods establishes the areas of the city that have chronic hot spots. Emerging issues will manifest themselves over the 30-, 60-, and 90-day periods. If the colors begin to change between 30-day periods, then a pattern or series may be surfacing. This will require an in-depth analysis of the issues plaguing the street segments to determine if a response is required. Comparing those segments to the one-year and three-year maps is also helpful as it can assist with determining what kind of problem is occurring. Focus police resources on the "hottest" areas with chronic problems; this will create a more effective police force.

The sixth step—evaluation—is a little more complicated as an untrained analyst may not be able to perform the statistical analysis. A phone call to a local university can lead to an academic partnership and assistance with the evaluation. Targeting, testing, and *tracking* interventions is an important component of evidence based policing. Tracking requires analyzing the outcomes to determine if the intervention was successful (Sherman, 2013). I argue that it is unethical to apply social interventions to a community without evaluating the impact on the community (Mitchell and Lewis, 2017). Without testing and tracking police interventions, we remain ignorant about the consequences of our actions. We need to understand whether our interventions unintentionally cause harm or create a benefit for those involved (McCord, 2003). For policing to become truly professional, we need to test our beliefs about "what works" and "what does not" in policing to achieve crime reduction with the least possible harm to the community.

Hot spots policing can be a simple and effective crime control strategy once the basics are understood. Indeed, the steps listed in this chapter only require an analyst and a willing area commander. Furthermore, although the initial street maps can be tricky to create, once an analyst masters ArcGIS, the maps are easily created. At the start, I suggest picking a few hot spots within the city, testing a hot spot strategy that is specific and focused, and seeing if it works in the locality and on the particular problems. Once this strategy proves successful, agencies can scale up the hot spots strategy citywide.

Notes

[1] A word of caution: while useful for many types of offences, the hot spot approach is not a remedy for all police problems, and in-depth problem analysis is required before a solution is applied.

[2] The Maryland Scientific Methods Scale (SMS) assists scholars, policymakers, and practitioners by creating a simplified numerical way of determining whether the research that they are reviewing is rigorous. The scale is heavily based on Cook and Campbell (1979) and ranges from 1 to 5, with 1 being the least rigorous and a 5 being the most rigorous (Farrington et al, 2002).

References

Ariel, B., Weinborn, C., and Sherman, L.W. (2016) "'Soft' policing at hot spots—do police community support officers work? A randomized controlled trial," *Journal of Experimental Criminology*, 12(3): 277–317.

Bottoms, A. (2007) "Place, space, crime, and disorder," in M. Maguire, R. Morgan and R. Reiner (eds) *The Oxford handbook of criminology*, 4th edn, New York: Oxford University Press, pp 528–574.

Braga, A.A., Papachristos, A.V., and Hureau, D.M. (2014) "The effects of hot spots policing on crime: An updated systematic review and meta-analysis," *Justice Quarterly*, 31(4): 633–663.

Braga, A.A., Turchan, B., Hureau, D., and Papachristos, A.V. (2017) "Hot spots policing and crime prevention: an updated systematic review and meta-analysis," paper presented at the annual meeting of the American Society of Criminology, November, Philadelphia, Pennsylvania.

Cohen, L.E. and Felson, M. (1979) "Social change and crime rate trends: A routine activity approach," *American Sociological Review*, 44(4): 588–608.

Cook, T.D. and Campbell, D.T. (1979) *Quasi-experimentation: Design and analysis for field settings* (Vol. 3). Chicago: Rand McNally.

Center for Evidence-Based Crime Policy (n.d.) "Evidence-based policing matrix." Retrieved August 3, 2018 from http://cebcp.org/evidence-based-policing/the-matrix/

Farrington, D.P., Gottfredson, D.C., Sherman, L.W., and Welsh, B.C. (2002) "The Maryland Scientific Methods Scale," *Evidence Based Crime Prevention*, pp 13–21.

Gibson, C., Slothower, M., and Sherman, L. (2017) "Sweet spots for hot spots? A cost-effectiveness comparison of two patrol strategies," *Cambridge Journal of Evidence based Policing*, 1(4): 225–43.

Groff, E.R., Ratcliffe, J.H., Haberman, C.P., Sorg, E.T., Joyce, N.M., and Taylor, R.B. (2015) "Does what police do at hot spots matter? The Philadelphia policing tactics experiment," *Criminology*, 53(1): 23–53.

Kochel, T.R., Burruss, G.W., and Weisburd, D. (2015) *St. Louis County hot spots in residential areas (SCHIRA) final report: Assessing the effects of hot spots policing strategies on police legitimacy, crime, and collective efficacy*, Southern Illinois University.

Lum, C., Koper, C.S., and Telep, C.W. (2011) "The evidence based policing matrix," *Journal of Experimental Criminology*, 7(1): 3–26.

Mazerolle, L.G., Ready, J., Terrill, W., and Waring, E. (2000) "Problem-oriented policing in public housing: The Jersey City evaluation," *Justice Quarterly*, 17(1): 129–158.

Mazerolle, L.G., Roehl, J., and Kadleck, C. (1998) "Controlling social disorder using civil remedies: Results from a randomized field experiment in Oakland, California," in L.G. Mazerolle and J. Roehl (eds) *Civil remedies and crime prevention: Crime prevention studies* (vol 9), Monsey, NY: Criminal Justice Press, pp 141–60.

McCord, J. (2003) "Cures that harm: unanticipated outcomes of crime prevention programs," *The Annals of the American Academy of Political and Social Science*, 587(1): 16–30.

Mitchell, R.J. (2017a) "Frequency versus duration of police patrol visits for reducing crime in hot spots: non-experimental findings from the Sacramento Hot Spots Experiment," *Cambridge Journal of Evidence based Policing*, Vol 1: 22–37.

Mitchell, R.J. (2017b) "The Sacramento Hot Spot Experiment: an extension and sensitivity analysis," unpublished PhD dissertation, Institute of Criminology, University of Cambridge.

Mitchell, R.J. and Lewis, S. (2017) "Intention is not method, belief is not evidence, rank is not proof: ethical policing needs evidence based decision making," *International Journal of Emergency Services*, 6(3): 188–99. Available at: https://doi.org/10.1108/IJES-04-2017-0018

Morton, V. and Torgerson, D.J. (2005) "Regression to the mean: treatment effect without the intervention," *Journal of Evaluation in Clinical Practice*, 11(1): 59–65.

Nagin, D.S., Solow, R.M., and Lum, C. (2015) "Deterrence, criminal opportunities, and police," *Criminology*, 53(1): 74–100.

National Research Council (2004) *Fairness and effectiveness in policing: The evidence*, Washington, DC: The National Academies Press. Available at: https://doi.org/10.17226/10419

PERF (Police Executive Research Forum) (2008) *Violent crime in America: What we know about hot spots enforcement*, Washington, DC: Koper.

Ratcliffe, J.H., Taniguchi, T., Groff, E.R., and Wood, J.D. (2011) "The Philadelphia foot patrol experiment: a randomized controlled trial of police patrol effectiveness in violent crime hotspots," *Criminology*, 49(3): 795–831.

Sampson, R.J. and Cohen, J. (1988) "Deterrent effects of the police on crime: a replication and theoretical extension," *Law and Society Review*, 22(1): 163–89.

Santos, R.B. (2016) *Crime analysis with crime mapping*, Thousand Oaks, CA: Sage Publications.

Sherman, L.W. (2013) "The rise of evidence based policing: targeting, testing, and tracking," *Crime and Justice*, 42(1): 377–451.

Sherman, L.W., Gartin, P.R., and Buerger, M.E. (1989) "Hot spots of predatory crime: Routine activities and the criminology of place," *Criminology*, 27(1): 27–56.

Sherman, L.W. and Weisburd, D. (1995) "General deterrent effects of police patrol in crime 'hot spots': a randomized, controlled trial," *Justice Quarterly*, 12(4): 625–48.

Sherman, L.W., Williams, S., Ariel, B., Strang, L.R., Wain, N., Slothower, M. and Norton, A. (2014) "An integrated theory of hot spots patrol strategy: implementing prevention by scaling up and feeding back," *Journal of Contemporary Criminal Justice*, 30(2): 95–122.

Taylor, B., Koper, C.S., and Woods, D.J. (2011) "A randomized controlled trial of different policing strategies at hot spots of violent crime," *Journal of Experimental Criminology*, 7(2): 149–81.

Telep, C.W., Mitchell, R.J., and Weisburd, D. (2014) "How much time should the police spend at crime hot spots? Answers from a police agency directed randomized field trial in Sacramento, California," *Justice Quarterly*, 31(5): 905–33.

Tittle, C.R. and Rowe, A.R. (1974) "Certainty of arrest and crime rates: a further test of the deterrence hypothesis," *Social Forces*, 52(4): 455–62.

Weisburd, D. and Green, L. (1995) "Policing drug hot spots: the Jersey City drug market analysis experiment," *Justice Quarterly*, 12(4): 711–35.

Weisburd, D., Bushway, S., Lum, C., and Yang, S.M. (2004) "Trajectories of crime at places: A longitudinal study of street segments in the city of Seattle," *Criminology*, 42(2): 283–322.

Weisburd, D., Wyckoff, L.A., Ready, J., Eck, J.E., Hinkle, J.C., and Gajewski, F. (2006) "Does crime just move around the corner? A controlled study of spatial displacement and diffusion of crime control benefits," *Criminology*, 44(3): 549–92.

Weisburd, D., Hinkle, J.C., Famega, C., and Ready, J. (2011) "The possible 'backfire' effects of hot spots policing: an experimental assessment of impacts on legitimacy, fear and collective efficacy," *Journal of Experimental Criminology*, 7(4): 297–320.

13

The cost of mental health–related calls on police service: evidence from British Columbia

Adam D. Vaughan
Simon Fraser University

Martin A. Andresen
Simon Fraser University

Introduction

According to Statistics Canada (Mazowita and Greenland, 2016), in the 2014/15 fiscal year, the expenditures for police services in Canada were $13.9 billion.[1] These expenditures are comprised of salaries and wages (66%) for the roughly 69,000 police officers and 28,000 civilian employees across Canada's 10 provinces and three territories, followed by benefits (eg the employers' contribution to group medical plans and pension plans) (15%) and operating expenditures (eg equipment maintenance and office supplies) (19%). Canada's population is primarily policed by independent municipal police services, followed by the Royal Canadian Mounted Police (RCMP), which provides both municipal and provincial police services, and provincial police services in three provinces. Understanding where resources are allocated in various jurisdictions can be useful in developing an understanding of the local policing cost and trends over time, which may assist in projected budgeting and future resource deployment.

Literature review

Generally speaking, police budgets are managed at the local level, with a local community police board as well as other support staff working together to develop and amend a police department's budget. The amount of resources in these budgets is generated using a variety of factors, but at its most basic level, it can be reduced to revenue streams (eg taxation and traffic and other fines) and expenses (eg salaries and equipment). With police services falling under the broad umbrella of public safety, local police budgets are likely to be associated in some manner with local crime rates. These rates may be generated at the local level, but federally generated Uniform Crime Report (UCR) data may be used as a barometer for the crime trends in a given jurisdiction or more broadly in a province. Although these are not the only factors in police budgets, they can act as a measure of the demand for a portion of police resources. The relationship between crime rates/statistics and policing costs has also been included in these discussions, with some noting the differences in trends over the past 20 years. For example, in Canada, policing costs increased by 45.5% between 1986 and 2012, while *Criminal Code of Canada* incidents per police officer declined by 36.8% (Di Matteo, 2014). Other scholars also note the increase in police budgets over this time frame but highlight that other state services—health and education—have per capita rates that are, respectively, six and four times higher than police services and are increasing at similar rates (Institute for Canadian Urban Research Studies, 2014).

To say that police budgeting has become a topic of public debate in the early 21st century is an understatement. Debates often encompass greater political pressure for fiscal and operational accountability, the increasing costs of policing, declining police growth, and shrinking or stagnant police budgets (Griffiths et al, 2015). The expanding demands on police services are of particular concern because in some jurisdictions, like rural and remote locations, the police are the only state-funded option to respond to social issues. Moreover, the addition of more and more police duties to cover social problems that are not being addressed by other service providers, such as mental health, is important to consider in any discussion regarding police expenditures (Coleman and Cotton, 2010). In addition, Leuprecht (2014: 5) highlights that front-line uniformed officers in Canada spend a copious amount of time "waiting to give testimony in court, transcribing interviews, teaching CPR, transporting prisoners, or a hundred other duties that take them off the street." Additional costs for policing are likely to be found in rural and remote locations as, generally speaking, the costs associated with these locations are much higher than in urban settings and much higher than the national average cost for policing (Ruddell et al, 2014).

One of the challenges for estimating the cost of "other duties" through crime statistics like the UCR is that they are not well captured or identified at all. For example, previous research suggests that in police records management systems, roughly 20–30% of the police calls for service generated are reflected in some way in the UCR, with almost 70–80% of other police files not being captured in the UCR (Her Majesty's Inspectorate of Constabulary, 2012; Institute for Canadian Urban Research Studies, 2014). As a result, estimates of costs of all calls for service—criminal and non-criminal—are virtually absent in the literature.

Police responses to persons with severe mental illness

Since the early 1980s, an area that has increased the demand for police services is the response to persons with severe mental illness (PwSMI) (Cotton and Coleman, 2010). Not surprisingly, this increase has also resulted in the use of more police resources, with some studies suggesting that police interventions with PwSMI use 87% more resources compared to interventions with persons without mental illness (Charette et al, 2014). The range of police contacts, the different ways in which PwSMI can be found within police data, and the varying police contacts within Canada result in some wide-ranging effects on how much police work and subsequent labor costs are tied to this population (Livingston, 2016). In Canada, UCR data will capture the criminal activity of PwSMI, but there are a sizable number of police interactions with this population that are for non-criminal reasons (eg victimization and general assistance) (Vaughan et al, 2016). More generally, it has been established over a number of years that a large number of police encounters with PwSMI often do not involve law enforcement and "involve people who are neither a danger to themselves or others" (Chappell, 2010: 289). As a result, accounting for the amount of police work attributable to PwSMI is often anecdotal or based on a small subset of the available data. In the push for evidence based policing, a natural next step is to estimate the amount of resources that police use with this population longitudinally using empirical data.

Resource use has been operationalized as the use of police time and/ or the financial costs of responding to PwSMI. Studies from Canada suggest that the duration of a call involving PwSMI is approximately 90 minutes in length, though this duration can increase substantially when the police incident involves a criminal event (Charette et al, 2014). The Vancouver Police Department suggests that in 2012, their police officers were involved in 3,043 events that fell under the British Columbia (BC) Mental Health Act (herein referred to as the Act, or MHA), which consumed 21,000 on-scene police hours (Szkopek-Szkopowski et al, 2013). A recent study from the UK has taken an additional step and provides estimates of the cost for a variety of interventions through mental health and police services (Heslin et al, 2017). The authors suggest that in 2012, the cost per police incident with persons with enduring mental health needs was, on average, £522. The authors go on to model service enhancements to represent alternative care pathways for patients in order to test the impact of a change in decision-making on the overall cost of response. Findings indicate that enhancing services may decrease per incident costs by 8%, but in other cases, the costs may increase by 6%. Clearly, there can be cost and benefits to changing the way PwSMI are serviced by health and policing services but it is crucial that any new programming and/or policy not only reduces recidivism (eg admissions to the Emergency Department (ED) and police contacts), but is also cost-effective for taxpayers.

The goal of this chapter extends this recent work to provide various estimates of the use of police resources when they respond to PwSMI. Using a longitudinal data set covering multiple policing jurisdictions, the aim of this chapter is to provide estimates of:

1. the amount of resources that police use to respond to PwSMI who fall under the Act;
2. the amount of resources used when police services respond to all calls with PwSMI; and
3. the resources consumed when police respond to "heavy users" or persons who habitually cycle through police custody.

Methods

Study area

The Fraser Health Authority (FHA) is a large health region in the south-west section of BC, Canada. This area currently contains approximately 1.7 million of the BC population. The majority of the population resides along a major east–west highway. To the east of this catchment area lies Vancouver. To the north and west of the FHA are less densely populated rural areas followed by Washington State, which buttresses the southern portion.

Data for analysis

Data for this project were provided by all police services contained within the FHA. Within this catchment area, there are five independent municipal police agencies, a regional transit police agency, and various contracted police forces by the RCMP. All police services in BC use the same records management systems for storing and maintaining their call-for-service data. Various data sets were created for analysis using the same initial number of PwSMI subjects ($n = 37,000$). For research question 1, we looked only at MHA events, and for research questions 2 and 3, we considered all police contacts that a participant may have had. All data used in this study were for a seven-year period from January 1, 2009 to December 31, 2015.

Costing model

For this chapter, resource usage is operationalized using multiple perspectives. We use costing estimates in terms of dollars spent on a call, the full-time equivalent (FTE) of the number of full-time police officers in a year, and per capita cost estimates. Given the fact that pay scales can vary dramatically both within and between police services in Canada, and that the data for analysis cover six regional or municipal police departments and 13 RCMP departments, the costing and FTE rates were standardized. However, the formulas used for calculating resources can be reused in other jurisdictions with proportional adjustments.

The recent Statistics Canada report on policing services was used as a guide to produce costing estimates for police-involved calls for service with PwSMI (Mazowita and Greenland, 2016: 11), which suggests that policing expenditures are comprised of "salaries and wages (66%), benefits (15%), and other operating expenditures (19%)." Here, benefits refer to all payments made to employees that are not a component of their salary or wages, for example, a police department's contribution to employment insurance, health insurance, clothing allowances, and severance pay. Operating expenditures includes, but are not limited to: office furniture, vehicle purchases, building and equipment rentals, and professional services contracts. Using these expenditure proportions, we extended this model to generate a per-hour cost estimate for police services:

$$C = (X + Y + Z)T,$$

where X represents the cost of one officer with benefits and operating expenses to respond to a call for service. In 2015, the hourly cost for a first-class constable (three years of experience) in one of the municipalities in this study was $44.31/hour. Their associated benefits and operating expenses were $10.07 and $12.75, respectively. Therefore, the total estimated hourly cost of one officer in 2015 was approximately $67.13. T represents the duration of a call for service measured in hours, as recorded in the computer-aided dispatch (CAD). In roughly 10% of the calls for service in this study, the duration exceeded a single shift (12 hours). For example, missing persons cases could take several days or longer to complete. To reduce the spread of the duration of calls to generate conservative estimates of cost, we truncated all long-duration calls to a length of 12 hours. Y represents the cost for support and supervision for MHA. As calls that fall under the Act are known to be resource-dependent (Szkopek-Szkopowski et al, 2013), this additional cost was estimated to be 50% of A. This cost is intended to cover civilian support, clerical staff, dispatchers, overtime, and other uniformed staff that may have been involved indirectly with a call (eg supervisors and mental health liaison officers). The 50% support cost of A in 2015 is approximately $33.57/hour. Z

represents the cost for support and supervision for all calls for service. Given the wide range of calls that the police respond to, we chose to use a more conservative proportion to account for support services. In 2015, we estimate that, on average, 25% of X will be needed for a police response, which is $16.78/hour. Finally, C represents the total estimated cost for a police officer to respond to a call for service with support services. Previous research by Heslin et al (2017) suggests that in 2012/11, it cost roughly £58.24/hour for police to respond to a S.136 call for service, which is similar to a S.28 Act apprehension. The currency conversion translates to roughly $95/hour. As such, we have indexed C based on the Canadian inflation rate, which in 2012, produces a comparable rate of $96.42/hour.

In order to estimate the number of full-time police officers required to respond to Act-related calls for police service, we consider one FTE officer to work 1,720 hours per year. This number accounts for annual holidays, sick leave, and statutory holidays, and is based on a shift rotation of four days on and four days off.[2] The per capita estimate is simply the cost divided by the population. The population in the FHA in 2015 was approximately 1.7 million. Population estimates for the FHA were obtained from BC Statistics.[3]

Results

Of the sample of PwSMI (n = 36,893), they were involved in 76,310 Act calls. The yearly increase was about 9.70% per year. As a consequence, the number of policing hours associated with these calls has also increased, but at a slightly higher rate (11.84% per year). The resulting cost to the police service and per capita costs are highlighted in Figure 13.1. Using C, the most expensive year for policing was 2015, where we estimate the cost to be $4.79 million across all police agencies, with an average annual increase of roughly 13.56% (range 3.75–20.43%). In 2009, the per capita cost was $1.37 per person who resided in the FHA. In 2015, that amount doubles to $2.74 per person. In comparison to the national per capita costs for policing in Canada of $320 per person (Mazowita and Greenland, 2016: 11), these amounts are relatively small. However, the fact that the per capita costs for policing PwSMI in Canada have doubled over a seven-year period is concerning considering that since "2009/2010, operating expenditures have generally been declining, including a 0.9% decrease in 2014/2015" (Mazowita and Greenland, 2016: 11). Furthermore, although these calls for service do occur, the strict guidelines as written in the Act ensure that police officers only use the legislation when a patient is in danger of harming themselves or others.

The number of FTE police officers needed to enforce the Act over the seven-year period ranges from as low as 13.73 in 2009 to as high as 26.53 in 2015 (see Figure 13.2). Much like the per capita estimates, we see a doubling

Figure 13.1: Policing and per capita cost to enforce the MHA

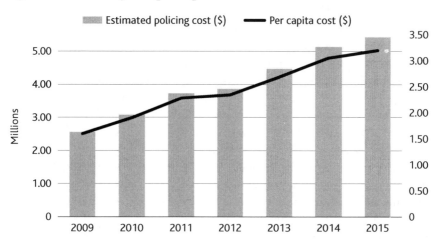

of the required police resources over the seven years of data. Although 26.53 police officers may not sound like a lot (Surrey alone, the largest municipality in the FHA, has an authorized strength of over 600 police officers), this is still a sizeable number of police officers, for example, this is one half of the authorized strength of Port Moody, a small municipality in the FHA region and part of Metro Vancouver.

Knowing that police work with PwSMI involves a wide array of calls for service, we considered all of the police interactions for the PwSMI sample. This sample was involved in approximately 564,691 event files, which is roughly

Figure 13.2: Number of police officer hours and equivalent number of full-time police officers to respond to all calls for service with PwSMI

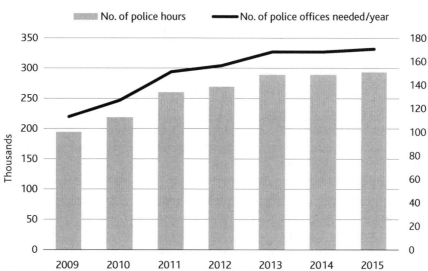

15.5% of all Police Records Information Management Environment – British Columbia (PRIME-BC) event files within the FHA. This rate is slightly higher than in previous research, which suggests that 12% of all calls for police service involve the patient's mental health care pathway (Livingston, 2016). With each patient having roughly six to seven additional police contacts on top of their MHA interaction, the cost for police services also increases. Using C, we estimate that at its lowest level in 2009, the cost to policing services of responding to all calls for service with PwSMI across the FHA was roughly $14.8 million. Much like the other upward trends in the data, in 2015, the estimated cost increased to $24.6 million.

Given the large number of police hours associated with all calls for service, FTE estimates suggest that in 2009 and 2015, it would have taken roughly 113 and 170.5 police officers across all of the police services within the FHA, working full time, to respond to all calls associated with PwSMI. This is a large number of police officers who are "dedicated" to responding to a relatively small portion of the population. In order to provide some context, the City of Port Moody has a population that is approximately the same size as the PwSMI sample in our analysis. The Port Moody Police Department has an authorized strength of 51 sworn police officers. The number of officers in the FHA region as of 2015 to respond to this population is 3.33 times the authorized strength of the Port Moody Police Department. This is very clearly an expensive sub-population to serve.

With many programs and policies placing heavy emphasis on reducing recidivism and improving the well-being of PwSMI who are "frequent fliers" or "heavy users" of police services (Akins et al, 2016), we selected the top 10 most frequent users in the data set to estimate their police resource usage and to explore some of the basic trends in this group in terms of the types of police services that they are accessing. Table 13.1 provides a general overview of the demographics of this group, the total number of police interactions, their mobility patterns (ie the number of different police services that they were serviced by), the resources used, and the nature of their police interaction. It is important to note that all heavy users had continual contact with the police over the data-collection period and, along with the high number of police contacts, we can predict that these patients were not incarcerated or hospitalized for any prolonged period.

Although the patterns of the heavy users should not be interpreted as the trends for the population, there are some early indicators that there are differences of police contact in this group. For example, participant 29485, a middle-aged man with slightly fewer than 100 contacts per year, has had many encounters with the police for substance use, such as public intoxication and other liquor-related problems. Participant 36330 is a middle-aged female with roughly the same total number of contacts with the police. However, roughly two thirds of her police contacts are non-criminal in nature, or the police were not enforcing or using criminal law. With all participants, the number

Table 13.1: Cost estimates for PwSMI who are heavy users of police services

ID#	Sex	Age	# of unique police departments	#of events MHA	# of events crime	# of events non-crime	# of missing persons/ assist	# of substance use events	Total # of events	Total number of hours	FTE @ 17.20 hr/yr
11016	M	26–32	8	41	514	230	492	10	1,287	4,214.51	2.45
29485	M	46–52	5	13	224	68	128	234	667	1,620.4	.94
36330	F	45–51	8	23	166	409	33	3	634	1,633.1	.95
15160	F	54–60	5	1	368	48	63	85	565	1,709.2	.99
15896	M	51–57	2	2	183	257	40	2	484	1,566.3	.91
36776	F	41–47	8	2	274	128	55	2	464	1,031.6	.60
7558	M	32–38	4	6	209	179	34	5	433	1,310.6	.76
30414	M	8–14	7	3	171	38	211	2	431	1,188.1	.69
29222	M	46–52	7	36	182	131	67	7	423	1,096.6	.64
3228	M	50–56	5	4	148	85	35	143	415	1,179.2	.69
Total				131	2,439	1,573	1,158	496	579	16,549.6	9.6

of Act events was relatively modest. Over the 10 participants, we found only about 2.25% of their contacts were associated with the Act.

Notwithstanding the high volume of calls for service that all heavy users have, the longitudinal pattern of participant 30414 is particularly concerning given his first contact with police occurred at age eight. Comparable to other life-course research in criminology (Moffitt et al, 2002), previous research on the developmental etiology of criminality among persons with mental disorders results in three typologies: early starters, adolescent-limited offenders, and late- or adult-start offenders (Hodgins and Janson, 2002). At a quick glance, one may suggest that participant 30414 is an "early starter" as his patterns of criminal behavior have been stable in childhood to early adolescence. However, if we only include his criminal events, we overlook that roughly 49% of his other interactions with the police were calls for assistance and/or missing persons. In other words, his spectrum of criminal justice system involvement is multifaceted, going beyond crime and the direct application of the Act, and like most of the other heavy users in this study, he interacted with multiple (seven) police departments.

Of particular concern with this group is that, on average, each one of them requires their own full-time police officer to respond to their calls for police service, broadly speaking. The range is 0.6 to 2.5, so even having to require one half of a full-time police officer is a huge economic cost. This points to the importance of considering increased, and more cost-effective, social services for this population aside from policing.

Discussion

It should be clear that the PwSMI population places a significant cost on our police services. Moreover, this population is involved with a disproportionate number of calls for police service and a corresponding number of police officers to respond to their calls for police service. Regardless of how the budgets change and crime rates decrease, the counts, costs, and proportion of budgets that go toward responding to MHA calls has been going up over time. The slopes of the cost per year of the trend line in Figures 13.1 and 13.2 are always increasing. Heavy users consume an enormous amount of resources, and implementing problem-solving/collaborative programs is crucial for reducing recidivism and getting them into a treatment plan that works for them. The 10 heavy users had many similar features but many more features that differed. As such, having different programs available, especially ones that do not require that a patient be already involved in the court/correction system, would likely work more effectively. Of course, there is also an ethical issue here given that the provision of mental health services should not only come after someone has been involved in the criminal justice system.

Although instructive, our analyses are not without limitations. First, we used truncated data (calls were capped at 12 hours/call). This was done to limit the time spent by a police officer to be an entire shift. Although this may be considered a long time for any given event, there will also be calls for police service that require continued attention by the police. Second, our cost estimates only include direct policing costs. We do not include any other costs (dollar costs or hours spent/FTE equivalents) associated with the services of other emergency personnel: hospitals, paramedics, the fire department, and so on. We also do not consider the influence of substance use. Finally, we estimate the values of C as 1.5 for Act calls and 1.25 for all other calls based on the number of officers necessary to address each of these types of call for police service. Future research should investigate exactly how many members responded to a call for service and how much time each call consumed as cases where a patient barricades himself into a house or threatens to commit suicide will likely take up more than 1.5 or 1.25 members.

Despite these limitations, our estimates of costs and FTE police officers for the population of PwSMI in the FHA have shown to be instructive. Our estimates are at the lower bound because they only consider direct policing costs and assume only one member/event responds. Moreover, despite the relatively low percentage of police calls for service that are direct responses to mental health (2%), all of their interactions with the police comprise approximately 15% of their calls for service. Based purely on the population of the FHA, the mental health-related calls for police service from this population is proportional to the number of calls to the police (both are approximately 2%). However, we must remember that a fraction of the population actually consumes any police services and that 2% of the FHA population accounts for 15% of the police calls for service when all of their police interactions are considered. This is a significant overrepresentation in police workload that deserves future considerations.

Notes

[1] All prices given throughout this chapter are in Canadian dollars.
[2] Holidays were calculated considering an RCMP member with five to 10 years of service (20 days) (see: http://www.rcmp-grc.gc.ca/en/salary-and-benefits); paid sick days are based on the Canadian average (see: https://www.canada.ca/en/treasury-board-secretariat/services/innovation/human-resources-statistics/average-paid-unpaid-sick-leave-usage-organization.html).
[3] See: http://www2.gov.bc.ca/gov/content/data/statistics/people-population-community/population/population-estimates

References

Akins, S., Burkhardt, B.C., and Lanfear, C. (2016) "Law enforcement response to 'frequent fliers': an examination of high-frequency contacts between police and justice-involved persons with mental Illness," *Criminal Justice Policy Review*, 27(1): 97–114.

Chappell, D. (2010) "From sorcery to stun guns and suicide: the eclectic and global challenges of policing and the mentally ill," *Police Practice and Research: An International Journal*, 11(4): 289–300.

Charette, Y., Crocker, A.G., and Billette, I. (2014) "Police encounters involving citizens with mental illness: use of resources and outcomes," *Psychiatric Services*, 65(4): 511–16.

Coleman, T.G. and Cotton, D. (2010) *Police interactions with persons with a mental illness: Police learning in the environment of contemporary policing*, Ottawa, ON: Mental Health Commission of Canada.

Cotton, D. and Coleman, T.G. (2010) "Canadian police agencies and their interactions with persons with a mental illness: a systems approach," *Police Practice and Research*, 11(4): 301–14.

Di Matteo, L. (2014) *Police and crime rates in Canada: A comparison of resources and outcomes*, Vancouver, BC: Fraser Institute.

Griffiths, C.T., Pollard, N., and Stamatakis, T. (2015) "Assessing the effectiveness and efficiency of a police service: the analytics of operational reviews," *Police Practice and Research*, 16(2): 175–87.

Her Majesty's Inspectorate of Constabulary (2012) *Taking time for crime: A study of how police officers prevent crime in the field*, London: Her Majesty's Inspectorate of Constabulary.

Heslin, M., Callaghan, L., Barrett, B., Lea, S., Eick, S., Morgan, J., Bolt, M., Thornicroft, G., Rose, D., Healey, A., and Patel, A. (2017) "Costs of the police service and mental healthcare pathways experienced by individuals with enduring mental health needs," *The British Journal of Psychiatry: The Journal of Mental Science*, 210(2): 157–64.

Hodgins, S. and Janson, C. (2002) *Criminality and violence among the mentally disordered: The Stockholm metropolitan project*, Cambridge and New York, NY: Cambridge University Press.

Institute for Canadian Urban Research Studies (2014) *Economics of policing: Complexity and costs in Canada*, Burnaby, BC: Institute for Canadian Urban Research Studies.

Leuprecht, C. (2014) *The blue line or the bottom line of police services in Canada? Arresting runaway growth in costs*, Ottawa, ON: MacDonald Laurier Institute.

Livingston, J.D. (2016) "Contact between police and people with mental disorders: a review of rates," *Psychiatric Services*, 67(8): 850–7.

Mazowita, B. and Greenland, J. (2016) *Police resources in Canada*, Ottawa, ON: Statistics Canada, Canadian Centre for Justice Statistics.

Moffitt, T.E., Caspi, A., Harrington, H., and Milne, B.J. (2002) "Males on the life-course-persistent and adolescence-limited antisocial pathways: follow-up at age 26 years," *Development and Psychopathology*, 14(1): 179–207.

Ruddell, R., Lithopolous, S., and Jones, N.A. (2014) "Crime, costs, and well being: policing Canadian aboriginal communities," *Policing: An International Journal of Police Strategies & Management*, 37(4): 779–93.

Szkopek-Szkppowski, T., Palmer, A., Lepard, D., Robinson, D., Pauw, R., and Tran, H. (2013) *Vancouver's mental health crisis: An update report*, Vancouver, BC: Vancouver Police Department.

Vaughan, A.D., Hewitt, A.N., Andresen, M.A., and Brantingham, P.L. (2016) "Exploring the role of the environmental context in the spatial distribution of calls-for-service associated with emotionally disturbed persons," *Policing: A Journal of Policy and Practice*, 10(2): 121–33.

14

Using body-worn cameras to create an evidence based de-escalation training program

Natalie Todak

University of Alabama at Birmingham

Introduction

E fforts to improve police–community relations have been stunted by a lack of consensus on what comprises good police work. How do police officers, agencies, and the general public define good policing? What do these behaviors look like? What are their outcome goals? How can agencies promote these behaviors in their officers? With the exception of the body of work on procedural justice (eg Sunshine and Tyler, 2003; Mazerolle et al, 2013), these questions have remained unanswered in research for decades. Indeed, there has been a clear focus among scholars on "bad" police behaviors, such as misconduct (eg Kappeler et al, 1998; Fyfe and Kane, 2006), corruption (eg Sherman, 1978; Punch, 2009), excessive force (eg Skolnick and Fyfe, 1993), and racially biased policing (eg Brunson, 2010; White and Fradella, 2016; Fridell, 2017). There is also a growing body of work focused on best practices for holding officers accountable for misconduct (eg Walker and Archbold, 2014).

As Kane and White (2013: 165–6) argued, however:

> in discussions of ... police accountability, we often focus on redressing and/or preventing misconduct ... and although we generally know that we do not want corrupt or overly violent

police officers, we often do not know exactly what we do want in our police.

Good policing is not simply the opposite of bad policing (Fyfe, 1993). The techniques used by agencies to weed out problem officers will not automatically result in a police force of high-performing officers. The intervention systems in place to uncover misconduct will not incentivize officers to perform "above and beyond the call of duty." For example, these mechanisms will not encourage officers to communicate with citizens in procedurally just ways, or use expert verbal tactics to calm down agitated citizens. They will not teach officers to avoid using force when it is unnecessary, yet justified. Understanding how agencies can systematically promote these behaviors requires a separate inquiry, beyond existing efforts to minimize unprofessional police behavior. A lack of systematic knowledge about good police work is frustrating for both citizens, who deserve a high-functioning police force, and police officers striving to earn legitimacy in the eyes of a public who are not fully clear on what it is that they want from police.

Body-worn cameras (BWCs) have emerged as a technology that many believe can assist with persisting issues in policing. The technology diffused across the US between 2014 and 2015 following high-profile controversies surrounding police use of force. Agencies were motivated to adopt BWCs quickly to demonstrate a willingness to be transparent. Moreover, it is believed that BWCs will provide better evidence of what transpired during controversial cases, which are usually plagued by the proverbial "he said/she said" problem. The central premise of this chapter is that BWCs may also be used to study good policing. Coupled with a vigorous nationwide enthusiasm for enhanced police training focused on de-escalation tactics, it is an ideal time for agencies to embark on this quest. In this chapter, I draw on existing research to provide a framework for studying good police work using BWCs, and describe how agencies can use BWCs to develop an evidence based de-escalation training program.

Good policing

To understand how scholars conceptualize good police work, we must look back to early research. Scholars such as Banton (1964), Bittner (1967), and Muir (1977) described the skilled police officer not as a rigorous enforcer of the law, but as an ad hoc peacekeeper. Bittner (1967) observed that officers working on Skid Row in the Los Angeles Police Department were more effective if they developed a "particularization of knowledge," where they assembled a detailed understanding of their beats, fostered relationships with community members, business owners, and frequent offenders, and used this familiarity to keep peace in the community. A second technique was the "restricted relevance of culpability," in which arrest alternatives were used, especially in minor situations. Officers did not enact the law for the sake of enforcement, but only when the act of arrest or issuing a citation prevented the problem from escalating. Finally, Bittner (1967) described the "background of ad hoc decision making," where Skid Row officers made on-the-job decisions in the broader pursuit of maintaining peace in the community. This technique was made possible because the officer had a deep understanding of the events and people in the community, and knew how his actions would affect the larger environment.

Skolnick and Fyfe (1993) similarly proposed that a good officer is one who does not enforce the law for its own sake, but rather makes decisions in the interest of saving the most lives. They gave the example of a patrol officer who, when interested in protecting human life, may think twice before issuing a speeding driver a ticket if it is discovered that the driver has an emergency and is headed to the hospital. Fyfe's lifetime body of work often emphasized this human life philosophy. For example, his research on police shooting policies (Fyfe, 1979) was instrumental in showing that shooting fleeing felons as they escaped was an ineffectual crime-control strategy and only resulted in the needless loss of human life. Muir (1977) likewise described the skilled officer as one with passion (reconciled with using coercive force when needed) and empathy (an understanding of the human condition). Those officers who Muir (1977) considered as less than professional were the enforcers (who had only passion), reciprocators (who had only empathy), and avoiders (who had neither). Specific to potentially violent situations, Klockars (1996) defined the skilled police officer as one who used physical force only when necessary, but who often found tactical or verbal ways to avoid it (see also Fyfe, 1986).

These theories of highly skilled police work are clearly dated. Indeed, some of the skills and behaviors described earlier are more difficult for police to use today as communities are larger and more diverse, and officers are responsible for covering exponentially more ground in their patrol cars. A modern police officer would find it difficult to develop the "particularization of knowledge" to the extent that Bittner describes as so few are afforded the necessary time to be on foot engaging with the public. In some jurisdictions, officers spend the bulk of their time jumping from call to call, finding time to fit in paperwork and a bite to eat when they can. This leaves very few opportunities for the majority of patrol officers to get to know residents on a personal level.

It is also illogical to expect the modern police officer to possess detailed information about a call prior to arriving on scene. Most officers today know nothing about the people involved before arriving and asking questions. It is particularly problematic when a false-positive error is made by the caller or by the radio dispatcher—the officer is told that the person has a weapon and, in reality, he or she does not. Dispatch information contributes heavily to officers' decisions at the scene, and when the information is incorrect, officers may be more likely to erroneously shoot a citizen (Binder and Scharf, 1980).

New theories of highly skilled police behaviors must take into account the realities of policing in the 21st century. Police officers frequently interact with diverse and special populations, including some who have very low levels of trust in police. Making things more difficult, modern police are often called to situations with people whom they have had no prior contact with, and are responsible for resolving symptoms of deep-seated issues in short spans of time.

Despite these challenges, early theories about skilled police work can provide a foundation for current research on this topic, and for promoting these behaviors in 21st-century policing. The assertion from Skolnick and Fyfe (1993) that good policing involves, above all, the protection of human life provides a clear outcome goal of good policing. Early scholars asserted that the role of the skilled police officer is to use the law not for its own sake, but for the purposes of de-escalating conflict and protecting public safety. A large body of research stemming from Tyler's (2006) propositions regarding "why people obey the law" has further confirmed the importance of engaging with citizens in procedurally just ways to build a reservoir of police legitimacy that ensures citizens' future cooperation with law enforcement. It is important to note that these ideals contradict the premise of "tough on crime" and zero-tolerance approaches to policing—that if officers enforce the law indiscriminately for minor offenses, this will prevent more serious crime. As White (2010) argued, the tough on crime approach may do more harm than good for crime control and community relations efforts. Moving forward, a framework for studying good police work therefore involves the use of tactics geared toward de-escalating immediate conflicts, and decisions made in the broader interests of protecting public safety and preserving or improving the legitimacy of the police.

Police–citizen transactions

A second area of research provides additional insights for building a good policing framework. In the study of police–citizen transactions, researchers adopt social-interactionist theories (eg Tedeschi and Felson, 1994) to understand how the outcomes of police–citizen encounters occur as products of step-by-step interactions between the citizen and the officer. Goffman (1956) theorized that interactions between persons are made up of a series of exchange rituals, where it is expected that each person will be respectful to the other, and that each is treated as an equal player. Tedeschi and Felson (1994) further underscore the importance of situational and ecological factors that shape interactions and their outcomes.

In a policing context, the social expectations described by Goffman (1956) are not always upheld because of the power differential between officers and citizens (Sykes and Clark, 1975). Out of respect for the officer's responsibility to protect public safety, the citizen is expected to show deference that is not expected to be returned by the officer, and officers are trained to take strategic steps to maintain their advantage throughout (Van Maanen, 1978; Sykes and Brent, 1980; Alpert and Dunham, 2004). Alpert and Dunham's (2004) study demonstrates how the power differential can lead to violence in some cases. They observed that in encounters where officers used force, the interactions often devolved when the officers' efforts to assert control incited the citizen to react aggressively.

Terrill (2005) looked at whether officer use of force behaviors were proportionate given citizen behaviors, and how the officer proceeded incrementally along the use of force continuum. He theorized that use of force that falls within the proscribed force continuum structure is likely to have been used for the purposes of gaining control. Since justified force is *only* that which is used to control the subject, behaviors that fall outside the use of force continuum structure may have been employed for some other purpose, and, in some circumstances, signify excessive force. In the vast majority of the cases, officers refrained from escalating up the use of force continuum, even though they would have been warranted in doing so considering the citizen's behavior. However, in 20% of cases, officers escalated their use of force response with non-resisting citizens, including one officer who hit a non-resisting person in the head with a flashlight. He found that escalation was more common when officers were dealing with drunk or intoxicated individuals, suggesting that officers used force out of frustration rather than to control a resisting suspect.

Beyond the interactions between officer and citizen, Binder and Scharf (1980) observed that the police–citizen encounter begins long before the officer makes contact with the citizen. They distinguished four stages that make up all police–citizen encounters, each with a set of common activities, and each with implications for the final outcome. The first is the *phase of anticipation*, or the moment when the officer becomes aware of the problem. The nature of the problem and indicators of its seriousness as relayed to the officer can heavily influence his or her actions on scene. The second is the *phase of entry*, during which the officer arrives on the scene and makes an initial assessment of the situation. The officer also uses the entry phase to establish police authority, establish the tone of the police response, and clarify expectations to citizens. The third is the *phase of information exchange*, where officers gather facts from suspects, victims, and witnesses. Finally, the *phase of final decision* occurs when the officer diagnoses the problem and employs a solution. This phase includes the officer's decision of whether or not to use force.

This body of work offers numerous insights for studying and training officers in violence de-escalation tactics. Police–citizen interactions, and particularly those that have the potential to turn violent, are complex processes involving an intricate pattern of actions and reactions (Alpert and Dunham,

2004; Terrill, 2005). It is not enough to know only the final actions of the citizen that led to the use of force (Fyfe, 1986). To understand these situations in ways that uncover more opportunities for de-escalation, we must assess what fully transpired from the moment the call came in (Binder and Scharf, 1980). BWCs are useful tools that could assist agencies in using a transactional approach to understand and promote good police behaviors, including skilled tactics in de-escalation.

Using BWCs to create an evidence based de-escalation training program

While BWCs have been lauded as a tool for holding police accountable, their broader utility is in their ability to capture police–citizen interactions from close range and to provide evidence for writing reports, making decisions about legal cases, and internal review purposes. Certainly, a video recorded from the focal point of a police officer's chest will not provide a 360-degree view of the entire scenario. Nevertheless, the ability to observe and listen to hundreds of thousands of interactions between police officers and citizens with some clarity and proximity has never before been available. Thus far, there has been surprisingly little enthusiasm about, or guidance on, how BWCs can be used for data and training purposes.

Our understandings of police–citizen encounters rarely take into account micro-processes, such as how short statements, movements, or intricate gestures can affect people's feelings and reactions about what is going on (Terrill, 2005). Scenarios in which force is used often involve a citizen who responds to police authority in anger, and begins to resist police (Alpert and Dunham, 2004). Certainly, it is a complex task to understand why some people respond in some ways and others do not. However, by examining larger samples of encounters on BWC videos, and focusing on how the interactions play out to the final decision, we can better understand patterns and identify tactics for preventing situations from escalating. It is just as important to study officer behaviors. What behaviors or words seem to foster a negative tone in interactions or anger citizens? Why do some officers decide to escalate up the use of force continuum, whereas other times they de-escalate their response? How do these actions affect the final outcome? These are all factors that can be analyzed deeply on BWC video.

BWCs also provide insight into the different stages of police–citizen encounters and how events that occur within each stage affect the final outcome. Most evaluations of police use of force tend to center on the final seconds of the encounter, with the focal point on the suspect's behavior at the exact moment when the officer takes physical action (Fyfe, 1986). However, the research reviewed earlier suggests that the events that occur up to this point are vitally important. By looking for patterns on BWC video, agencies can uncover opportunities for de-escalation. In the anticipation phase, for example, getting the information correct up front may reduce the use of unnecessary force, as well as perceptual errors that lead to erroneous shooting decisions. It is important to note that in order to best assess the events that occur during the anticipation phase, agencies must require officers to activate cameras as soon as the call comes in so that the conversations had between dispatch and officers are captured for analysis.

BWCs can also provide situational and ecological context unique to the agency's own community, which shape individual interactions (Tedeschi and Felson, 1994), and can assist officers in deciding how to best respond to a problem (Bittner, 1967). Watching videos showing real-life interactions may uncover systematic problems in the community not shown in official reports. For example, officers in one agency may adhere to procedural and legal criteria for conducting stop, question, and frisks (SQF), *and* draw on their procedural justice training during the stop, but still generate complaints from citizens. By watching videos of these encounters, agencies might see that citizens become enraged after being stopped several times per month for what appears to be no reason—even if they are treated with dignity and respect during these stops. With this information, the agency may rethink the use of SQFs if it is found to be overly damaging to community perceptions of police. More broadly, by watching videos of interactions, agencies may begin to understand what behaviors signify good police work, as perceived by the citizens in their own community.

To use Ariel's words in Chapter Ten of this text, de-escalation in policing is "uncharted territory," so much so that the field lacks even a clear definition of what is meant by the term (Todak and James, in press). As such, agencies need to spend time exploring the concept with their officers, affected stakeholders, and members of the community before developing and testing a training program. A good way to start exploring the topic is to have conversations with these groups and define the tactics and goals of de-escalation, keeping in mind the content reviewed in this chapter. Agencies should then encourage patrol teams to engage in debriefs of BWC videos recorded by fellow officers in the field. When an officer records a call in which they used de-escalation, the video can be tagged and forwarded to the sergeant for debrief by the whole team. The protocol used by Todak (2017) in her focus group study of de-escalation can be used to guide these exploratory discussions. In this study, officers watched BWC videos and were asked to discuss the nature of the call and the expected mindset of the officer on the way to the call. They were asked to discuss what minute behaviors or words used by officers appeared to de-escalate a situation and what tactics actually seemed to escalate, rather than de-escalate, problems. Focus should be given to opportunities for de-escalation even prior to the officer's arrival on scene, and throughout the entirety of the interactions that transpired between officer and citizen.

Agencies should offer incentives to officers for participating in the video forwarding and debrief process (perhaps a merit based system for forwarding videos that leads to a commendation for de-escalation). It is also important to watch both good and bad examples of de-escalation, so a non-punitive policy should be adopted for officers who forward videos where their actions escalated, rather than de-escalated, the problem. Patrol teams might also decide to review all use of force cases as a group and watch for any missed opportunities to de-escalate. In all cases, teams should discuss how the nature and challenges of the call made de-escalation more difficult for the officer.

Through this exploratory process, the department can begin to assemble a collection of exemplar videos showing effective and ineffective de-escalation tactics, and forward these to the training division so that they may eventually be used to create a pilot de-escalation training program. Team discussions about each call should be documented and included in pilot training development. At this point, the department might also decide to engage a research team to assist. Researchers offer expert skills for organizing focus group discussions of videos with officers, systematically analyzing BWC videos and focus group discussion transcripts, and providing digestible information to the training division that would assist in the development of an evidence based de-escalation training program that meets the unique needs of the community.

Once a pilot training program is developed, it should be offered to a sample of police officers. Feedback should be solicited from the officers and, optimally, the citizens with whom they come into contact. Preliminary inquiries should be made about the impact of the training for use of force, citizen complaints, and officer perceptions of their interactions with citizens. Ultimately, the training program should be improved and finalized, and then, with the assistance of researchers and input from impacted stakeholders, tested using experimental methods. Most importantly, an effective de-escalation training program is one that is grounded in a transactional approach to police–citizen encounters, and that encourages good policing from the perspective of the officers in that agency and the needs of the surrounding community. The program should also be developed, tested, and improved using empirical evidence about the impacts of the training for officers and citizens. As shown in this chapter, BWCs are an underused tool that can provide the best data for creating an effective, evidence based de-escalation training program.

References

Alpert, G.P. and Dunham, R.G. (2004) *Understanding police use of force: Officers, suspects, and reciprocity*, Cambridge: Cambridge University Press.

Banton, M. (1964) *The policeman in the community*, New York, NY: Basic Books.

Binder, A. and Scharf, P. (1980) "The violent police–citizen encounter," *The Annals of the American Academy of Political and Social Science*, 452(1): 111–21.

Bittner, E. (1967) "The police on skid-row: a study of peace keeping," *American Sociological Review*, 32(5): 699–715.

Brunson, R.K. (2010) "Beyond stop rates: using qualitative methods to examine racially biased policing," in S.K. Rice and M.D. White (eds) *Race, ethnicity, and policing: New and essential readings*, New York, NY, and London: New York University Press.

Fridell, L. (2017) "Explaining the disparity in results across studies: assessing disparity in police use of force: a research note," *American Journal of Criminal Justice*, 42(3): 502–13.

Fyfe, J.J. (1979) "Administrative interventions on police shooting discretion: an empirical examination," *Journal of Criminal Justice*, 7(4): 309–24.

Fyfe, J.J. (1986) "The split-second syndrome and other determinants of police violence," in A. Campbell and J.J. Gibbs (eds) *Violent transactions*, Oxford: Basil Blackwell, pp 207–25.

Fyfe, J.J. (1993) "'Good' policing," in B. Forst (ed) *The socio-economics of crime and justice*, New York, NY: M.E. Sharpe.

Fyfe, J.J. (1996) "Training to reduce police–citizen violence," in W.A. Geller and H. Toch (eds) *Police violence: Understanding and controlling police abuse of force*, New Haven, CT: Yale University Press.

Fyfe, J.J. and Kane, R.J. (2006) *Bad cops: A study of career-ending misconduct among New York City police officers*, NCJ No. 215795, Washington, DC: US Department of Justice, National Institute of Justice.

Goffman, E. (1956) "The nature of deference and demeanor," *American Anthropologist*, 58(3): 473–502.

Kane, R.J. and White, M.D. (2013) *Jammed up: An examination of career-ending police misconduct*, New York, NY: NYU Press.

Kappeler, V.E., Sluder, R.D., and Alpert, G.P. (1998) *Forces of deviance: Understanding the dark side of policing* (2nd edn), Long Grove, IL: Waveland Press.

Klockars, C.B. (1996) "A theory of excessive force and its control," in W.A. Geller and H. Toch (eds) *Police violence: Understanding and controlling police abuse of force*, New Haven, CT: Yale University Press, pp 1–22.

Mazerolle, L., Antrobus, E., Bennett, S., and Tyler, T.R. (2013) "Shaping citizen perceptions of police legitimacy: a randomized field trial of procedural justice," *Criminology*, 51(1): 33–63.

Muir, W.K. (1977) *Police: Streetcorner politicians*, Chicago, IL: University of Chicago Press.

Punch, M. (2009) *Police corruption: Deviance, accountability and reform in policing*, Portland, OR: Willan Publishing.

Sherman, L.W. (1978) *Scandal and reform: Controlling police corruption*, Berkeley, CA: University of California Press.

Skolnick, J.H. and Fyfe, J.J. (1993) *Above the law: Police and the excessive use of force*, New York, NY: The Free Press.

Sunshine, J. and Tyler, T.R. (2003) "The role of procedural justice and legitimacy in shaping public support for policing," *Law & Society Review*, 37(3): 513–48.

Sykes, R.E. and Brent, E.E. (1980) "The regulation of interaction by police—a systems view of taking charge," *Criminology*, 18: 182.

Sykes, R.E. and Clark, J.P. (1975) "A theory of deference exchange in police–civilian encounters," *American Journal of Sociology*, 81(3): 584–600.

Tedeschi, J.T. and Felson, R.B. (1994) *Violence, aggression, and coercive actions*, Washington, DC: American Psychological Association.

Terrill, W. (2005) "Police use of force: a transactional approach," *Justice Quarterly*, 22(1): 107–38.

Todak, N. (2017) "De-escalation in police–citizen encounters: a mixed methods study of a misunderstood policing strategy," dissertation, June, Arizona State University, Phoenix, AZ.

Todak, N. and James, L. (in press) "A systematic social observation study of police de-escalation tactics," *Police Quarterly*. Available at: https://doi-org.ezproxy1.lib.asu.edu/10.1177/1098611118784007

Tyler, T.R. (2006) *Why people obey the law*, Princeton, NJ: Princeton University Press.

Van Maanen, J. (1978) "The asshole," in P.K. Manning and J. Van Maanen (eds) *Policing: A view from the street*, Santa Monica, CA: Goodyear, pp 221–38.

Walker, S. and Archbold, C.A. (2014) *The new world of police accountability*, Thousand Oaks, CA: Sage Publications.

White, M.D. (2010) "Jim Longstreet, Mike Marshall, and the lost art of policing Skid Row," *Criminology & Public Policy*, 9(4): 883–96.

White, M.D. and Fradella, H.F. (2016) *Stop and frisk: The use and abuse of a controversial policing tactic*, New York, NY: New York University Press.

SECTION IV:
Experiences in evidence based policing

15

Moving to the inevitability of evidence based policing

Peter Martin

Queensland Corrective Services, University of Queensland,
and Australia and New Zealand Society of Evidence Based Policing

Introduction

For a couple of centuries now, "modern" policing has been both commissioning and deploying resources to prevent and control significant community problems. Police officers have done this mostly in good faith, using intuition and historical practice to guide their deployment and response decisions. Importantly, though, policing has developed almost entirely as a craft-oriented occupation, with an absence of science or any systematic evaluative mechanism to guide practice.

This chapter explores how police agencies are likely to transition into being science-driven agencies. I will argue that both now and increasingly into the future, policing will be driven by the desire not only to "do good," but also to be efficient and responsible in the way we use resources. I will show that, as with other fields such as medicine, education, and engineering, which have embraced over time scientific methods and utilized research to guide and shape practice, policing is likely to move with increased pace to use science to guide future practice.

Understanding evidence based policing

The term "evidence based policing" (EBP) can be confusing. For those not familiar with the term, it can conjure up notions of either evidence that guides a prosecution or, alternatively, forensic evidence that points to guilt by an individual, which ultimately forms physical evidence. However, what is EBP? It may mean different things to different people and it is important to acknowledge that there are various definitions. Sherman (2015: 11) offers the following definition:

> Evidence based policing is a method of making decisions about "what works" in policing: which practices and strategies accomplish police missions most cost-effectively? In contrast to basing decisions on theory, assumptions, tradition, or convention, an evidence based approach continuously tests hypotheses with empirical research findings.

EBP is a departure from that which was a common and predominant policing style in the mid-1970s, described as the "three R's": *random patrol, rapid response*, and *reactive investigations* (Berkow, 2011). Sherman (2015) advocates a more evidence based future state, focusing on the "three T's": *targeting, testing*, and *tracking*.

EBP is the converse of "policy based evidence making" (PBEM). PBEM is an attempt to use evaluative methods or interpret existing research to "prove" that the policy or practice is actually effective (Sanderson, 2002). Such an approach could be, and arguably should be, highly criticized because of the obvious implications for bias shaping the potentially preconceived "research" outcome.

Contemporary policing challenges

Leading an evidence based police agency is easier said than done (Martin and Mazerolle, 2015). Police leaders face rapid changes in society that arise from a myriad of issues, including: competing demands for resources; competing priorities; changes of policy direction; economic and social factors impacting communities; technological investments; terrorism; organized crime; changing dynamics of crime; community demands, including community engagement; political expectations; and, of course, there are many others. Public funding for functions of government is highly competitive and police budgets are generally under great stress.

Against the previously mentioned backdrop of change, the contemporary police leader needs to be articulate, innovative, adaptable, communicative, and informed. This leader needs to understand research methods, be receptive of research findings, and be capable of applying (translating) these into real-world applications. Importantly, Weisburd and Neyroud (2011) state that it is now time for police to "own their science."

Police owning the science will present opportunities and challenges. For many police agencies and their leaders, the rhetoric of being evidence based far outstrips the reality (Martin and Mazerolle, 2015). For the whole lifecycle of research to be realized in the policing context, it will require: leaders espousing the importance of EBP; officers embracing the philosophy; investment in research; the translation of research into outcomes; and a host of others things that will be discussed later.

In terms of the challenges associated with implementing EBP. Lum and Koper (2015: 263) argue that EBP's principles of decision-making can be in conflict with an "organisational culture in which decisions are influenced by other philosophies and processes." Lum (2009) indicates that these include: hunches and best guesses; traditions and habits; anecdotes and stories; emotions, feelings, whims, and stereotypes; political pressures or moral panics; opinions about best practices; or just the fad of the day. It is important to understand, however, that what is often described as the "craft" of policing (Wilson, 1978) can sit comfortably with science, and EBP does not herald the death of officer intuition.

The Police–Research Organizational Investment and Maturity Continuum

Introduction and overview of the model

In considering *how* police organizations are likely to mature into EBP agencies, I argue that it is important to consider where policing has come from, where it is heading, and the realization, as has already been stated, that EBP is progressing to a future eventuality. I propose a model that I will call the "Police-Research Organizational Investment and Maturity Continuum." This model consists of three key component parts, described as: (1) existing police practice; (2) the realization and opportunity for EBP; and (3) the actuality.

The "existing police practice" component

Policing is, as has already been described, a complex endeavor. The police role is also difficult to identify and define precisely. Although there are key elements of policing that have transcended time, the reality is that policing is changing and evolving due to a number of factors that have been previously discussed. Police have had and will continue to have some opportunity to shape their own future. This is a future not only about what they do and where they do it, but also, importantly, about how they do it. Policing of the future would be well served to understand and respond to the following key issues. First, there is a paucity of research available to guide police practice (National Research Council, 2004; Weisburd and Eck, 2004; Martin and Mazerolle, 2015). Second, the research that *is* available remains largely unknown to the

Figure 15.1: Evidence based policing and the organizational maturity continuum

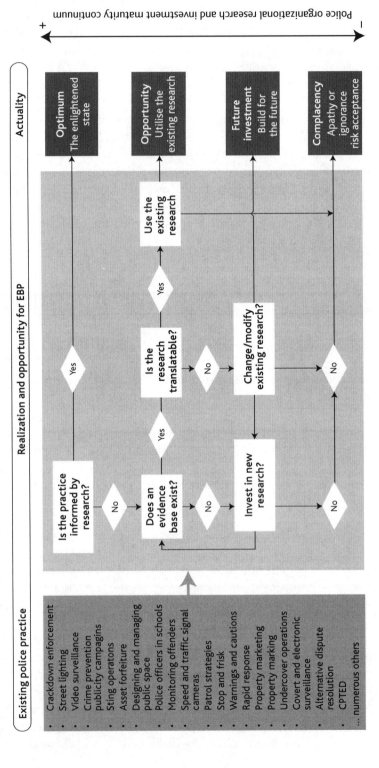

police. Lastly, that research which is available and known is not capable of being translated into changed behavior "on the ground." Given the scope and complexity of the police mandate and the paucity of the research, as previously identified, police research might still be provocatively described as "fertile ground" to further invest in and explore.

There are numerous strategies that police regularly employ in responding to a particular policing problem. Scott's (2016) unpublished list of common responses to policing problems identifies those responses that are commonly employed by police to address a variety of crime and disorder problems (as distinct from rarely employed responses or responses that are specific to a particular problem):

1. Crackdown enforcement.
2. Street lighting (eg residential and commercial streets, around buildings, and other places).
3. Closing streets and alleys.
4. Video surveillance (eg in public and private places).
5. Crime prevention publicity campaigns.
6. Sting operations.
7. Asset forfeiture.
8. Designing and managing parks (eg in urban and suburban parks).
9. Assigning police officers to schools.
10. Monitoring offenders on conditional release.
11. Civil actions against property.
12. Automated vehicle license systems.
13. Speed and traffic-signal cameras.
14. Patrol (eg random preventive, directed, vehicle, foot, mounted, etc).
15. Arrest and deterrence (some already covered by police enforcement crackdowns).
16. Stop and frisk.
17. Warnings and cautions.
18. Rapid response.
19. Mobilizing citizens (eg neighborhood watch, citizen patrol, etc).
20. Property marking.
21. Offender marking (eg smart water).
22. Monitoring social media networks.
23. Informants and tip lines (eg could be subsection of mobilizing citizens).
24. Undercover operations (eg infiltration, surveillance, sting operations).
25. Covert electronic surveillance (eg wiretaps, pen registers, video).
26. Checkpoints (traffic, drug, weapons).
27. Security rating/grading schemes.
28. Background checks of potential offenders.
29. Alternative dispute resolution (eg mediation, arbitration, negotiation).
30. Geographical restrictions on offenders.

31. Informing the public (eg warning/alerting, reassuring, encouraging law compliance, etc).
32. Follow-up criminal investigations.
33. Encouraging/reinforcing informal social control.
34. Crime Prevention Through Environmental Design (CPTED).
35. Others actions.

The "realization and opportunity" component

A way of describing this key component of the model is through the posing of six key questions or propositions that are then considered within the context of three case studies. These questions are:

- Is the police practice informed by research?
- Does an evidence base exist for the practice?
- Is the research translatable (or implementable)?
- Does the police agency use the existing research?
- Is there the need to change/modify the existing research to make it implementable?
- Does the police agency invest in the creation of new research?

We now consider these questions within the context of the three aforementioned case studies.

Case study: enthusiastic adopter

Sherman (2015) refers to the early adopters of science as "evidence cops." There are, however, a small number of police agencies that not only understand the importance of EBP, but are mature in their adoption of the concept, and are demonstrably moving to embed this into their new organizational paradigm. I will refer to such agencies as "Enthusiastic Adopter Agencies."

With reference to the key questions laid out earlier, Enthusiastic Adopter Agencies are those that:

- inquire whether police practice is informed by research;

- seek out the available research and promulgate that research;

- interrogate the research to identify that which is translatable;

- are open to replication of research in different contexts in order to build knowledge for the future; and

- partner with research institutions and researchers, and build relationships between the next generations of police practitioners and researchers.

Case study: cautious pedestrian

There are those individuals and police agencies that are undecided about EBP, and most police agencies fall into this category. They are neither strenuously opposed nor overtly supportive; they remain patently agnostic about EBP. Perhaps their cautiousness stems from waiting to see whether EBP is the next criminological "flash in the pan." There could be other obstacles to embracing the concept fully, such as: not wanting to commit organizational resources; challenging past practice; and ambivalence to challenging the status quo and doing things differently. This case study acknowledges that scientific evidence is not a significant priority for most police organizations (Chan et al, 2003). Of the three case studies, the majority of agencies are in this category. Disappointingly, even where the scientific evidence exists, and the research findings are unambiguous, they are ignored by most police agencies (Weisburd and Neyroud, 2011). I will refer to such organizations as "Cautious Pedestrian Agencies."

With reference, again, to the key questions laid out earlier, Cautious Pedestrian Agencies are likely to:

- be ambivalent about evaluative methods applied to policing activity;

- be more guided by intuition, past practice, and convention than aggressively seeking out research;

- be aware of research but skeptical of the ability to operationalize that research;

- be politely ambivalent to approaches from researchers and research institutions—engaging in the conversation but being non-committal when it comes to resourcing and organizational investment; and

- be pleasant in the police–researcher relationship but not overly committed to sustainable and mutually beneficial outcomes.

Case study: affirmative abstainer

There are police agencies that are vehemently opposed to EBP. It is difficult to know whether they are opposed to EBP *per se* or whether they are opposed to any change. EBP is not without its critics (Sparrow, 2016). In cases where agencies are opposed to research, I will refer to them as "Affirmative Abstainer Agencies."

With reference to the key questions laid out earlier, Affirmative Abstainer Agencies are likely to:

- resist change and find comfort in replicating past practice;

- oppose attempts to enquire into the operations of the agency;

- not value existing research or actively undermine the research (ie organizational defaults such as "we already tried that," "we currently do that," or "that is not relevant to our context");

- react negatively to undertaking research, facilitating replication projects, or implementing research outcomes; and

- resist researcher "interference" and reject any form of police–researcher partnerships.

The actuality component of the model

The last component of the model is the "actuality" phase, which is the identification of four key states that exist on, what I describe as, the "Police Organizational Research and Investment Maturity Continuum." At the mature or positive end on this continuum is what is described as the "Optimum or Enlightened State." This is the utopian state in which police practice is informed by research and research informs the execution of the strategy. The qualities articulated previously in the Enthusiastic Adopter Agency are relevant to this state. In a perfect world and with sufficient commitment, time, and the right resourcing and focus, all police agencies would be at this point or at least demonstrably be charting a course in this direction.

The second state along the aforementioned continuum is what has been described as the "Opportunity" state, where research is identified and considered for use. The use or rather partial use of the research is informed by an understanding that some evidence basis exists and that the outcomes, or some outcomes at least, are capable of translation. This state is concerned with organizational understanding of that research which does exist and seeking opportunities for the implementation of EBP practice. For the very reasons stated previously in the "Actuality" phase, that is, commitment, time, and resources, EBP maturity will remain an elusive proposition. Perhaps it will therefore be analogous to "work–life balance"—where the journey is as important as the destination and where wanting it and striving for it is as important as the end point.

The third state is referred to as "Future Investment" and involves creating future opportunities by building research opportunities but with a future focus. In this state, the research is not advanced and there is largely an absence of research to guide practice. There may well, however, be an opportunity to build on previous research, to change or alter the methodology to make it applicable, and to facilitate a future experiment or commission new research that will contribute to future learning. In this state, the benefit will not be materialized quickly and the research–translation lag will be a consideration.

The fourth and last state is referred to as "Complacency," otherwise described as apathy, ignorance, or risk acceptance. For many police organizations, this might be familiar. This is historically where police have operated—perhaps unwittingly or, in other cases, accepting of the status quo and not wanting to innovate, test, or challenge. This is at the lowest end of the continuum. The opportunity presented here is for police research activity to be moved along this continuum towards the higher-order ambitions of "Optimum" or at least "Opportunity" (see Figure 15.1). This end of the model is identified in the previous case studies as the "Affirmative Abstainer Agency."

What would it take to embed EBP in a police organization?

A challenge and opportunity is to embed EBP in a police organization and to do so in such a way that it takes hold, is difficult to retreat from, and ultimately becomes part of the very DNA of a police organization. For EBP to "metastasize" within a police agency will require organizational commitment, cultural change, and investment.

Sherman (2015) has identified 10 key strategies, which he claims will create a "tipping point" in building an EBP agency. With some adaptations, these are:

1. the creation of an EBP unit;
2. EBP training at recruit, in-service, and leadership levels;
3. leaders to undertake master's-level training;
4. a central registry of EBP projects;
5. regular internal invitations for experiments to be conducted;
6. a peer-review process for policing experiments;
7. embedded criminologists with PhD-level EBP expertise in police agencies;

8. a public EBP website of evidence;
9. "evidence cops" who make sure police practice is in line with evidence; and
10. annual EBP prizes.

In 2015, the executive leadership team of the Queensland Police Service, Australia, in a facilitated conversation with senior researchers from the University of Queensland, also grappled with what that jurisdiction would have to do to embed EBP in a policing organization and, as well as affirming Sherman's (2015) 10 ideas, identified a further 10 such ideas. These include the following:

11. facilitate research internships within work units coordinated by the Evidence Based Policing Unit (EBPU);
12. require commissioned officers to contribute to publishing their science;
13. systemize the relationship between the EBPU and operational units;
14. create data labs and recruit high-end quantitative analysts;
15. identify an "EBP ambassador" (someone with gravitas and status);
16. engage external change auditors to design and manage change management;
17. establish a change agent network via the existing Talent Identification Program;
18. embed EBP in everyday business—experiments tied to performance development agreements and/or Comp-Stat-like processes;
19. network nationally and internationally with other EBP agencies; and
20. initiate, stimulate, and foster community demand for EBP.

There are other initiatives, however; some of these are linked to the 20 issues identified earlier, but, for clarity and in the interests of completeness, they are recorded herewith. These include:

21. a strong statement of organizational support for EBP from the commissioner/chief and executive;
22. the development of a police research committee;
23. the identification and promulgation of police agency research priorities;
24. the utilization of existing resources to orientate labor to the creation and dissemination of new knowledge (eg librarians, statistical analysts, etc);
25. organizational support for societies of EBP;
26. appointing police officers as visiting fellows to key universities;
27. partnering with universities to develop social-analytic laboratories (resourced with police primary data); and
28. diverting significant discretionary funding to contribute to research outcomes.

EBP strategy maturity hierarchy

This identified list of now 28 key initiatives is not in any hierarchy of importance. Other key success factors or dependencies are not linked with each of these initiatives. They are listed merely as a "shopping list" of issues to invest in and pursue. Police organizations desirous of moving to a rational and mature position with respect to EBP might also want to implement some of these strategies before others. Having regard for issues associated with resourcing and organizational cultural change, deciding to take an incremental approach to implementation might be more beneficial.

I acknowledge that not all police agencies will have the desire or the resources to implement each of these aforementioned strategies. Rather than take a revolutionary approach, something closer to an evolutionary one might be warranted. Applying each of these 28 identified strategies to a policing organization and considering the complexity from a resourcing and organizational change perspective might see an incremental, stepped, or tiered approach appear as the following (see also Figure 15.2):

- Tier 1: Basic:
  - build EBP in an introductory way into recruit, in-service, and leadership training (Strategy 2);
  - "evidence cops" who make sure police practice is in line with evidence (Strategy 9);
  - identify an "EBP ambassador" (someone with gravitas and status) (Strategy 15);
  - network nationally and internationally with other EBP agencies (Strategy 19);
  - strong statement of organizational support for EBP from the commissioner/chief and executive (Strategy 21);
  - development of a police research committee (Strategy 22);
  - identification and promulgation of police agency research priorities (Strategy 23); and
  - organizational support for societies of EBP (see later) (Strategy 25).

- Tier 2: Intermediate. All strategies identified in Tier 1 as well as:
  - somewhere within the agency to coordinate research requests (Strategy 1);
  - leaders to undertake master's-level training (Strategy 3);
  - regular internal invitations for experiments to be conducted (Strategy 5);
  - public EBP website on evidence (Strategy 8);
  - annual EBP prizes (Strategy 10);
  - require commissioned officers to contribute to publishing their science (Strategy 12);
  - engage external change auditors to design and manage change management (Strategy 16);

Figure 15.2: Evidence-Based Policing Maturity Taxonomy

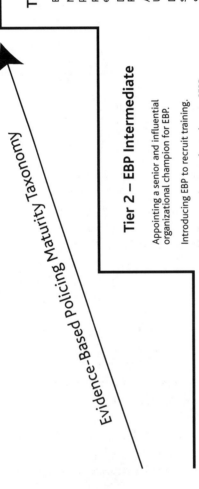

Evidence-Based Policing Maturity Taxonomy

Tier 3 – EBP Organizational maturity

Experimentation involving research methods.

Mainstreaming evaluation methodology applied to policing initiatives.

Performance management systems value and measure extent of research guiding practice.

Developing mature and sustainable partnerships with Research Institutions domestically and internationally.

Appointment of Senior Officers as Visting Fellows to Universities.

Developing specialist in-house research capability e.g. statisticians, criminologists, etc.

Systematizing and embedding research outcomes into BAU policing.

All officers are responsible for innovating and creating new knowledge.

All personnel are trained and professionally developed in EBP.

Leaders/managers held accountable for creation of new knowledge (expectation of contributing to the science of their craft)

Creation of a permanent innovation and research structure.

Employment of an embedded criminologist (perhaps a Director of Crimonology).

Significant proportion of discretionary funding utilized for research and other evaluative methods.

Tier 2 – EBP Intermediate

Appointing a senior and influential organizational champion for EBP.

Introducing EBP to recruit training.

Active recruitment of members to SEPBs.

Partnering with research community to undertake research.

Promulgating research outcomes throughout the police organization.

Professionally developing senior leaders in EBP.

Organizational expectation that senior leaders/managers can contribute to the science of their craft.

Identification of an organizatonal structure to coordinate research.

Rewarding and recognizing effort towards EBP.

Tier 1 – EBP Basic

Organizational introduction to EBP concepts.

Organizational support for SEBPs.

Developing and promulgating organizational research priorities.

Developing an organizational Research Committee.

Utilization of specific personnel, such as librarians, to utilize existing research.

    – establish a change agent network via the existing talent identification program (Strategy 17); and

    – utilize existing resources to orientate labor to the creation and dissemination of new knowledge (eg librarians, statistical analysts, etc) (Strategy 24).

• Tier 3: Mature. All strategies identified in Tiers 1 and 2 as well as:
    – build an EBP unit within the police agency (Strategy 1);
    – peer-review process for policing experiments (Strategy 6);
    – embedded criminologists with PhD-level EBP expertise (Strategy 7);
    – facilitate research internships (Strategy 11);
    – partnering with universities to develop social-analytic laboratories (resourced with police primary data) (Strategy 14);
    – employ highly skilled quantitative analysts (Strategy 14);
    – embed EBP into everyday business—experiments tied to performance development agreements and/or Comp-Stat-like processes (Strategy 18);
    – initiate, stimulate, and foster community demand for EBP (Strategy 20);
    – appoint police officers as visiting fellows to key universities (Strategy 26); and
    – divert significant discretionary funding to contribute to research outcomes (Strategy 28).

Some of the strategies identified, particularly those in Tiers 2 and 3, will require considerable organizational commitment and, indeed, resourcing. However, it is argued that the rewards are potentially significant and are likely to move the individual police organization forward considerably, as well as contribute to the positive movement forward of EBP and policing as a field of endeavor more broadly. These benefits are reasonably expected to include, but are not limited to, the following: greater focus on research leading to better understanding and utilization; mainstreaming this into policing functions to a greater degree; better utilization of existing resources; better, more productive, and professional police–researcher partnerships; next generation trained and committed and ready to challenge; leaders who are engaged, committed, and well respected by the workforce; better and more defensible business (and government) investment decisions; and an organizational focus on efficiency (and, at the very least, not doing any harm) (Martin and Mazerolle, 2015; Martin, 2016).

Conclusion

This chapter has explored how EBP is likely to mature as an important and defining philosophy for contemporary and future policing. A realistic assessment of where police science is currently positioned has been discussed and, importantly, those strategies that are likely to propel policing forward to truly making EBP part of the DNA of police organizations have been identified and advocated for. I have proposed a model for assessing organizational maturity based upon the police response to various contextual policing issues and the status of the research.

Despite the quantum of police research over a number of decades, the reality is that this research has arguably not led to significant positive change within policing. Perhaps this is because of the lack of organizational will to change, or that research is not accessible to the police audience or, alternatively, that research outcomes are equivocal, not clear in their outcomes, and just not sympathetic to implementation. A significant proportion of research is written from the perspective of a person who will never have the responsibility of operationalizing the research findings but there are positive changes occurring within research institutions in this regard (Rojek et al, 2014).

Policing is on an evolutionary journey when it comes to embracing evidence. There are currently positive signals that there is movement forward toward science or evidence. Whether we are at a "tipping point"—that point at which it requires less energy to go forward than to retreat backwards—is debatable. However, it is argued that, as with other fields such as medicine and engineering, which have embraced over time scientific methods and utilized research to guide and shape practice, policing will also continue to move with increased pace in this future scientific direction. There is positive movement in this direction and the strategies and signposts for success are becoming clear. As with those other previously mentioned disciplines, once you start down the scientific road, there is no turning back!

References

Berkow, M. (2011) "Lecture to the National Police Academy," Hyderabad, India, June 10.

Chan, J., Devery, C., and Doran, S. (2003) *Fair cop: Learning the art of policing*, Toronto: University of Toronto Press.

Lum, C. (2009) "Translating Police Research into Practice," *Ideas in American Policing*, 11 (August): 2–10.

Lum, C. and Koper, C.S. (2015) "Evidence based policing," in R. Dunham and G Alpert (eds) *Critical issues in policing* (7th edn), Longrove, IL: Waveland Press, pp 260–274.

Martin, P. (2016) "Moving beyond the rhetoric of evidence based policing?" Presentation to the ANZSEBP Conference—EBP Symposia, AIPM, Manly, Sydney, NSW.

Martin, P. and Mazerolle, L. (2015) "Police leadership in fostering evidence based agency reform," *Policing: A Journal of Policy and Practice*, 10(1): 34–43.

National Research Council (2004) "Effectiveness of police activity in reducing crime, disorder and fear," in W. Skogan and K. Frydl (eds) *Fairness and effectiveness in policing: The evidence*, Committee to Review Research on Police Policy and Practices, Committee on Law and Justice, Division of Behavioral and Social Sciences and Education, Washington, DC: The National Academies Press, pp 217–51.

Rojek, J., Martin, P., and Alpert, G. (2014) "Developing and maintaining police–research partnerships to facilitate research use: a comparative analysis," translational monograph, George Mason University, Fairfax, Virginia, US.

Sanderson, I. (2002) "Evaluation, policy learning and evidence based policy making," *Public Administration*, 80: 1–22.

Scott, M. (2016) "List of strategies frequently used by police," unpublished paper.

Sherman, L.W. (2015) "A tipping point for 'totally evidence policing': ten ideas for building an evidence based police agency," *International Criminal Justice Review*, 25(1): 11–29.

Sparrow, M. (2016) *Handcuffed: What holds policing back, and the keys to reform*, Washington, DC: The Brookings Institution.

Weisburd, D. and Eck, J.E. (2004) "What can police do to reduce crime, disorder, and fear?" *The Annals of the American Academy of Political and Social Science*, 593: 42–65.

Weisburd, D. and Neyroud, P. (2011) "Police science: towards a new paradigm," *New Perspectives in Policing*, January: 1–23.

Wilson, J.Q. (1978) *Varieties of police behavior: The management of law and order in eight communities*, Cambridge: Harvard University Press.

16

Why is evidence based policing growing and what challenges lie ahead?

Alex Murray

West Midlands Police and Society of Evidence Based Policing

Introduction

What is evidence based policing (EBP)? In overused academic parlance, this is a contested concept involving many different actors and contexts. However, this chapter will try to cut through what are often unhelpful debates by returning to an article that arguably kick-started EBP.

In 1998, Lawrence Sherman (Sherman et al, 1998) published "Preventing crime: what works, what doesn't and what looks promising," within which he applied to policing the philosophies that underpin the scientific method. For Sherman, EBP is a process that begins with a willingness to enter a workplace and pose what can often be a challenging question: "Why do we do that?" Asking and answering this question requires having the scientific discipline to move beyond opinion or even experience and, instead, to look for the actual evidence that supports (or not) what the police do. Here, evidence does not mean what an officer presents before a court; rather, it means understanding what question you are trying to ask and then using the best research methodology available to get the best answer. Many of the "What?"-type questions will require a quantitative approach; many of the "Why?"-based questions require a qualitative approach. Whichever it is, it must be rigorous and transparent, with the elimination of as much bias as possible.

Police officers are rightly subject to a huge number of laws around the admissibility of evidence before a court: "How was the evidence obtained?"; "Was the police officer being impartial?"; "Did the officer ask leading questions?"; "Have they established continuity of the exhibits?"; and, in the UK context, "Have they highlighted to the defense all the evidence that *undermines* the prosecution case?" Weigh, then, these rules of court-based evidence against the rules we use for creating police policy. The truth is that there are no rules for creating police policy. Instead, policy creation typically relies more on experience or judgment, or ideology or politics. Then compare the amount of time that an officer spends in court against the amount of time that they are engaged in using policy—the difference is significant. The policing mission is not about going to court (though that is important). Rather, the Peelian principle that still has traction today is one of prevention: to not have victims or offenders in the first place. This gap between court evidence and policy evidence is unsettling. A small amount of police work (prosecution) has many rules; the larger role has none. EBP, for reasons of effectiveness, is filling this gap.

Sherman (2013) has recently provided a helpful summary of his understanding of EBP. He describes policing as moving away from its historical "three R" approach of *reactive* investigation, *random* patrol, and *responding*, toward a "three T" approach: using the best methods to understand where we should *target* our resources, *test* what is effective, and then *track* police interventions. When the approach is blended with invaluable experience, police officers have started on the journey of being evidence based.

This chapter is split into three sections. In the first, we will examine what factors have led to the increase in appetite to be evidence based. Second, we will examine how the concepts are spreading. Finally, we will examine what challenges the spread of an evidence based approach.

What causes EBP?[1]

What is the evidence that police forces are becoming more evidence based? It feels like there are several proxies that, when taken together, provide a good basis for arguing that EBP is increasing. The second T that Sherman refers to—that of *testing*—is helpful here. Say that the police want to engage in a tactic, but before they do, they would want to test its effectiveness. A good way of doing that is by developing a randomized controlled trial (RCT),[2] one of the forms of research methodology extolled through EBP teachings. Recent research by Neyroud (2017) has tracked the growth of RCTs in policing, and given the promotion of RCTs in EBP, this growth likely tells us something indicative of the extent to which there has been greater adoption of EBP.

While Figure 16.1 demonstrates the increased use of this evidence based method, the actual number of RCTs is likely to be higher. Why? The graph

Figure 16.1: RCTs in policing, 1970–2015

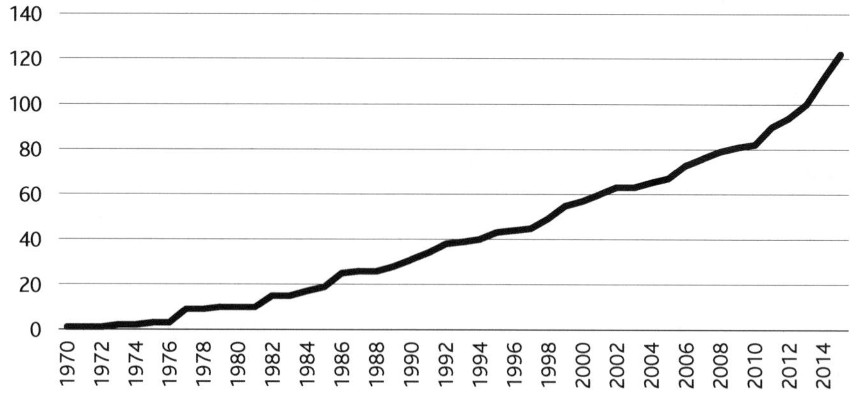

Note: N = 122.

Source: Neyroud (2017)

tracked only those RCTs that were published. Many RCTs will have served their purpose in providing insight to those who conducted them, but the same practitioner will not have the time to go through the process of publishing it in a peer-reviewed journal.

Further to the spread of the RCTs, in the UK, the College of Policing has spent £10 million on the Police Knowledge Fund.[3] This fund aims to link professional researchers with police officers in order to create better policy. The Society of Evidence Based Policing is a movement largely run by police officers, whose members seek to use, communicate, and produce the best research evidence. There are now similar societies in Australia and New Zealand, Canada, and the US, with Scandinavia and Spain just starting.[4] There are also new journals populated with applied research from "pracademics" (practitioners who are also academics), such as *Police Science* in Australia or the *Cambridge Journal of Evidence based Policing*. Although it is, as yet, impossible to measure the growth of EBP, it is clear that it is on the move, and it is worth trying to understand why. I would like to argue that the confluence of five factors has created an appetite to be evidence based, which are outlined in the following sections.

Austerity

In the UK, police funding has been cut by 20%, with a reduction of 34,100 staff.[5] At the same time, crime is increasing, with the UK seeing a substantial increase in crime in 2017.[6] Further, crime is increasing in non-traditional areas that are not subject to industrious crime-recording practices, like cyber-dependent and -enabled crime. Demand is also increasing as there is the increasing desire to police risk (Loader and Sparks, 2007), like sex and violent offenders and the protection of the vulnerable. At the same time, there is a growing demand to police the past, with public enquiries and historical allegations on the rise. There are simply less resources to focus on an undiminished appetite to reduce crime. Austerity then becomes a drive to understand the impact of every taxpayer's penny. What is the effectiveness of every police tactic? Does it really work? It is no longer acceptable to do what *may* be effective and, more importantly, we must stop doing what causes harm. The only way to understand these impacts of our actions is to be evidence based.

Maturing performance regimes

In the 1990s, the UK saw what has been termed the rise of *new public management*, where public services were subject to performance indicators (McLaughlin and Hughes, 2001). While sometimes beneficial, there have also been many recorded cases of perverse incentives, for example, the criminalization of the young to achieve better detection rates or the unethical non-recording of crime to demonstrate reductions. The performance focus was coupled with an immature focus on statistics. Binary comparisons led to spurious claims (Guilfoyle, 2013). Now, there is a focus on crime data integrity, a more effective and nuanced detection regime, and, importantly, a sophisticated approach to understanding when a trend really is a trend. For example, "Signals from Noise" is an automated crime analysis tool that will highlight a trend so that natural fluctuations in crime can be ignored.[7] These developments allow for a culture in policing where genuine improvements in public safety are sought instead of arbitrary performance indicators. This requirement drives a police service to become evidence based.

Integrity

Ethics should rightly be at the center of what motivates police. This has historically meant not being corrupt, racist, violent, or dishonest. However, when we combine the effects of austerity and a mature understanding of performance, so our interpretation of integrity should also mature.

The title page of Cloud (2006) describes integrity as "having the courage to meet the demands of reality." For police officers, this is interpreted to mean that we should be evidence based (Murray, 2013): "What is truly going on, on the ground?"; "What beneficial effect or otherwise did a policing intervention have?"; "What difference did I make?"; and "What claims am I going to make about that difference?" A police leader often states that crime has gone down under their police leadership, but when it goes up, they will point to all sorts of other socio-economic influences, such as the economy. With integrity at the heart of what we do and say, it is no longer tenable to have it both ways—it lacks integrity. All our claims should be evidenced.

Geek chic and a desire for professionalism

How did police officers think in the past? How do they think now? How do we want them to think in the future? Going back to the genesis of UK policing, Robert Peel argued that a service was needed that was independent of politics—it needed to be impartial and only the servant of the law. For this reason, he argued, policing was not an occupation for a gentleman—because of their inherent biases (Blair, 2005). This birthed the culture of policing as blue-collar and the pejorative title of *plod*. Gradually, things are changing as a result of the increasing complexity of policing. For example, the UK College of Policing recently proposed that all officers should carry a degree rising to a master's degree for chief officers.[8]

Somewhere along the line, there has been a shift in emphasis from brawn-only to include the brain. The value of tactical communications and rapport building, for example, has been recognized, and now we are potentially seeing the value of understanding the scientific method. "What algorithms best predict crime?"; "Can we trust these statistics?"; and "How do we harness artificial intelligence?"—such questions require cognitive power, which is a trend that has been recognized internationally in other domains of public life. For example, Bill Gates, Steve Jobs, and Mark Zuckerberg are respected for their innovative thinking, and historic figures like Alan Turing are receiving more attention. As a result, commentators opine that geek is the new cool.[9] The rise of geek chic will, and should, also touch policing.

These traits should not be preferred over each other; rather, there should be a leveling of the field, where the attributes of strength are seen in a similar way to the attributes of rapport building and cognition. Whereas this would once have been seen as absurd, there is now a sense that having these skills is seen as beneficial to policing. Syed (2015: 158–9) quotes Professor Dave Lane, as follows: "In coming decade's success will not be just about intelligence and talent. They should never overshadow the significance of understanding what is going wrong and evolving. Organisations that foster the growth of knowledge will dominate."

Capability

It is not enough to want to become evidence based. It is not even enough to have officers who have the ability to be evidence based. You also need tools that leverage that desire and ability. These tools come in two forms.

Advances in data analytics

A multiple regression looks at the relationship between many variables to see how one affects the other. It could examine the characteristics of a population (age, gender, time in a location, and contact with the police) and establish how each variable predicts propensity to commit crime, or to have confidence in the police. The utility of a multiple regression is clear: it can inform one as to where to concentrate scarce police resources. Statistics become a salient tactical tool.

In the 1960s, to do a multiple regression would take months of handwritten mathematics. Today, software programs allow computations to be completed immediately and on much bigger and cleaner data sets. There is hardly a police force now that is not interested in merging and mining data sources. Difficult questions that were previously unthinkable to answer can now be answered accurately and with relative ease. For instance:

> Computer, provide me a list of criminal recruiters within this area.

> Computer, provide me with a list of people who are on a journey to become a gang member (so that I can intervene early and prevent it happening).[10]

> Computer, where should I place my staff to maximize the opportunity for preventing the next burglary?

Data analytics allow the first T (targeting) of EBP to be easily realized:

> Computer, I have engaged in a new intervention for 100 offenders—I want to compare the effect against another 100, a control group. Please understand the effect of that intervention. I want to understand how the outcomes compare.

The second T (testing) is now easier:

> Computer, are my police officers in the spaces that will maximize their crime preventing capabilities?

> Tell me how much drug testing we are doing?

> Who are the officers I should be concerned about in relation to stress or use of force?

The final T (tracking) is now easier. The digital revolution is one of the greatest enablers of EBP.

Partnerships

Good police officers rarely have the skills to conduct complex research methods and professional researchers may not be the best people to tackle a volatile domestic violence incident. There is a natural symbiosis that occurs when the two come together: researchers need data, they need access, and they need to publish; and evidence based police officers needs analysis, they need to get close to cause and effect, and they need the ability to crunch their data. There are now hundreds of examples of both formal and informal collaborations between professional researchers and police forces. Dr Barak Ariel, an experienced experimental criminologist from Cambridge University, has conducted over 30 RCTs with police forces all over the world. The College of Policing in the UK has seed-funded evidence based academic partnerships,[11] each having a focus on producing research evidence that directly affects policy.

The confluence of these five areas creates the opportunity for EBP to flourish, but opportunity is not enough. Something else must happen. The second section attempts to identify how ideas associated with EBP are spreading.

How does EBP spread?

Gladwell (2006) contends that the ways in which ideas spread are incredibly similar. It is possible to overlay the spread of an EBP approach with the three factors that he suggests are important. First, you need the "Law of the Few," where well-connected individuals spread and sell the concept. Second, he defines the "stickiness factor," which enables ideas to remain in the consciousness, often because they are counterintuitive. For EBP, this is particularly strong as empirical analysis can turn conventional wisdom on its head, for example, look at the effectiveness of restorative justice (Strang et al, 2013) or cognitive behavioral therapy (Smedslund et al, 2007), or the ineffectiveness of alternative education programs (Cox et al, 1995). Finally, context is important as it conspires to make or break idea contagion. For EBP, the context is austerity, professionalization, and capability.

There are, then, four methods for the spread of EBP:

1. professionals drive it from the bottom up;
2. corporate institutions support it from the top down;
3. the utility of EBP is realized as a management tool; and
4. the utility of EBP is realized as a method of testing anything, even the ludicrous.

Bottom up

Within this context, it is worth considering what the Society for Evidence Based Policing (SEBP) has achieved. The SEBP is made up of officers and professional researchers who are desperate to see change through the use of evidence based practice. EBP is not an end, but the means to an end—that being better outcomes for victims, less crime, reduced reoffending, safer streets, and safer digital spaces. The SEBP has been able to communicate what EBP is and has tapped into a feeling of uneasiness within policing, where staff know that there must be more than just conducting business in the normal way. Conferences disseminate the latest evidence and regional leads bring interested parties together to communicate what works and pull together ideas around what could be tested next. The SEBP is not well led, organized, slick, or well endowed, but it works because there is a thirst for increased knowledge from police officers who are not happy with receiving the conventional wisdom. The SEBP is an example of how ideas spread from the bottom—where key influencers pass ideas onto others.

Top down

In 2013, the UK government was keen to build policy on "what works"[12]— for "what works," read "evidence based." To that end, it created seven "what works" centers in the UK, ranging from the Early Intervention Foundation (for younger years) to the National Institute for Clinical Excellence (for health). The College of Policing in the UK is the "what works" center for crime and it has been a significant driver in the journey to become evidence based. Systematic reviews that evaluate interventions are listed on the "What Works Centre" web pages. It runs evidence based boot camps and creates promotion frameworks that ask questions like "How have you been involved in evidence based policing?" Similar initiatives exist elsewhere, with, for example, the New Zealand government funding academic partnerships between the police and universities.[13]

EBP as a form of management

Sherman (2013) describes the third facet of EBP as tracking. In this context, tracking can mean one of two things. First, tracking can refer to the effect of an intervention that you are testing. Second, when you already understand what works, it can refer to tracking your staff to make sure that they are actually doing it.

The former is obvious; the latter requires some explanation. The efficacy of hot spot policing is now largely undeniable (Braga, 2005). However, actually making an officer stay in a hot spot is a challenge. This is perhaps because officers long to be *hunters, not sentinels* (Sherman, 2015). If you instruct officers on the tenets of procedural justice (treat the citizen with dignity, demonstrate your motivation is good, and give the citizen a voice), most officers will consider this obvious. Yet, Mazerolle et al (2012) demonstrated that when officers used a procedural justice checklist for breath tests on drivers, the difference was stark compared to a control group.[14] This then comes back to a driver for EBP being integrity. If we as leaders want to make a difference, we need the ability to track delivery against what works—discretion up to a point, but not beyond what works.

The ability to innovate and test even the ludicrous

The story of the lemon cure for scurvy is well known. James Lancaster worked for the East India Company, and on a journey to India from the UK, he experimented by giving one of his four ships lemons. On that ship, none died from scurvy compared to the other ships (Lind, 1772). If you apply rigorous testing, then all ideas are worth attempting. In a recent set of trials by the West Midlands Police (WMP), six interventions based on behavioral insights were tested using RCTs (Behavioural Insights Team, 2016). Some worked, some looked promising, and others failed. When sending out fines for speeding, normal legal letters were compared to more simplified letters where data on child fatalities were highlighted with the picture of a roadside memorial. Court appearances from the fines reduced by 41% and reoffending by 20%. This is an example of a trial that worked.

The WMP then trialed scrawling *growth mindset* graffiti on cell walls to impact on reoffending. Figures 16.2 and 16.3, respectively, show the wording that appeared on a cell wall with and without the graffiti.

The reoffending rates were then compared and showed a marginal, but statistically insignificant, improvement. The idea did not work.

In summary, the fourth reason why EBP ideas spread is that it allows you to test anything and failure is not seen as failure, but as learning what does not work. In a non-evidence based police service, these ideas would be subject to either ridicule or success (in the way that most police operations are doomed to succeed) depending on the credibility of the leader.

When the drivers and benefits seem so clear, it would be easy to assume that the spread of EBP is inevitable, but it is not. The following sections highlight who is trying to control the spread of EBP and why.

Figure 16.2: The cell wall before the graffiti

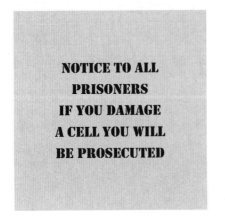

Figure 16.3: The cell wall after the graffiti

People think what they do makes them who they are. It doesn't.

When I was sitting here, I thought this was me. I thought I'd just keep coming back. Thought it was just meant to be that way. Couldn't change.

But the thing is, we do stuff for lots of reasons. We do stuff because our mates did it, because we got angry, because we thought it felt good, or just didn't think

I had my own reasons. You probably do too.

I was pretty good at blaming others. But when I was here last time, I realised this is on me. What I do is my choice. And it's time I chose something else.

When I left, I said I would do things differently and I did. It took effort, I won't lie, but it paid off. If I've got one piece of advice, it's that the first step is the hardest, so make it small.

Think what's the thing you can do to make sure you don't end up back here?

Remember it, and when the door opens, do it.

It's never too late.

C

What are the challenges to EBP?

Ideology and experience

Daniel Kahneman (2011), the Nobel prize-winning economist, describes decisions based on *system 1* and *system 2 thinking*. System 1 is an evolutionary, experience based decision. The decision is immediate and intuitive. System 1 comes naturally to police officers. System 2 is a more data-driven approach, based on systematic analysis. Sometimes, system 1 is right and sometimes it is wrong. Many police officers will tell you that we should always arrest for domestic abuse. They would also tell you that the criminal justice system needs to offer stronger deterrents. Yet, when the data are examined, all these assumptions are, at best, questionable. Sherman and Harris (2015) have shown that death rates increased by 64% for those domestic abuse perpetrators who were arrested as opposed to warned during a period in 1988 in Milwaulkee. Cullen et al (2011) will describe how pushing people through court (particularly younger individuals) has a criminogenic effect (it makes them worse). Famously, McCord (1992) showed that a mentoring scheme for delinquent youths backfired on every variable. Reactions to this can be interesting. Do the data challenge liberal/conservative/democratic/ Left/Right viewpoints? If they do, then we are experiencing the friction between ideology and evidence. We inherently know best because of our beliefs or experience, in the same way that doctors knew that prescribing thalidomide was beneficial for curing sickness in pregnancy, or blood-letting assisted infection, or trepanning[15] cured peculiar behavior. While experience and ideology can be valuable, their utility becomes much stronger when grounded in empirical evidence.

This challenge of ideology and experience can combine with an anti-academic rhetoric within policing. There are phrases that refer to officers engaged in research as "living in an ivory tower" or "all brain, no common sense." Real officers come from the "school of life." These reactions are sometimes understandable; however, there does not seem to be this reaction in medicine, an occupation that (like policing) has to make life and death decisions and, as such, relies on evidence based practice.

This tribal dichotomy is false and needs to be challenged. A good senior officer is one who works with their experience and common sense and merges it with the best research evidence. What matters is not where someone is from, but the impact that they make, and you need common sense, experience, and an appreciation of evidence to be a good senior leader.

Finally, many police officers will have been subject to policing trends over their service. Many of these trends have come and gone, and, as a result, it is understandable that any new approach to policing will be seen within the context of an ebb and flow of senior officer initiatives. Sooner or later, EBP will be sacrificed at the expense of the next large policing initiative. Many officers may therefore choose to ignore it as, after a while, it will fade away.

The methods war

The second challenge is even starker and could be defined as the *methods war*. Inherently, academics are more proficient at research methods than the police and so police officers look up to them for understanding how to evaluate impact. Police may even assume a sense of rationality in the corridors of academe. Sometimes, this is not the case. Often, academics build their professional career and identity using their preferred research method. Any challenge to that method can be seen as a challenge to their identity, and here starts the backlash. Tomes have been written proffering the advantages of one research method over another. Many academics spend a considerable amount of time critiquing EBP. There is a place for challenging method but the scale, obfuscation, and quantity of literature on this subject can leave a police officer bewildered and cause them to eventually return to doing what they have always done. It is also worth stating that some proponents of evidence based methods are equally guilty in their critiques of more qualitative approaches.

This, though, is a chapter about EBP that does have an empirical slant as, so often, the question is "What works?" rather than "Why is something happening?" This is the heart of the methods debate. The "Why?" question is often referred to as the *mechanism*. If you can discover the mechanism behind why something does or does not work, it is helpful, but the *why* without the *what* is less so.

The final battle in the methods war concerns arguments around the RCT, proponents of which are sometimes classified as *randomistas* (for a summary of the critique of EBP, see Sparrow, 2011). Often, those who denigrate EBP choose to see it through the lens of conducting RCTs. Some RCTs are simple to run and some are incredibly complex. Many RCTs have failed because implementation has been difficult to achieve (you have to ensure that the test group gets the intervention as defined by the experiment and the control group does not). Many have attempted an RCT that has subsequently failed, and opponents will seize on this as a demonstration that EBP is not relevant to the field of social science. The answer to this is that an RCT is not right for everything and does not define what EBP is; however, where RCTs are achievable, they set high standards for understanding what works. The Birmingham Scale of Effectiveness in Police Experiments is a useful guide here (Murray, 2013).

The way through must be the following:

- What is the research question?
- Which method best answers that question?
- Use that method.

Conclusion

The police journey to become evidence based is still in its infancy. It is still a marginal process. This chapter goes a small way toward understanding what EBP is, why it spreads, and what challenges lie ahead. The need for integrity in what we do and the need to reduce crime with less money become the driver for understanding what works. When coupled with new capabilities arising out of big, clean data and partnerships with academics who are remunerated more on community impact than on theoretical advancement, we find the perfect environment for EBP to flourish. If police practitioners and researchers can overcome the challenges of pride and nostalgia and focus instead on demonstrating an impact on the reduction of harm, then the foundations of an evidence based approach to policing will be set not as a trend, but as a fundamental approach to operating effectively.

Notes

[1] The assertions made here are assumptions. There has been no primary research that has underpinned this chapter; instead, there is a reporting of some facts, some correlations, and some claims to causal inferences—all which should be subject to rigorous testing.

[2] For a full understanding of RCTs and the Maryland Scale, see Sherman (1997).

[3] See: www.college.police.uk/News/College-News/Pages/Police-Knowedge-Fund.aspx

[4] See: www.sebp.police.uk; www.anzsebp.com; www.can-sebp.net; and www.americansebp.org/

[5] See: www.politics.co.uk/reference/police-funding

[6] See: https://www.theguardian.com/uk-news/2017/jul/20/official-figures-show-biggest-rise-crime-in-a-decade

[7] See: www.lightfootsolutions.com

[8] See: http://www.college.police.uk/What-we-do/Learning/Policing-Education-Qualifications-Framework/Pages/Policing-Education-Qualifications-Framework.aspx

[9] See: http://www.bbc.com/news/magazine-20325517

[10] West Midlands Police, UK, has answered these questions with their Data Driven Insights (DDI) program.

[11] See: http://www.college.police.uk/News/College-news/Pages/Police-Knowledge-Fund.aspx

[12] See: https://www.gov.uk/guidance/what-works-network

[13] See: http://www.stuff.co.nz/national/crime/88319987/police-and-university-of-waikato-form-research-partnership-to-tackle-crime

[14] You can listen to a podcast on this experiment at: www.sebp.police.uk/videos-podcasts

[15] The process of drilling into the scull of a live patient.

References

Behavioural Insights Team (2016) *The Behavioural Insights Team: Update report 2015–16*, London: Behavioural Insights Team.

Blair, I. (2005) *The Richard Dimbleby lecture.* Available at: http://www.bbc.co.uk/pressoffice/pressreleases/stories/2005/11_november/16/dimbleby.shtml

Braga, A.A. (2005) "Hot spots policing and crime prevention: a systematic review of randomized control trials," *Journal of Experimental Criminology*, 1(3): 317–442.

Cloud, H. (2006) *Integrity: The courage to meet the demands of reality*, New York, NY: Harper Collins.

Cox, S.M., Davidson, W.S., and Bynum, T.S. (1995) "A meta-analytic assessment of delinquency-related outcomes of alternative education programs," *NCCD News*, 41(2): 219–34.

Cullen, F.T., Jonson, C.L., and Nagin, D.S. (2011) "Prisons do not reduce recidivism: the high cost of ignoring science," *The Prison Journal*, 91(3): 48S–65S.

Gladwell, M. (2006) *The tipping point: How little things can make a big difference*, New York, NY: Little, Brown and Company.

Guilfoyle, S. (2013) *Intelligent policing: How systems thinking eclipse conventional management practice*, Axeminster: Triarchy Press.

Kahneman, D. (2011) *Thinking fast and slow*, New York, NY: Macmillan.

Lind, J. (1772) *A treatise on the scurvy* (3rd edn), London: S. Crowder, D. Wilson, G. Nicholls, T. Cadell, T. Beket and Co.

Loader, I. and Sparks, R. (2007) "Contemporary landscapes of crime, order and control: governance, risk, and globalization," in M. Maguire, R. Morgan, and R. Reiner (eds) *The Oxford handbook of criminology*, Oxford: Oxford University Press.

Mazerolle, L., Bennet, S., Antrobus, E., and Eggins, E. (2012) "Procedural justice, routine encounters and citizen perceptions of police: main findings from the Queensland Community Engagement Trial (QCET)," *Journal of Experimental Criminology*, 8(4): 343–67.

McCord, J. (1992) "The Cambridge–Somerville Study: a pioneering longitudinal experimental study of delinquency prevention," in J. McCord and R.E. Tremblay (eds) *Preventing antisocial behavior: Interventions from birth through adolescence*, New York, NY: Guilford Press, pp 196–206.

McLaughlin, E.J. and Hughes, G. (2001) "The permanent revolution: New Labour, new public management and the modernisation of criminal justice," *Criminal Justice*, 1(3): 301–18.

Murray, A. (2013) "Evidence based policing and integrity," *Translational Criminology*, Fall issue: 4–6.

Neyroud, P.W. (2017) "Learning to field test in policing: using an analysis of completed randomised controlled trials involving the police to develop a grounded theory on the factors contributing to high levels of treatment integrity in police field experiments," unpublished PhD thesis, University of Cambridge.

Sherman, L.W. (1997) *Preventing crime: What works, what doesn't, what's promising: A report to the United States Congress*, Washington, DC: US Department of Justice, Office of Justice Programs.

Sherman, L.W. (2013) "The rise of evidence based policing: targeting, testing and tracking," *Crime and Justice*, 42(1): 377–451.

Sherman, L.W. (2015) "Hotspot policing: Beating back crime in the Caribbean." Available at: www.enterprise.cam.ac.uk/case-studies/hot-spot-policing/

Sherman, L.W. and Harris, H.M. (2015) "Increased death rates of domestic violence victims from arresting vs warning suspects in the Milwaukee Domestic Violence Experiment (MilDVE)," *Journal of Experimental Criminology*, 11(1): 1–20.

Sherman, L.W., Gottfredson, D.C., MaxKenzie D.L., Reuter, P., and Bushway, S.D. (1998) "Preventing crime, what works, what doesn't and what looks promising," *Research in Brief*, National Institute of Justice.

Smedslund, G., Dalsbø, T.K., Steiro, A., Winsvold, A., and Clench-Aas, J. (2007) "Cognitive behavioural therapy for men who physically abuse their female partner," *The Cochrane Database of Systematic Reviews*, 18(3): CD006048.

Sparrow, M.K. (2011) *Governing science: New perspectives in policing*, Washington, DC: Department of Justice, National Institute of Justice.

Strang, H., Sherman, L.W., Mayo-Wilson, E., Woods, D., and Ariel, B. (2013) "Restorative justice conferencing (RJC) using face-to-face meetings of offenders and victims: effects on offender recidivism and victim satisfaction. A systematic review," *Campbell Systematic Reviews*, DOI: 10.4073/csr.2013.10.

Syed, M. (2015) *Black box thinking: The surprising truth about success*, London: John Murray.

17

A practical approach to evidence based policing

Gary Cordner

Professor Emeritus, Kutztown University and Eastern Kentucky University

Introduction

The National Institute of Justice (NIJ) is the research and science agency of the US Department of Justice. It encourages the adoption of evidence based crime control and criminal justice practices, and has supported and promoted police–researcher partnerships for over 20 years. Currently, the NIJ has a Law Enforcement Advancing Data and Science (LEADS) Agencies Program that seeks to assist agencies in developing their own capacity to use data and research to improve performance and effectiveness.

The LEADS Agencies Program uses a framework that is modest and yet demanding. It embraces the view that "police practices should be based on scientific evidence about what works best" (Sherman, 1998: 2) and that "[r]esearch, evaluation, analysis, and scientific processes should have a 'seat at the table' in law enforcement decision making about tactics, strategies, and policies" (Lum and Koper, 2017: 3–4). Consistent with the "seat at the table" perspective, the LEADS Agencies Program emphasizes evidence based policing while also recognizing that police decisions at various levels are influenced, properly so, by law, ethics, values, experience, and professional judgment. In other words, data and science have a lot to contribute to making policing as effective and fair as possible, but they are not the sole determinants of police practice, and should not be. Police are part of a government that is, ultimately, "of the people" not "of science."

It is sobering to note that the idea that research and science can benefit policing is not new. Scientific criminal investigation got underway in the 1800s, and by the early 1900s, the police chief in Berkeley, California, August Vollmer, was promoting the social and physical sciences as valuable contributors to police training, education, and practice (Oliver, 2017). In the mid-1900s, in the book *Police planning*, Vollmer's protégé, O.W. Wilson (1957: 7), observed that "research is needed before the relative merits of many alternative police procedures may be accurately appraised. Controlled experiments will provide basic data from which sound conclusions may be drawn." Conducting research into police effectiveness, including experiments, got well underway in the 1970s and has continued to the present (Wilson, 1980; Cordner and Hale, 1992; Skogan and Frydl, 2004; Weisburd and Majimundar, 2017).

A practical approach

It seems important, in fact, necessary, to develop and present the concept of evidence based policing in a way that makes it understandable, compelling, and non-threatening. In addition, it needs to be clearly connected to things that matter to police practitioners, or else it is likely to be regarded as nothing more than the latest fad foisted on police by academics and politicians. A further challenge is that adopting evidence based policing cannot be accomplished merely by purchasing technology, installing advanced software, or hiring some analysts.

For starters, a practical approach to evidence based policing ought to be based on some agreed-upon tenets:

- This is not something new. It has been actively developing for at least 40 years.
- Saying that police decisions and practices should be evidence based is not a rejection of experience or professional judgment. It is a recognition that policing should be as evidence based as possible, just as medicine, engineering, teaching, and social work should be as evidence based as possible.
- The purpose of improving data, analysis, research, and science in policing is to make policing more effective. That is, evidence based policing is not a way of promoting research for its own sake. Rather, it is all about finding the best ways to deliver police services to make communities safer, more orderly, and more just.
- Evidence based policing is not the next version of policing, ready to replace community policing, problem-oriented policing, intelligence-led policing, predictive policing, or any other "fill in the blank" variety of policing. Instead, it is an approach to police planning and police administration that

is committed to identifying and implementing the most effective practices, whatever they are.

• Finally, evidence based policing is a mindset and a practice that is as equally relevant for the New York Police Department, the Iowa State Patrol, and police in a small town. Law enforcement agencies of all types and sizes need good situational awareness, need to identify their own trends and problems, and need to draw upon the scientific knowledge base of the police profession when making decisions and designing programs. How they do it, how much data they have, whether they have analysts, whether they do their own research, and whether a study done somewhere else is readily transferable to them—these details will all vary across agencies, especially between big and small ones. Thus, doing evidence based policing will not follow a "one size fits all" template, but will rather need to be tailored and customized. This responds to the realities of policing and reinforces the important role of experience and professional judgment.

A systematic and thorough approach

Any police agency determined to take a scientific and evidence based approach to its business needs several types of information: (1) data and analysis about conditions, trends, and problems in the community (crime, disorder, fear, trust, etc); (2) data and analysis about matters inside the agency (safety, wellness, morale, etc); (3) credible information about how well the agency's current policies, programs, and strategies are working, that is, their effectiveness; and (4) knowledge from elsewhere in the profession about the effectiveness of contemporary police practices. These are the key ingredients of evidence based policing. It should be emphasized, though, that having the proper ingredients is not enough—they have to be used. An agency that has all this information, data, analysis, and knowledge but does not use it to inform its decisions and practices is not doing evidence based policing; it is just posing.

Not specifically mentioned in the preceding paragraph is research. Research is what you do when you have an important question that cannot be answered by looking it up, "Googling" it, or calling some colleagues. The line between research and analysis is fuzzy, but research is generally more involved and in-depth. For example, if a hot spots patrol was applied to a problem location, analysis could tell you whether targeted crimes went down, by how much, and whether the impact was greater on certain offenses or at certain times of the day. However, if you wanted to know for sure whether it was the hot spots patrol that caused crime to go down, versus mere chance or some other cause, a more elaborate study would be needed, probably involving comparison or control groups. In other words, research would be involved.

We have a tendency to think of research as a higher-level activity than merely using data or doing analysis, and we tend to think of an experimental study (often referred to as a randomized controlled trial [RCT]) as the best form of research. This is an important topic to address because some proponents of evidence based policing glorify randomized experiments as the only source of valid scientific knowledge. Due to that tendency, some in the policing world have gotten the impression that doing evidence based policing means doing RCTs, period. This is unfortunate for many reasons, not the least of which is that most police and most agencies will never do a randomized experiment, and thus would be excluded from the evidence based fraternity.

The LEADS Agencies Program takes a more expansive and inclusive view of evidence based policing. This is not because doing research is too demanding or too hard for police agencies; it is not a way of watering down or dumbing down evidence based policing. Rather, it reflects the reality that a serious commitment to evidence based policing requires a much more thorough and systematic approach than merely looking for opportunities to do an experiment. A police agency could not carry out a hot spots experiment without good data. It would not even know that it had a hot spot without analysis. Moreover, figuring out if fear of crime is elevated in certain neighborhoods, if public trust is lower among some segments of the population than others, if use of force is increasing, if morale really is the lowest it has ever been, or if more officers are wearing their seatbelts requires data and perhaps analysis, but not an experiment.

The next section introduces seven domains of evidence based policing and identifies quite a few specific activities within each. Doing research, including experiments, is one of the domains, but only one. The total list of activities is daunting and may seem overwhelming. If nothing else, it drives home the point that policing is a big, complicated business. This is not a new revelation, but since policing and police administration are so multifaceted, doing them in an evidence based way requires a systematic and thorough framework.

Domains of evidence based policing

The LEADS Agencies framework identifies seven domains of activity that collectively comprise evidence based policing. The domains reflect the gamut of data, analysis, research, and evidence utilization corresponding to the police mission and the responsibilities of police administration.

Agency outcomes

The first domain highlights the primary outcomes of policing. It has long been a challenge to identify the main goals of policing and/or the principal components of the police mission. While the purpose of policing can be summarized simply as "keeping the peace" or "protect and serve," it is also possible to list an extensive number of functions and objectives. As a practical matter, one or two very vague goals do not provide much guidance and are nearly impossible to measure and track. At the other extreme, a lengthy list tends to exceed our attention span and become more of a data drudge than a guiding light. Moore and Braga (2003) found the sweet spot between these two poles with their seven dimensions of "the bottom line of policing":

- Reducing serious crime.
- Holding serious offenders to account.
- Maintaining safety and order in public places.
- Making people feel safe.
- Providing quality services.
- Using force and authority fairly and effectively.
- Using resources effectively and efficiently.

The beauty of this typology of policing outcomes is that it includes the one that tends to dominate most discussions (reducing crime), as well as the one that has proven most demanding in recent years (using force and authority fairly), plus it incorporates several other outcomes that are universal and timeless yet often overlooked when assessing how well a law enforcement agency is performing. Holding offenders to account (solving crimes and enforcing the law) matters greatly to crime victims and is a prerequisite for specific and general deterrence, but it is often ignored in lofty debates about police effectiveness. Similarly, police performance in the furtherance of traffic safety is obviously of great significance to life and limb, but it is rarely mentioned by policing big thinkers. The same can be said for responding quickly and appropriately to calls for service, providing services to vulnerable individuals, and making the public feel safe. These are things that people expect from the police—they are important dimensions of police performance that cannot be taken for granted.

These outcomes should play an important role in evidence based policing. All of the activities in a law enforcement agency associated with data, analysis, research, and the utilization of scientific evidence should be aligned with these outcomes, or, in other words, with improving the effectiveness of the agency. An evidence based agency should systematically measure how well it is achieving each of the outcomes, watch for any slippages or weaknesses, and continuously look for ways to improve.

Measuring external conditions

This domain and the two that follow are mainly about data or, in contemporary jargon, metrics. They highlight the importance of situational awareness. Front-line personnel, supervisors, managers, and executives all need valid and reliable information in order to know what is going on, what is going well, and what is not. There is overlap with the "agency outcomes" domain but these next three domains go into more detail.

This second domain focuses on the kinds of data needed to measure and track *external* conditions, that is, incidents and problems in the community that are pertinent to police. These data, simply as information without any particular analysis or research, may be essential for identifying trouble spots, setting priorities, and making decisions. When an agency uses these data to guide and inform its operations, it can claim to be "data-driven." Naturally, there are situations in which the data do not "speak for themselves," in which analysis and/or research are needed to reveal relationships and causal factors and to avoid misinterpreting raw data or short-term fluctuations. Even in these situations, though, taking a scientific and evidence based approach has to start with the data.

Twelve components or categories of widely applicable external conditions are listed in the following. Any full-service law enforcement agency should want to have data on each one. Some are harder to obtain than others, requiring special data-collection efforts. While it is true that resources are always limited, a telling indicator of an agency's real commitment to effective and evidence based policing is the effort it makes to obtain the whole range of data on the following:

- Crime.
- Disorder.
- Drug abuse.
- Vulnerable people.
- Calls for service.
- Gangs and gang members.
- Parolees, probationers, and registered offenders.
- Traffic crashes.
- Fear of crime.
- Client satisfaction.
- Citizen complaints.
- Public trust/citizen attitudes toward the police.

Measuring internal conditions

The next domain focuses on data needed to measure and track *internal* conditions, that is, conditions within the law enforcement agency. These may be of particular interest to executives and other administrators since they are most responsible for leading and managing their organizations and personnel.

This domain might seem to fall outside the realm of evidence based policing since it applies more to police administration than to police operations or the outcomes of policing. However, a law enforcement agency cannot do (implement) evidence based policing if its personnel do not have the skills and knowledge needed to carry out modern policing practices, if they are unsafe in performing their duties, if they actively resist management priorities, if supervisors do not support and encourage effective tactics, and so forth. A strong case can be made for the "inside-out" approach to effective policing—the agency needs to deal with its employees effectively before it can realistically expect them to deal with the public effectively (Wycoff and Skogan, 1993). Ignoring internal conditions is highly likely to result in the weak implementation of policies and programs, if not outright resistance.

Ten categories of internal organizational conditions are cited in the following. These are all pertinent for a law enforcement leader's "situational awareness" of conditions within their agency that might influence the implementation of effective and evidence based practices, and therefore might deserve careful attention:

- Officer safety.
- Officer/employee health and wellness.
- Officer/employee attitudes toward the public.
- Officer/employee work-related attitudes.
- Officer/employee knowledge, skills, and talents.
- Discipline.
- Grievances.
- Quantity and quality of applicants.
- Quantity and characteristics of new hires.
- Quality and effectiveness of training.

Measuring performance

This domain focuses on data needed to measure and track the performance of individuals, units, programs, strategies, and the organization as a whole. This mainly pertains to outputs, as opposed to outcomes. While it is absolutely true that, in the end, it is agency outcomes that really matter most, performance measures such as response time to emergency calls, the proportion of vehicle searches that result in seizures, the conviction rate for drunk driving arrests, the proportion of new recruits who successfully pass field training, the proportion of 911 calls answered before the second ring, and the annual cost of civil judgments are presumed to be related to important outcomes. Carefully designed performance measures should communicate to members of the organization the kinds of actions and behaviors that are expected to result in positive outcomes for the agency.

As noted earlier, the range of such data could be huge—in particular, data pertinent to the performance of each different unit in a police department might vary (the training unit, the property/evidence unit, the detention unit, etc). Striking a good balance between having a comprehensive set of measures and having too many is always difficult. One of the most important considerations is to craft measures that reflect quality, not just quantity, for the kinds of performance listed in the following:

- Arrests.
- Citations.
- Vehicle stops and searches.
- Pedestrian stops and searches.
- Public contacts.
- Community engagement.
- Problem solving.
- Response time.
- Crime clearances.
- Judicial outcomes.
- Use of force.
- Pursuits.
- Civil suits and judgments.
- Individual performance appraisals.
- Unit performance.
- Program performance.

Identifying and analyzing problems

The main reason to measure external conditions, internal conditions, and performance is to achieve thorough and accurate situational awareness. This enables the organization to recognize when things are going well, but also, and perhaps more importantly, to recognize when they are not. When data are consistently and systematically available, the organization can spot problems that may need attention—in the community (such as crime), within the organization (such as officer safety or use of force), and in performance (such as a low conviction rate for DUI cases).

Data and metrics are essential for identifying problems, but they do not usually reveal *why* the problems are occurring. The key purpose of analysis is to answer "Why?" questions—"Why is the problem occurring?"; "Why now?"; "Why here?"; "Why in this form?" and so on—because these are often crucial insights into how to solve the problems. This domain emphasizes the important role played by analysis. Topics in this domain mirror many of those introduced in the three previous domains but with a focus on trends, patterns, and "Why?" questions.

Any of the analyses on the following long list, or others not listed, might be needed by a law enforcement agency. Importantly, however, that does not suggest that an evidence based agency has to be engaged in doing all these analyses all the time. If the agency has the kinds of data identified in previous domains, it will be able to scan for problems more or less continuously. Only when that scanning identifies a problem, such as a spike in convenience store robberies or a downward trend in the police academy graduation rate, would an analysis be called for:

- Crime analysis.
- Problem analysis.
- Drug abuse analysis.
- Hot spots analysis.
- Intelligence analysis.
- Social network analysis.
- Workload analysis.
- Analyzing client satisfaction.
- Analyzing public trust.
- Analyzing officer safety.
- Analyzing officer/employee health and wellness.
- Analyzing officer/employee attitudes.
- Analyzing grievances.
- Analyzing citizen complaints.
- Analyzing civil litigation.
- Analyzing officer activity.
- Analyzing use of force.
- Analyzing pursuits.
- Analyzing vehicle stops and searches.
- Analyzing pedestrian stops and searches.
- Analyzing recruitment.
- Analyzing selection.
- Analyzing training.

Evaluating practices and testing alternatives

This is the domain in which research comes into play (as noted earlier, the line between analysis and research is not always clear-cut, so some of what gets done in analysis could also be called research). The research focus here is mainly on what works. This applies to policies, programs, and strategies that the police organization is currently using, as well as to any situation in which a decision is made to try something different. Some agencies will have the capacity to conduct such studies themselves, whereas others may need assistance from research partners or consultants.

A law enforcement agency striving to be as evidence based as possible should constantly be assessing the way it does business, looking for ways to improve. It is common, for example, to have programs that were initiated years ago that may have been effective at first; however, as times and personnel have changed, no ongoing evaluations have been conducted to determine if they continue to be effective. Such programs may have fallen into the category of "we've always done it this way," which is a clear signal that they should be assessed. It is possible that they continue to produce the outcomes for which they were first created, but it is also possible that they are no longer effective at all, or that they could be more effective with some changes.

Similarly, implementing a new program or policy presents an ideal opportunity for evaluation. The new practice is presumably being adopted to address some problem or other need, so it is only logical to watch carefully to see if it succeeds. Launching something new normally makes it possible to establish a pre-implementation baseline, which is crucial for learning if anything changes. Also, a new program or policy can sometimes be implemented in an experimental way, such as targeting some hot spots but not others, providing a stronger case for any subsequent conclusions about how well or poorly it worked.

The core feature of this domain is a commitment to evaluating and testing the agency's practices, rather than settling for the presumption that everything is working just fine. A law enforcement agency should always be asking its managers and other employees "How are things going?" and, whatever the response, coming back with "Based on what?" The more that the answers are based on data, analysis, and careful testing and evaluation, the more likely that practices are informed by evidence, not just opinion or convenience.

Using evidence

None of this measuring, analyzing, and testing has much value unless the results are used by the law enforcement agency in making decisions and adopting/ revising practices. Besides research conducted in the agency itself, studies have been and are being done in lots of other agencies, both by practitioners and by researchers, with results available in journals, professional magazines, monographs, reports, and online. Collectively, all these studies comprise "the evidence" available about policing, including what works. Being evidence based means finding and using this evidence.

At the same time, it is understood that law enforcement leaders are frequently constrained by resources, politics, legislation, collective bargaining agreements, and other practical matters that limit their ability to make rational decisions based solely on professional and scientific knowledge. In addition, the results of analyses and research are not always clear, nor are their implications always obvious or straightforward. As noted at the outset, one of the obligations of professional police is to use their experience and judgment in concert with whatever scientific knowledge may be available in order to make the best possible decisions, defined as those that maximize the outcomes and effectiveness of their agencies.

A commitment to actually using evidence requires top executives of law enforcement agencies to look for organizational mechanisms that will support and encourage evidence based policing, beyond just collecting data, having an analyst, and doing some studies. This might involve enhancements to the education and training of agency personnel, encouraging membership in evidence based policing societies, recognizing and rewarding examples of evidence based policing, assigning someone to be the "chief evidence officer," creating a committee or process with the responsibility of imposing an "evidence based lens" on decisions, policies, and programs, or some other techniques not yet identified.

A way forward

The NIJ's LEADS Agencies Program is presently developing this framework for "practical evidence based policing" with input from numerous practitioners and experts. It is anticipated that a "self-assessment tool" will be produced that law enforcement agencies can use to assess their current strengths and weaknesses related to data, analysis, research, and using evidence. A companion guidebook will help explain each of the domains and specific components of evidence based policing, provide some information about how to implement each one, and point agencies to further information and assistance. The NIJ is also working directly with a handful of agencies around the country to field-test some elements of the framework and collect examples of good practice.

Ultimately, it seems that the mindset and components of evidence based policing need to be inserted into the executive development systems that prepare current and future law enforcement leaders. This does not mean that future chiefs and sheriffs must be trained to design and execute randomized experiments, but it does mean that they need a full understanding of the multifaceted policing bottom line, a keen awareness of the kinds of data and analyses that should inform decision-making, familiarity with the circumstances under which practices should be tested and evaluated, and a savvy grasp of the ways in which evidence should be used to improve police effectiveness. It will be very helpful if programs such as the Federal Bureau of Investigation's National Academy, the Police Executive Research Forum's Senior Management Institute for Police, the Southern Police Institute, and all the other state and national providers of advanced education for police recognize the need to make evidence based policing one of the core components of their courses of study.

References

Cordner, G. and Hale, D. (eds) (1992) *What works in policing? Operations and administration examined*, Cincinnati, OH: Anderson Publishing.

Lum, C. and Koper, C. (2017) *Evidence based policing: Translating research into practice*, Oxford: Oxford University Press.

Moore, M. and Braga, A. (2003) *The bottom line of policing: What citizens should value (and measure) in police performance*. Washington, DC: Police Executive Research Forum. Available at: http://www.policeforum.org/assets/docs/Free_Online_Documents/Police_Evaluation/the%20bottom%20line%20of%20policing%202003.pdf

Oliver, W. (2017) *August Vollmer: The father of American policing*, Durham, NC: Carolina Academic Press.

Sherman, L. (1998) "Evidence based policing," *Ideas in American policing*, Washington, DC: Police Foundation. Available at: https://www.policefoundation.org/publication/evidence-based-policing/

Skogan, W. and Frydl, K. (2004) *Fairness and effectiveness in policing: The evidence*, Washington, DC: The National Academies Press.

Weisburd, D. and Majimundar, M. (eds) (2017) *Proactive policing: Effects on crime and communities*, Washington, DC: The National Academies Press. Available at: https://www.nap.edu/catalog/24928/proactive-policing-effects-on-crime-and-communities

Wilson, J. (1980) "Police research and experimentation," in R. Staufenberger (ed) *Progress in policing: Essays on change*, Cambridge, MA: Ballinger, pp 129–52.

Wilson, O. (1957) *Police planning* (2nd edn), Springfield, IL: Charles C Thomas.

Wycoff, M. and Skogan, W. (1993) *Community policing in Madison: Quality from the inside out*, Washington, DC: National Institute of Justice. Available at: https://www.ncjrs.gov/pdffiles1/Digitization/144390NCJRS.pdf

Index

References to figures and tables are in *italics*